Contents

List of contributors

Anne Bannister is a social worker who is also a Dramatherapist and Psychodramatist. She is currently the Manager of the NSPCC/Greater Manchester Authority's Child Sexual Abuse Unit and has specialised in child sexual abuse work, especially with children, since 1981.

Harry Blagg has been involved in research and writing in the areas of crime, social policy and social work since 1981. This has included work on multi-agency co-operation, victim–offender mediation and youth/child related social work. He is Lecturer in Social Administration and Director of the Centre for Child Policy Research at Lancaster University.

Julian Boon graduated in psychology from Aberdeen University and later gained a PhD on the topic of eye witness testimony from the same university. He is currently a Research Fellow at Glasgow College working on child witnesses. He has written on memory and child witnesses.

Eileen Craig joined as a Team Member of Rochdale NSPCC in 1986, she was previously working in a Local Authority and specialising in child care. She has been developing the treatment of sexually abused children in both individual and group settings.

Marcus Erooga is a team member of Rochdale NSPCC. He gained an MA in Social Work at Manchester University in 1983. Before joining the Rochdale Child Protection Team in 1987 he worked as Probation Officer in Manchester specialising in juvenile offenders. He has led teams working with the mothers of sexually abused children and is currently involved in a treatment group for perpetrators.

Rhona Flin graduated from Glasgow university and gained a PhD from the University of Aberdeen. From 1981-5 she was a postdoctoral Research Fellow at Aberdeen University. She is currently a Lecturer in Organisational Psychology at Robert Gordon's Institute of Technology, Aberdeen. She has published widely on the psychology of memory and visual recognition, particularly in relation to children and adolescents and has just completed a research project on child witnesses for the Criminological Research Branch of the Scottish Home and Health Department.

David Glasgow is Lecturer in Forensic Clinical Psychology at the University of Liverpool. He graduated from Leicester University in Psychology and worked at Special Hospitals on Merseyside before training in Clinical Psychology at Liverpool University. After qualification he worked for the Merseyside Regional Forensic Psychology Service developing assessments acceptable to court proceedings. He is currently developing a course in Forensic Behavioural Science.

John A. Hughes is Reader in Sociology, University of Lancaster. He has published widely on research methodology, the philosophy of social research, and, latterly, practical decision-making in a variety of institutional contexts including business, air traffic control and in the police use of information technology. He is currently involved in a project on the social organisation of the disclosure process.

Tony Kilkerr is Detective Chief Superintendant in charge of the Crime Policy Unit at Scotland Yard. He is also Chairman of the Metropolitan Child Abuse Working Party which produced the Code of Practice. The majority of his 29 years as a police officer have been spent as a detective working in the inner divisions of London.

Norma Martin is currently Lecturer in Law at the University of Leeds specialising in family and child welfare law. She graduated from Oxford and also gained an LLM from Harvard University. She is working on public inquiries and legalism.

Tony Morrison is Team Manager for the Rochdale Child Protection Team. He qualified in Social Work at Manchester University in 1977 and then worked in the Salford Probation Office specialising in groupwork programmes with adolescent delinquents. In 1980 he joined the newly formed NSPCC Rochdale team and focussed on assessing dangerousness and, more recently, work with perpetrators. He is a co-author of *Dangerous Families* and has also written on teamwork, stress, groupwork with perpetrators and parental participation in case conferences.

Eileen Shearer is Deputy Team Leader, Rochdale NSPCC. She has been a social worker since 1974 after qualification with an MSc at Oxford University. After a period as a local authority social worker she co-led the first Rochdale treatment group for sexual perpetrators. Her interests include professional self-care, TA and gestalt based therapies.

Paul Stubbs was Visiting Research Fellow at Lancaster University and now works for the Family Services Unit in Liverpool. He has a PhD for research on race and adoption and has written widely on aspects of race and social policy.

Mai Walton has been a social worker in both voluntary and public agencies. She is currently Teaching Fellow on the Child Protection Course at Lancaster University. Prior to this she was a team member in the NSPCC's Child Sexual Abuse Unit in Manchester with additional responsibilities for training and statistical research. Her research interests are in child protection policy.

Corinne Wattam is a researcher and child protection officer with the NSPCC managing a project on the child's perspective of the disclosure of child sexual abuse in the North of England. She has previously worked as a lecturer in social work, and in Social Services as a social worker, and is currently Honorary Research Fellow in the Department of Sociology at Lancaster University.

Jeannie Wells was co-ordinator of a volunteers' bureau and for South Clwyd Women's Aid. In the 1980s she became professionally qualified in social work and began work for a Social Services Child Abuse Unit as a long-term caseworker. She has worked for the NSPCC for the last three years. She has contributed articles for and co-founded a community newspaper, and written for *Comunity Care* and *Child Abuse Review*.

Acknowledgements

Chapter 1. I would like to acknowledge the help of Mary Seguss, Daisy-Mae Morrison, and Paul Stubbs in the preparation of this chapter.

Chapter 2. Thanks are due to Margaret Moren, Jean Horn, Sue DeLecea and the rest of the team for all their help and forbearance in the writing of this chapter.

Chapter 4. With acknowlegements to Ed Mason and Wilf Roberts — our co-team members at the Rochdale NSPCC Child Protection Team.

Chapter 6. I would like to thank Lena Dominelli, Brenda Ryan and Harry Blagg for their support in helping to formulate many of the ideas presented here, and for their comments on earlier versions of this chapter.

Chapter 7. Thanks and acknowledgements to Peter Gwynn, Kathy Byrne, Pauline Oliver, Manjula Kavina, Ken Day, Jim Carr, Jim Bailey, who gave time and commitment to the detail of a protracted and ongoing project.

Foreword

The latest NSPCC research 'Child Abuse Trends in England and Wales 1983–87' shows that the number of children registered for sexual abuse has increased twelvefold during the period 1983 to 1987. As professionals have gained experience of helping sexually abused children so the confusion which so often characterised early professional intervention has given way to a more informed, considered and planned response to protecting children from sexual abuse. The chapters in this book, derived from practice and research, provide insights which form the foundation of such an approach.

Effective communication with abused children is an essential component of child protection. The reliance on what children say is greater when (as in sexual abuse) the abuse may display few physical signs and takes place as an unobserved private event.

This book examines a number of the problems that professionals face and provides a clearer understanding of the issues involved, and at times indicates the likely direction of possible solutions. Drawing contributors from a range of disciplines, the chapters in this book look at how professionals perceive and respond to child sexual abuse within professional, organisational and social contexts, and explore the meaning of the concept of a child-centred approach.

There is an increasing professional awareness of how interventions by professional agencies can mirror the abuse of power and trust which children experience when they are sexually abused. Preventing such 'secondary abuse' means adopting an approach which recognises and validates the child's perspective. An understanding of the power relationship between adults and children is an essential prerequisite for helping sexually abused children.

Listening to children and hearing what they say requires that professionals understand pressures placed on the child by the abuser to maintain the secret of the abuse and the possible consequences for the child if they tell their story. Children must feel safe and protected from the abuser if they are to talk freely about what happened and give expression to their fears and anxieties.

Children's understanding of the world is quantitatively and qualitatively different to that of adults, and to understand the child's experience practitioners need to make the leap of imagination necessary to place themselves in the position of the child. From this understanding skills and techniques need to be developed which enable the child to express their distress in a way that can be understood and validated by the professional without being damaging to the child. Several contributors discuss the use of such techniques and the part that they can play in assessment and therapy.

Improvements in procedures governing inter-agency co-operation, changes in the law and court process, along with improved investigation and assessment skills are all vital to protecting children. Unless communication with children is effective and meaningful, children will remain vulnerable to abuse and will continue to suffer. Without the techniques and skills to listen to children and to hear what they say, it is doubtful the professionals will be able to develop a truly child-centred approach. Effective communication between children and adults is essential if professionals are to be successful in putting children first.

Dr A. GILMORE, CBE
Director of The National Society for the Prevention
of Cruelty to Children

Introduction: Discovering a child centred approach

Harry Blagg, John A. Hughes, Corinne Wattam

Although this book is concerned with British experiences of dealing with child sexual abuse, the problem is not, of course, unique to this country. In the United States, Europe and Australasia, professionals concerned with the health and welfare of children are reporting substantial increases in the incidents of the sexual abuse of children (Baker and Duncan, 1986). Of course, these are a collection of states which have well-established systems of official statistical recording and it would be unwise to conclude that sexual abuse is confined to countries such as these or, indeed, that the increase in reported incidents has nothing to do with the growing sensitivity of reporting agencies to child sexual abuse itself. However, as the latest NSPCC report suggests (Creighton and Noyes, 1989), the effects of greater public awareness need not be straightforward. The figures post-Cleveland of registered children show a 5% drop from an increasing rate prior to those events which may indicate a growing reluctance to report suspected sexual abuse cases. Nevertheless, and despite the general problems of inferring from official aggregate statistics to the 'real' extent of some phenomenon, from what is known it appears that child sexual abuse is not confined to a small 'less respectable' section of the community but is evident in all socio-economic groups (Finkelhor, 1984; Baker and Duncan, 1985; La Fontaine, 1988). As far as this country is concerned, and accepting all the problems of sampling, variable rates of disclosure and varying definitions and conceptions, an estimate of 1 in 10 children being sexually abused is widely accepted by professionals as a not implausible 'true' rate (Baker and Duncan, 1986; La Fontaine, 1988).

Despite the widespread prevalence of child sexual abuse, and reasonably widespread commonsensical agreement about what sort of things constitute such abuse, there is more than just a lingering suspicion that variations, between countries, between regions, between administrative districts, and so on, are, to an unknown degree, artifacts of the difficulties involved in operationalising definitions, be they legal, medical, social, commonsensical, of sexual abuse. Definitions are, of course, not simply about words but about practices involved in effecting their meaning and use in practical circumstances; practices which could, and do, 'at the coal face' produce disagreements. One has only to think of the sometimes overlapping, sometimes divergent, sometimes clear, sometimes vague applications of the notions of physical abuse, sexual abuse, and emotional abuse to see a little of the problem here; a problem that has a bearing on some of the dramatic failure of — some — practitioners and agencies to determine and deal with cases that, in the event, can be seen as representing an horrific and tragic collapse of the faith that professional practice can, and will, reduce the rate and the extent of the abuse of children. Further, and perhaps the crux of the problem, the justifiable application of such labels in official contexts, would seem to require an agreed upon guiding definition and unequivocal symptomology that is conspicuously lacking. The most commonly adopted definition, quoted by Kempe and Kempe (1978), 'Sexual abuse is defined as the involvement of dependent, developmentally immature children and adolescents in sexual activity they do not truly comprehend, to which they are unable to give informed consent, or that violate the social taboos of family roles' is, in many respects, too overly abstract for describing what is for practitioners, such as social workers, the police, lawyers, teachers, and so on, a very practical problem that they have to deal with as part of their daily work. If Cleveland, on the other hand, were to be a measure, then this offers far too narrow a definition centering largely on incest and anal abuse and putatively standard medical symptoms of such abuse. In other words, and the practical problem just referred to, practitioners have to assemble a bricolage of children's statements, physical symptoms, if any, family circumstances and family history, parental claims, or counter claims, behavioural displays, and more, into a justifiable basis for the *fact* of sexual abuse, or not, and any actions that follow from whatever determination is made. As with many crimes, child sexual abuse is generally witnessed only by the offender and the victim with the result that the evidence of the events that took place is hard won and surrounded by delicacies of interpretation and judgement to which few other crimes are subject.

For our part, as editors we refrained from imposing on contributors an all-embracing definition. All have long experience, either as practitioners or as researchers, sometimes both, of the problems of child sexual abuse, one of which is the fact that it is an inexact construct. It is 'inexact' in a number of ways including a diverse assortment of medical, psychiatric, feminist, legal and sociological conceptions, not to mention the diversity introduced by varying moral stances, the lack of well-defined and widely accepted presenting symptomology, and the sheer range of possible behaviours that could be construable as sexual abuse.

However, the point is not to bemoan the lack of agreed upon definitions, or, and perhaps of more practical help, how to apply these, or to complain about the 'failure' of experts and scholars, from whatever field, to tell us what child sexual abuse is, let alone its causes, as if the lack of agreement were the result of idleness or the perfidy of experts. After all, many of the concepts in the human sciences are inexact; a feature that has much to do with their infancy, the supposed complexity of their phenomena, as it has to do with the quality, or otherwise, of scholarship. Commonsensically, and as indicated earlier, few would have much difficulty in proposing the kind of activities that constitute child sexual abuse. But in the practical contexts of particular cases and children where evidence, judgements, procedures, and the rest, have to be justifiably employed, matters become less than clear and straightforward. It is important, accordingly, to try to recognise why there are such differences in perceptions and definitions and what the ramifications are for practitioners, children and for their families. Imposing strict definitional exactitude to encompass all that may be construable as child sexual abuse is not only likely to prove to be a Sisyphean endeavour but one that may, in the end, conceal problems that will not go away simply because they are no longer visible; ruled out, as it were, by definitional fiat. In significant respects, differences in definition and, more importantly perhaps, differences in practice and aims, have much to do not only with the differences among the various disciplines concerned with child sexual abuse but also with the varying institutional contexts within which it is dealt. The difficulties many commentators have noted about providing an all-embracing definition of child sexual abuse have much to do with the institutional frameworks within which child sexual abuse has to be determined, be they medical, legal, social work, psychiatric, or whatever, and how it enters into the activities that constitute the work of those who staff such institutions. The fact of abuse is not established definitionally but has to be assembled as a very practical set of activities of 'doing the work' of responding to, for example and as Wattam details, a referral. Only later in the process, as Flin and Boon explore, and as Martin details in her exposition of the current and likely legal position regarding child abuse, does the issue of legal definitions and making a case come to the fore bringing with it what may be a very different set of concerns and relevances. There is, too, and again as a number of contributors point out, the tensions between therapy, a concern for the welfare of the child, and the requirements that a crime be detected and dealt with through the due process of the law. Though, perhaps, it may be that the legal context constitutes a 'background' set of considerations which infuse, by way of anticipation, the initial investigation so shaping, as it were, what turn out to be the 'facts of the matter'. Further, and again as a number of contributors point out in various ways, definitions, and not just of child sexual abuse but of all the related ideals, concepts, beliefs, and so on, attached to it, may come to be seen as imposed 'from above' by professionals who, for whatever reason, lose sight of the point of view of the child.

Of course, collecting and analysing statistical information on abuse requires a level of definitional exactitude that may, as it turns out, bear only tangentially on the kind of categories practitioners have to use in the course of their work. As Martin's account of the current legal position regarding child abuse points to, local authorities and agencies in trying to secure protection for the child are, in terms of the law, faced with strategic choices as to which might prove to be the most effective way of achieving this goal. Whichever happens to be chosen has a bearing on the official figures and what they are capable of telling us. At the end of the day, of course, there ought to be a reasonably firm connection between the figures produced and the work done, but as is well known from various criticisms of official statistics, this is not always easy to achieve, to say no more than that. Nonetheless, as Walton argues, the differences shown in statistical information, if questioned sensibly, can be extremely suggestive as to variations in practice, and, through this, extremely helpful to practitioners in, among other matters, making claims for effective resourcing. However, our main point is that all-embracing definitions, though serving some purpose, by their nature fail to grip onto the practical circumstances of dealing with abuse.

It verges on a truism to point out that conceptions of child sexual abuse are subject to broader cultural and moral changes in notions of childhood, sexuality, abuse, adult-child relationships, and so on; changes reflected, though not uniformly or consistently, in public attitudes, the law and social welfare practice (see Gordon, 1989 for an analysis of the changing conceptions of child sexual abuse in the United States over the last 120 years). These are not changes which are easy to understand or which shift in isolation from other aspects of our culture and our social arrangements. As Stubbs discusses, Britain's emergence, since the 1950s, as a multi-racial and multi-cultural society has meant that practitioners and researchers alike must need become more sensitive to this dimension of practice and, as important, translate this sensitivity into methods and procedures which recognise that child abuse does not occur in separation from a web of other concerns. In other words, the sexual abuse of children is not a series of isolated acts but is situated within a complex of social and cultural arrangements and understandings rooted within the very fundamentals of our society. Among these we can include what we deem to be private and what public, the organisation of the varieties of the family, the moral organisation of sexuality, the social organisation of gender identities, those of race, the rights and obligations of parents and those of children, those of professional practitioners and their responsibilities to various clienteles, and more, all cross-cutting in complicated ways that defy easy categorisation, description or generalisation.

An emphasis on the practical circumstances in which practitioners have to work is important since it recognises the gap between prescription and practice; the gap in which a more child centred approach has to find room. Listening to the child means exactly that even when, as must happen at times, arguably there may be 'good reasons' for treating what the child says with caution. This will inevitably require changes in attitudes and a self-consciousness about practice that might be, for many, unusual. The experiences of Craig et al. recounted in chapter 4 give an insight into one team's response to the problems child sexual abuse creates, both for the victims and for the families, perpetrators and also for those whose task it is to deal with such abuse. Perhaps not every team can develop the necessary means to scrutinise their practice with such an assiduousness, but, nonetheless, their account provides a more than useful indication of the very real stresses generated by work in this field and how it has responded to the problems child sexual abuse poses. At the time of writing, one local authority social services department has expressed concern about the added burden that the increase in child sexual abuse cases is placing on its staff (Guardian, 12 April 1989). Certainly, the task facing workers can be overwhelming and the danger is that some practitioners begin to take refuge in their organisational frameworks; refuge in what Faller refers to as 'denial' (1988). As she notes, a practitioner's response to a child can be infused with 'denial' in the sense that the child is too readily seen as lying or fantasising.

Hitherto, two perspectives on child sexual abuse have largely dominated recent debate in this country: the feminist and the family therapy/systems approach. Both have not only increased awareness of the problem but have also contributed much to our

understanding, little as it may be, of the nature of the problem. It is
not our intention to detract in any way from what each of these
perspectives has and can still contribute, although the limitations of
the family dysfunction model, which underpins much family
therapy, is debated in several contributions. Rather, our intention is
to focus much more on the child itself as the central figure in child
sexual abuse. At the same time, we also wanted to emphasise the
problems of a more child centred approach within the contexts in
which practitioners of all kinds have to work. It is all too easy for
proposals like the need to become more child centred to end up as
little more than well meaning slogans, as empty adornments to practices which are being carried on in much the same way as before.
This 'is not, let us hasten to add, an attack on practitioners of
whatever branch, but a recognition that, and for many reasons
including the very real difficulties of establishing just what is
effective and possible, social welfare practice is done within a
collection of bureaucratic, moral, legal, social, economic and political constraints. Of course, what we have just referred to as 'constraints' are not merely that. They also represent resources that
facilitate, to whatever degree, dealing with child sexual abuse. In any
event, pointing to the problems of practice is no argument against the
effort to try to improve matters as best they can be, though it might
be an argument against a too ready acceptance of new approaches as
panaceas that will transform matters, overnight as it were. Kilkerr's
chapter reviews, through the example of the response of the Metropolitan Police to child abuse, just how difficult it can be to effect,
through essential discussion and negotiation, long term changes in
attitudes and practices to the benefit of the child. Glasgow, too,
though in a different context, details some of the delicate balances
that have to be kept in carrying out effective assessments which not
only produce evidence acceptable to the courts but are also effective
in helping the child.

    As a result, it is by no means easy to work out what a 'child
centred approach' implies in all the various areas concerned. 'Listening to the child' is important, but how this can work as more than
just a programme, however well-intentioned, needs to be thought
about carefully.

    So, in this volume the contributors, chosen mainly because of
their experience of dealing with or researching into child sexual
abuse, have tried to explore, in different areas, what a more child
centred approach can mean for practitioners of all kinds, and the
kind of problems it raises that have to be faced and dealt with. It has
been no part of our remit as editors to specify in detail for the
contributors what is meant by a 'child centred approach'. All advocate listening to the child but also recognise that what this can and

might mean is likely to vary, particularly but not only in terms of professional viewpoints and institutional concerns, and legitimately so. The multi-agency character of dealing with child sexual abuse, as well as the different professional competences deployed, inevitably create misunderstandings, sometimes conflict and sometimes reasonable and justifiable differences of opinion. These issues are illustrated again in Kilkerr's discussion of the efforts of the Metropolitan Police to develop systems of liaison with other practitioners and a Code of Practice for dealing with abuse cases. The danger is, and one that is becoming more widely recognised as well as indicated by the exhortation to listen to the child, that the victim of sexual abuse becomes victimised again by the very procedures designed to provide help and succour.

One important idea for furthering our understanding and practice from a more child centred approach is that of the child as victim, a theme explored by Blagg. In some ways the terms 'victim' and 'abused' are, within our commonsense cultural conceptions, dependent upon each other — it is hard to imagine an abused child who is not a victim. Though as Blagg argues, it is possible to be sexually abused and not be considered as a 'deserving victim'. The conception of a victim of child sexual abuse has particular repercussions for responding to and helping children. Part of the public consternation about Cleveland, and about child sexual abuse generally, is that it is hard to accept sexuality in children. This is endorsed by the response of many schools to 'sex education', where there are doubts and arguments about when it is appropriate for children to learn such things, what influence parents, governing bodies and teachers should bring, along with understandable fears about sexualising children too early. Not only does this highlight the power relationship between adults and children, a point reinforced by many of the contributions to this book, including Wattam, Blagg, Stubbs, Bannister, and Wells, in that 'as we all know', adults can make decisions about what children should know about. It also displays a cultural attitude about sexuality in that it is considered to be an adult matter to which children can be introduced gradually as they learn about the ways of the world. There is a hard to face paradox here: denying children sexuality allows some of those who recognise it to abuse it. The repercussions for the child as a victim, to be assisted by those agencies set up to protect children, are profound, since, as Blagg argues, children who are sexualised are not always considered deserving victims. And as Wattam points out, denying children sexuality can also deny the context and meaning of their experience, such that children are left to deal with this part of themselves without the help of others.

What we have reviewed in this introduction, and what the contributors have done in much greater detail, is highlight many of the problems practitioners face in dealing with child sexual abuse. In doing so they have identified research areas which are important and necessary in order that these problems may be solved or, failing this rather tall order, seen a little more clearly. But, of course, research takes time, often many years before its fruits, if any, become available. Also, it is often many years of hard thinking, assessing the results, persuading, arguing, before many problems come to be seen for what they are. Matters become prolonged, too, because of the inevitably multi-disciplinary character of research on child sexual abuse. Meanwhile practitioners have to carry on as best they can.

However, many of the problems that have been identified are not so much matters of research in the sense of providing data or adequate theories on which improvements in practice can be based, but have to do with changes in attitudes, approach, becoming more sensitive to matters hitherto taken-for-granted, even ignored or not known about. As many contributors to this volume have pointed out, often passionately, one of the major problems in implementing a child centred approach in the area of child sexual abuse is, to put it briefly, understanding the point of view of the child. As Glasgow details, differences in verbal facilities between adults and children, the fact that, culturally, an interview is a strange occasion for the child but one, nevertheless, which will be made sense of, often by the child believing that she/he has done something wrong, indicate something of the kind of leap that is required to begin to understand the child's point of view. What is also apparent, and to repeat, it is hard to determine just what the 'point of view of the child' is, not simply because of the constraints and presuppositions of the different institutional, professional and organisational contexts in which sexual abuse is dealt with, but because of the important fact that it is adults who administer the system. The obviousness of this point should not be underrated.

Within our culture, we suspect most cultures, the social categories 'adult' and 'child' form a contrast set in the sense that one implies the other. However, there is more to this than just a logical point. Culturally what the distinction points to are the very different arrangements of rights, obligations, duties and responsibilities, assumptions about cognitive and moral capacities, and so on; in short, matters to do with the social-cum-moral identities of children and adults and the relationships between them. The categories in a significant sense reflect and embody the social organisation of many of our everyday relations. Further, we also know from the work of mainly historians, anthropologists and sociologists of the family, that conceptions of adult–child relations vary both historically and culturally (see, for example, Aries, 1973). For our own and other cultures we also know a great deal about how adults view children, conceptions influenced, for ourselves, by the vast literature on child development. What we know less about is how children themselves organise their experiences vis-à-vis adults in a world which, in effect, is largely administered by adults in most of its detail.

It would be easy to overdraw this point but for the sake of argument we live with this risk, and hazard two further observations. First, for children in our culture the category 'adult' is omnirelevant in ways that it is not for adults themselves. To put it briefly, all adults, and not just parents, have rights and obligations over all children. These rights and obligations are not, of course, the same for all adults equally but what it means is that for adults vis-à-vis children there is a generalised disposition to look out for, admonish, correct, warn, etc. children in ways that are not so generalisable to other adults. In which case, if there is any cogency at all in the notion of a children's culture, adults would loom large, whereas for adults themselves the fact that they are adults is largely unremarkable, their world organised much more in terms of other social identities to do with occupation, for example, and other relationships that properly and appropriately 'belong' to the adult society. Second, although adults were once children, socialisation and the increments of experience that are the product of 'growing up' means that the child's world is, to use a phrase from another context, a 'world we have lost'. What we felt like as children, what it means to look at the world through a child's eyes, so to speak, becomes part of our history, our memories, to be changed, modified, sifted as our interests and concerns change through life. Adults are, as it were, forced to look at children, recover a child's experiences through adult eyes, adult interests, and adult concerns.

Putting the issue in this way suggests an alternative conception of adult–child relationships, one which takes us away from the developmental picture which has largely dominated psychological, educational and sociological research to date. It is a viewpoint which conceptualises the adult and the child's worlds as, in effect, two different cultures each with its own relevances, concepts, meanings, experiences, etc.; in short, each with its own distinctive sense of what the world is like. This is not to say that each member of the respective cultures sees the world in exactly the same way, or that the child's culture and the adult's are so distinctive as to have nothing in common. But what it does emphasise is that within its own terms, each culture has an authentic voice. It is a conception which recognises that one culture, the adult, has hegemony over the other and that, again in effect, 'growing up' is a colonising process in which children are enculturated into the adult world and, as a result, lose their sense of and identification with their originating culture.

This is not the place to develop this perspective much more

except to say that it is not offered as an alternative to developmental models of socialisation or adult–child relationships. These are, after all, not only the dominating perspectives of child development studies from whatever discipline, but also predominantly part of our everyday conceptions of adult–child relationships. Our point is that the idea of a children's culture is a conception which offers practitioners a way of meeting some of the problems identified by many of the contributors to this volume — which is not to say that all would agree by any means with our way of putting it — of implementing a child centred approach to child sexual abuse. Trying to understand the child's world from a child's rather than an adult's point of view becomes akin to the anthropologist's problem of making sense of the world of an alien tribe. Of getting to see the world from the perspective of people who may have very different moral and ethical systems to our own, speak a different language, organise their relevances differently, structure their cognitive and affective concerns in what to us are strange ways, and so on. For the anthropologist an important part of gaining a foothold on the alien world is achieving some distance from his/her own society, own cultural presuppositions. Similarly, to apply analogously to the culture of children, this means that adults need to distance themselves from their world in an effort to recover, as far as practicable, the world of the child.

It is easy to make this seem an impossible task. It is to require that adults, as Blagg puts it in his contribution, become children again. While such an injunction becomes absurd if taken as anything other than an emphatic way of expressing one requirement of a child centred approach, it does point in a direction which can have practical implications.

It is fashionable these days to emphasise the esoteric character of research — and there is no doubt that it can be such — and to underrate the value of practical experience. And, it has to be admitted, and sometimes pointed out, that the connection between research and the application of that research to practice is never straightforward in the human sciences, just as it is not straightforward in the physical sciences. For some practitioners the relevance of research is often remote, hard to determine and detached from the practical circumstances they have to face daily in the course of their work. For others, though this is perhaps simplistically exaggerated, practice has to be derived from theory and research and nothing else is worth considering. For our part, we want to demur from both these positions if presented in an absolutist, either–or fashion. The human sciences are still very much in their infancy and we have few, if any, adequate theories that lend themselves to application anything like as well as theories in the physical sciences. There are, of course, many reasons for this and there is a good case to be made for the inappropriateness of comparing the physical and the human sciences. Be this as it may, and it is an enduring argument within the human sciences, the point we want to stress here is that a child centred approach to child sexual abuse will have to recognise that any changes in procedures, approaches and attitudes will, inevitably, have to be effected by particular practitioners working in particular settings and circumstances; a theme emphasised by Wattam and by Flin and Boon in the legal context. As always, general prescriptions and programmes, whether offered by governmental agencies, academics of whatever disciplinary persuasion, managements, and so on, will have to be implemented in respect of particular and, in important respects, unique configurations of social and environmental circumstances, management styles and policies, resources, organisational relevances and personalities. It is these mixtures of contingencies that will shape a more child centred approach. It will involve practitioners, be they social workers, health visitors, child care officers, teachers, lawyers, and so on, reflecting on their own, often taken-for-granted, postures on each and every occasion. It will involve trying to see the child as responding to the particularities of its own life, what is happening to it, and how it responds to the very procedures put in place to help. As Bannister and Wells show, it will require listening to the child on its own terms, as far as this is possible, and all the time remembering that children, like adults, are not all the same, not all homogeneous members of some category 'child'. It will involve trying to see the particular children as social actors, like all of us, trying to make sense of a world which can be alien, mysterious, strange yet sometimes malleable, clear and obvious, a world in which mistakes can happen, tragedies occur, success be achieved, disapointments felt, and not children as representatives of some theory. It will involve, to use our earlier metaphor, trying to recover the cultures of children by treating them as authentic representatives of what is, after all, their culture.

Child sexual abuse is an horrific violation of a person who happens also to be a child. It is this moral response which, inevitably and rightly, provides the context for any approach to the problem of child sexual abuse, as it does to any social problem. This also means that, again inevitably and rightly, dealing with child sexual abuse, its victims, the perpetrators, the families, and so on, requires the application of human judgement in particular circumstances and, from our point of view, it would be better if this judgement were exercised more with the child in mind.

1 Fighting the Stereotypes — 'ideal' victims in the inquiry process

Harry Blagg

There is a growing recognition that childhood is not, for many children, a 'golden age', safely quarantined from the traumas of the adult world. Child sexual abuse in particular has pushed the issue of childhood victimisation to the forefront of public and official debate. This interest has, however, to be set against an historical neglect of the problem of child victimisation by society. Despite the current concern with the victims of crime, the introduction of national and local crime surveys, the proliferation of victim support schemes, and the influential role 'victimology' has come to occupy in criminological theory and research, childhood experiences of victimisation have remained largely under-researched and uncharted. It constitutes what Maguire and Pointing refer to as an area of 'hidden crime' (Maguire and Pointing, 1988). This may seem strange given that, in many respects children, by virtue of their dependency and vulnerability, represent an obvious source of data for victimisation studies. Yet the victim movement and criminological research have remained largely silent on the issue, with children appearing only on the margins of studies dealing with domestic victimisation (see for example Maguire and Corbett, 1987).

In this chapter I will argue that the suffering of children remains 'invisible' to us because children are frequently submerged beneath a deluge of mystifying images which cloud our perceptions of the issues: images of how victims, not exclusively child victims, are meant to look and behave and images of the kinds of pathological or deviant familial and cultural backgrounds from which victims, and offenders, are assumed to be drawn. It is also important that we recognise the extent to which the system itself can play a role in the 'secondary victimisation' of children. In the child abuse field — and this is to some extent true of other forms of sexual violence — it is not always useful to make rigid distinctions between the private domain of the family or community as the site of abuse, and some neutral public domain of safety: such is the power that all adults have over children any relationship, even those intended to rescue a child, can easily become abusive. Sexually abused children are frequently held responsible for their own victimisation. I will argue that notions of 'deserving' and 'undeserving' victims operate with children as well as adults and such factors as the social class, age and gender of the child (race is discussed in chapter 6) may influence the kind of treatment they receive by the state agencies. For, whereas a child sexual abuse inquiry may determine that a child has been 'abused', this does not imply that the child will be accorded 'victim' status, for this status is achieved on the basis of the abused person's degree of responsibility in the act: it is, therefore, a judgement rather than an assessment. I shall also argue that this tendency to make moral judgement is common to all agencies who become involved with sexually abused children: differences in professional culture may be over-ridden by those images of 'good' and 'bad' victims mentioned above.

The material for this paper is drawn from my experiences both as an academic researcher and as a counsellor helping to run groups for teenage girl survivors of sexual abuse in the north west for a major voluntary agency.[1] The research side focussed upon the factors influencing the form and content of multi-agency work across a number of sites, including: crime prevention, juvenile liaison, drug abuse, racial harassment, domestic violence and child sexual abuse. The latter issue in particular became an important area for inter-agency work over the lifetime of the research (Blagg et al., 1988: Sampson et al., 1988)[2].

Stereotyped images of child victims

Until very recently it was generally assumed that children did not suffer long term traumatisation as a result of victimisation. The commonsense assumption that children are 'resilient' and 'get over things quickly' has acted to suppress interest in the particular ways in which children express internalised trauma through physical and behavioural disorders. It is only recently, for example, that such behaviour as self-mutilation by teenage girls or persistent running away from home have been seen as possible responses to abuse rather than as simply disturbed or delinquent behaviour. The psychoanalytic tradition has also been criticised for its tendency to misread disturbed behaviour as symptomatic of childhood fantasy rather than as a response to some real occurrence or experience (Masson, 1984). In many respects science and commonsense have reinforced one another in ways which have tended to underestimate the impact victimisation has on children, or has tended to interpret behavioural problems as manifestations of some internal disorder unrelated to real events. These tendencies have real implications for the ways in which child victims are treated: firstly, there is the tendency to minimise the impact of victimisation, and secondly, the tendency to punish children whose acting out behaviour is interpreted as 'attention seeking'.

The first tendency is reflected in the example of 'Tracy' whose father had a nervous breakdown following her disclosure of sexual abuse by her uncle. The family did not want to engage with the issue, to the extent of not wanting her to receive therapy (they did, though, send her to the parish priest to be absolved of her sin). On the other hand, her father eventually had a nervous breakdown (children, one assumes, do not have nerves to breakdown). She felt very angry about the fact that he received help when she had not received any:

> It's all right for him he got the pills and counselling. I was told I was young and that I'd get over it.

An example of the second tendency is the case of 'Sandra' who was admitted to a psychiatric unit because of persistent self harming. She was told by the psychiatrist, in the presence of her parents, to stop hurting them with her unreasonable behaviour — only after some months was it discovered that her father had been regularly sexually abusing her for several years.

There seems to be a widespread blindness when it comes to seeing child victimisaton and an incapacity to read the messages that children give us. In Sandra's case the psychiatric staff failed for months to make any links between the self-mutilating behaviour and child abuse, despite the fact that the child would methodically wound herself with razor blades after visits from her father. This blindness may seem particularly strange in view of the numerous images we have of childhood innocence in our culture. The Children In Need Appeal, and other such ventures, demonstrate that large numbers of people are quickly moved by the plight of the vulnerable child. However, I would like to suggest that these images of childhood innocence, and the ideologies embedded within them, themselves constitute a barrier between ourselves, as adults, and the real world of childhood victimisation. One reason for this may lie in the fact that the stereotype of the victimised child, powerful and emotive though it may be, has generally been subordinated to its conceptual opposite, the child as offender. Two equally extreme and equally idealised notions of childhood are in play: the abused child in need, whose plight sets the phone lines ringing, and the dangerous delinquent from whose menacing behaviour society needs protecting. It has been the latter concern which has tended to dominate the political and policy agenda. As Nigel Parton (1985) suggests:

> The primary concern with children has been in terms of the prevention of crime and anti-social behaviour.

The 'child as victim' stereotype has tended to exist in a subordinate relationship to the 'youth as folk devil' stereotype which has been given greater prominence because of its power as a political signifier of social decline and urban disorder (Hall and Jefferson, 1978). Indeed dominant perceptions of 'the victim' have been constructed in response to the lawless, vandalised, urban wastelands made uninhabitable by the crimes and 'incivilities' of the young. It is hardly surprising therefore that children, as Jan Morgan suggests, have found it difficult to, 'earn the status of victim' (Morgan, 1988). Unearthing them from beneath this deluge of urban abandonment has become a difficult task: children and young people generally have become victims of a global ignorance, fuelled by 'paranoid delusions' about the imminent collapse of urban civilisation as we know it. It is difficult to stimulate debate about the extent of victimisation of children and young people when they have been so roundly and comprehensively designated 'a problem' in our society.

Paradoxically, when children have been discussed by victimologists they appear as the 'completely innocent victim': the quintessential victim. For the founding father of victimology, Mendelsohn, they appear at the very top of the hierarchy of victims, next to those 'victimised while unconscious' (Nagel, 1974). The message is clear, children are the most passive, inert and unknowing of victims and therefore their degree of 'culpability' in their victimisation is zero: like the 'battered baby' the child victim is, by definition, helpless.

The problem is that, though in theory children are ideal victims, real children in real life cannot usually sustain this level of '*Playdoh*' like passivity and innocence. Indeed one generally finds that the more victimised a child is, the worse, in adult terms, the child behaves. Children who have endured protracted humiliation and suffering within their families are angry, betrayed and wary and they let us know this in ways which adults find difficult to cope with. They are usually anything but unconscious and appear anything but innocent. Indeed they appear anything but childlike. One consequence of sexual abuse is precisely to kill off childhood as a developmentally distinct state with its own particular sexual universe and to catapult the child into an adult sexual world from which they are utterly unprepared and ill equipped. The child may adapt to the murder of his or her child-world by playing out in terms of sexualised behaviour what he or she considers to be adult's expectations, and in ways which invite labelling and punishment from adults. There awaits the child a very different assortment of stereotyped categories: 'Little Lolitas', 'slags', 'sexually precocious', 'disruptive', 'delinquent': our culture is rich in denigrative terminology which serves to place distance between ourselves and the suffering of child victims. It is 'them' and their behaviour which becomes the focus of intervention, rather than the deeper unhappiness of which their behaviour may be a presenting symptom. Not only can this lead to what William Ryan called 'victim blaming' (Ryan, 1974): they can quickly lose their 'victim' status altogether when their behaviour is interpreted as the cause of the abuse rather than as a consequence. But they may very well need to, 'behave in ways which are nasty and difficult to live with' (Pithers, 1988), due to their betrayal by the adult world and it may take a long time for them to trust adults again.

These images of 'good', 'innocent', 'unconscious' children are dangerous. They implicitly legitimate punishment or indifference to real children, who cannot live out this 'damaged angel' stereotype built up on adult expectations of how 'good' children and 'good' victims are meant to behave. The paradox lies, then, in the gulf between such social images and a wider reality which defies crude stereotypes. Many of the current stereotypes of the classically abused child — that appear, for example, as visual backgrounds to television coverages of the issue: young children appearing with their faces hidden in a state of dreamlike disengagement from the world, or the toddler with that tell-tale expression of 'frozen watchfulness' — are not necessarily typical of the sexually abused child, who may instead be over-engaged with adults and have, what David Pithers calls, a 'pathological need for compliance' with adults (Pithers, 1988).

On the other hand seeming to be good and innocent (if it can be achieved), while it may help a child to gain sympathy from professionals, will not necessarily protect a child from abuse. The 'aura' of innocence and vulnerability that surrounds children may be the very quality that puts them at risk. For Alice Miller goodness and innocence are no protection from the rage and desire of adults, for it is precisely these attributes which, 'arouse feelings of power in insecure adults' and often makes them a 'preferred sexual object' (Miller, 1985). Indeed innocence is itself something of a fetish for male sexuality in general, as Kitzinger (1988) argues:

> Innocence . . . is a problematic concept because it is itself a sexual
> commodity and because a child who is anything less than 'an
> angel' may be seen as 'fair game', both by the courts and by other
> men who will avail themselves of a child they know has been
> abused.

Defending children from abuse requires that we struggle with the
web of stereotypes that entangle our perceptions of childhood. I have
suggested above that the status of victim has to be achieved; it is
accorded on the fulfilment of certain criteria and is not offered
unconditionally, even to children.

'Why didn't you say no?': the 'culpable' victim

Even when I knew I was helpless
and unable to stop
the gradual debasement of my soul
I long to believe I didn't succumb (Janssen, 1983)

The notion of 'culpability' is central to the social construction of the
'ideal victim' and it acts to deny sympathy to those who are deemed
to have been instrumental in their own abuse. Culpability raises particular difficulties in the area of sexual violence. Of course groups
like prostitutes have always found sympathy hard to come by when
subjected to violence from men, even when this results in horrific
murder (see Chadwick and Little, 1987). Women who have been
raped are often put on trial to determine whether they led their assail-
ant on. However even sexually abused children can be subjected to
interrogation to determine their degree of culpability: sexually active
teenagers may find themselves accused of seducing their fathers, or
giving the wrong signals to strangers, or just having 'asked for it'.
Time is spent in such circumstances establishing the child's 'innocence' through an examination of their sexual biographies and
uncovering how they reacted to the abuser. As in rape cases, children
can be deemed culpable if they did not do enough to 'resist' the
abuser or if they seemed to have actively encouraged the encounter
(see Waterman and Foss-Goodman, 1984; De Young, 1982). One
recent study of professional reactions to abused children found that:

> . . . children were not viewed as innocent victims simply by virtue
> of their age. Children who encouraged the encounter as well as
> those who remained passive during the interaction were viewed as
> sharing responsibility for their abuse with the perpetrator (Brous-
> sard and Wagner, 1988).

Despite a growing body of evidence suggesting that children are not

capable of giving *informed* consent to sexual encounters with adults
and that 'resistance' is frequently impossible anyway given the
degree of power adults, particularly parents, hold over children in
our society, cultural assumptions about responsibility in sexual relations are difficult to shift. Why is this the case? There is not room in
this paper to provide a full exploration of this complex issue but I
believe the answer may lie in our denial of child sexuality in general.
A society that does so much to suppress, and has so little knowledge
of, normal childhood sexuality (or any other for that matter), is not
well placed to understand or sympathise with patterns of sexuality
that differ from the norm. If children are not thought of as sexual
beings *any* manifestation of sexual curiosity of the kind which may
put a child at risk can be interpreted as a form of sexual deviance and
make the child a responsible accomplice. Most forms of sexual abuse
to children do not take place episodically or as random acts of sexual
violence but take place within a long term relationship in which the
child is literally overwhelmed by the power and authority of the
adult. It is a kind of incremental undermining of the child's life-
world rather than a sudden assault: one girl described it, with unsur-
passable simplicity, as 'rape slowed down'.

nightmare

Children become trapped in these relationships by promises,
threats, bribes and kindness and they are fooled into a kind of com-
plicity: 'let this be our little secret'. One of the most difficult dimensions of the abusive relationship for survivors to come to terms with
centres around their own feelings of responsibility: 'why didn't I say
no?' Perpetrators, in such situations, reassure the child that what
they are doing is normal and natural. This is made worse by the fact
that children do often get things out of the relationship: love, affec-
tion, sweets, money, attention from an adored adult, but they are
asked a high price for what they receive: *it is always more than they can
pay.*

guilt

Survivors need to work through the self-hate and self-anger left in
the wake of such a relationship. One teenage girl captured this legacy
excellently when she described her guilt in a collage under the head-
ing 'An important announcement':

> One of the reasons why I still feel guilty is when I look back on
> him giving me sweets. I feel that I was selling myself. It wasn't as
> if I simply just accepted them. If he offered me one I'd ask for
> two. I feel *very* angry with myself for this.

Some professionals respond to this kind of internalised guilt by reinforcing it. Some of the teenage survivors in the group mentioned that
the interviews following disclosure, although in the main sensitively
handled, dwelled on their own role in the abuse: 'why didn't you say
no?' 'why didn't you tell anyone?' 'why did you go back again', were

typical questions. In these interviews the police officers and social workers informed the child that these were the kinds of questions a court might ask and so the child had to be prepared for them. As other contributors to this volume observe, child sexual abuse inquiries are increasingly taking place in a context defined by 'legalism' and this demands both an emphasis on 'evidence gathering' and a need to establish the legal validity of the case. So, although the interviewers may begin by saying they believe the child, the actual process of legal verification may undermine the child's confidence in this belief and reinforce feelings of guilt, self-blame and worthlessness.

We should not underestimate the damage self-blame can inflict upon children. The girl who made the 'important announcement' was announcing her own feelings of responsibility. Even though she was only eight years old at the time of the abuse, she still felt that she shared responsibility for the abuse with the adult perpetrator. This tendency to assign responsibility to children is not restricted to the inquiry stage but can infiltrate into therapy as well. In Sandra's case the issue of her role in the abusive relationship, particularly why she consistently returned home to face certain abuse, when she was old enough to leave home, was a consistent topic for discussion at group therapy sessions run by psychiatric staff at the unit concerned. Family therapy, which has been criticised for its tendency to blame mothers in sexual abuse cases (Saraga and McCleod, 1988; Hooper, 1987; Nelson, 1987) can also impose burdens of guilt on children who are asked to 'accept responsibility' for 'their role' in the relationship[3].

The point I am trying to make in presenting this material is that real life sexual violence to children does not always conform to the patterns of a sudden rape. This does not mean that children 'share' responsibility: children's activity is circumscribed by the limitations of their particular developmental stages. They simply cannot know the implications and long-term consequences of their involvement in sexual relationships. For there to be responsibility there must be choice and children's will is never free in the sense of them having governorship over their, as yet, unformed sexual identities, or being able to make decisions about their needs free from the overwhelming influence of powerful adults. Perpetrators are often very skilled at making the child accept responsibility and feel responsible as an equal partner: the self-delusory system they inhabit is premised upon their need to make children accomplices and 'willing' partners.

I have suggested that the 'ideal' victim is one who is sexually unconscious. A child who is not can slip from the top of Mendelsohn's hierarchy to the slot reserved for those 'provoker' or 'impudent' victims who actively encourage their victimisation (Nagel, 1974; Schafer, 1977). This creates particular difficulties for child victims of sexual abuse who do not present themselves as damaged angels. Sexually active teenage girls, difficult and dangerous children, may find their root to victim status and protection blocked. As I mentioned earlier, being an abused child and being a victim of abuse are not the same thing. If the child is part of a 'pathological' or 'dangerous' family structure he or she may be considered abused but not necessarily a victim of abuse. It has been argued that the child is the 'state's hostage in the family' (Donzealot, 1980; Ennew, 1986), particularly so in working class families. Children from poor families may be 'believed' when concerns about abuse can reinforce already present images of a particular family as being deviant or pathological: however the resulting intervention may be punitive if it involves a wholesale deconstruction of the family unit and no attempt is made to identify a non-abusing parent or relative who could care for the child. The child in such families could be considered a responsible contributor, and the mother a 'colluder' when the family as a whole is believed to suffer some systemic dysfunction (Saraga and Macleod, 1988). This perspective is reinforced by some unproven, but nevertheless widespread, beliefs that abuse is a cyclical process, with those who are abused as children inevitably going on to repeat the abuse with their own children. Such theories compound the tendency to 'individuate' (Hearn, 1989) and desocialise the sexual abuse phenomenon to a product of particular types of dangerous family.

The gender dimension in work with child victims is also complexly interwoven with cultural stereotypes. Teenage girls, for example, may not be seen as 'children' in the eyes of adult professionals, especially if they are sexually active, whereas all but the very youngest of boys may find it difficult to earn the status of sexual abuse victim at all. Boys' virginity is not culturally prized by society and their involvement in sexual relationships with older men may be constructed as a form of initiation rather than abuse. The Broussard and Wagner (1988) study reveals that male professionals in particular were inclined to hold boy victims responsible for abuse:

> ... male respondents attributed significantly less responsibility to the perpetrator when the victim was male than when the victim was female (p.567).

and:

> ... male victims were penalised more by male respondents, and male victims who behaved in an encouraging manner were more likely to be penalised by respondents of both sexes (p.568).

One can only surmise as to why males are so unsympathetic to male victims, perhaps because they are more likely to, and have a greater need to, believe that male sexuality is always predatory rather than

passive allied to deeper anxieties about the security of their own mas-
culinity (for a discussion see Hearn, 1989). Whereas women may be
relatively more sympathetic because they have a greater awareness of
the dangers of sexual violence in general (a point which reinforces the
argument for only using women professionals in the initial assessment and inquiry stages of intervention — see below). It is, nevertheless, ironic that adult male sexist attitudes act to suppress concern for
the safety of other younger males.

Child sexual abuse victims in the inquiry system ✗

It is particularly important that whatever we do when intervening in
the lives of children does not further compound the trauma for the
child. I want to argue that knowing when to act is not a privilege of
superior professional knowledge alone but is a corollary of working
closely with children and understanding their needs: many forms of
child victimisation and particularly sexual abuse, cannot be 'assessed'
scientifically but can only be verified through a close relationship
with the child (Glasgow, 1988; Glaser and Frosch, 1988). One of the
many problems we face when confronted with a possible case of
abuse is that there are in fact very few objective indicators to which
we can turn for verification other, that is, than the child itself. It is
often impossible to prove that sexual abuse has taken place without
the child's own testimony: child sexual abuse, like many forms of
sexual violence, takes place in situations which leave the child as the
only witness. I would wish to go further than this and to suggest that
professionalism can not only get in the way of talking to children it
can provide a means of avoiding it altogether.

When a child discloses it generally creates a crisis for professionals. The crisis is not only one of what courses of action to take, it is
also a profoundly existential crisis, evoking a range of feelings which
are difficult to manage: including, fear, paralysis, anger, loathing
and an incapacity to believe (see Glaser and Froch, 1988). People
rush to the phone; withdraw behind the two-way mirror to find com-
fort in a liaison with colleagues 'about' the child; leap into the cup-
board to find the anatomically correct dolls; watch the child from
behind a video-camera; contact yet more professionals. Meanwhile
the child is left in limbo perhaps now regretful of having spoken.
There are so many pressures on us to 'bottle' the child's 'testimony'
that we can all too easily bottle up the child too and not provide
reassurance, confirmation and support at the critical moment. Professional technique can become a 'bolt hole' for adults who cannot
confront the appalling reality of sexual abuse to children. The sophisticated arsenal of technologies now available to investigators, dolls,
videos, etc., provide a means of retaining control in tense encounters

with victims and retaining a distance between ourselves and them. It is also a way of retaining power over the situation.

Here we can see the tendency I noted above for science to reinforce traditional adult practices of 'taking over' and further disempowering children. Professional power is expressed through the deployment of technique and the monopoly of knowledge, which requires that the object of intervention remains passive and receptive rather than active and involved in the process. Allowing children to talk about their experiences free from the mediating influence of professional techniques may undermine the foundations upon which professional intervention by powerful agencies is based. Indeed, the very notion of 'expertise' itself may be threatened by any process which places the child itself and his/her definitions at the centre of the inquiry. It is not only our status as professionals which is under threat here: maybe to engage with a child's feelings following abuse without the armour of professionalism may require us to share their powerlessness and their trauma, to become children ourselves.

The child's feelings are frequently sacrificed in inter-agency squabbles between different professionals, each anxious to exert its own power and display the infallibility of its particular repertoire or techniques. Nowhere has this problem been more apparent than in the Cleveland case and the problems of medical diagnoses of sexual abuse. The procedure for diagnosing sexual abuse has to some extent been grafted onto those developed in the physical abuse field where there is a clear hierarchy of physical presenting symptoms. This has given medicine a leading role in the inquiry process: and made doctors the most expert of expert witnesses in court. Paediatrics as a distinct branch of medicine grew in power and influence due to its colonisation of this area, achieving diagnostic power through innovations in such areas as brittle bone and the 'battered baby syndrome' (Parton, 1985). Sexual abuse, however, produces symptoms which are non-specific and involve socio-behavioural as well as physical signs (Independent Second Opinion Panel, 1987). This has increased the role of other professionals who concentrate on the child's testimony itself as the primary source of evidence. The attempts to construct a new medical diagnostic technique, such as the controversial anal dilatation technique pioneered by Doctors Hobbs and Wynne and adopted by Marietta Higgs and Geoffrey Wyatt in Cleveland, may in part be seen as an attempt to retain this pre-eminent position in the face of competition from other professional groups and diagnostic methods. The repercussions for children who become the object of such techniques may involve a truamatic re-enactment of the abusive event for those who have been abused and an unwarranted intrusion into the bodies of those who have not.

The damage caused to children in the inquiry system is not

confined to the medical sphere. The 'disclosure interview' (a contradiction in terms if ever there was one) has also become a source of
concern. This is not just the case when professionals disbelieve a
child who may have claimed that he/she has been abused but extends
also to situations where they believe abuse has taken place in the
absence of a clear disclosure — a tendency criticised in the Cleveland
inquiry. Here pressure may be exerted on the child to 'disclose'. The
most notorious example of this is provided by Ben-Tovim et al. in
their disclosure methods adopted at Great Ormond Street, where
pressure has been placed upon children 'blocking' some painful
truth, usually by denying that abuse has actually taken place:

> . . . such pressure is necessary to enable the child finally to make
> statements against another family member . . . *it is necessary to
> match the trauma which the child has suffered through the abuse by
> placing equal pressure on the child to talk about what has occurred*
> (Bentovim and Bingley, 1985, my emphasis).

This form of interview has been criticised on a variety of grounds: on
legal grounds because of the problematic status of evidence gained
under such pressure (Official Solicitor, 1988); on the grounds that
such investigations can themselves become 'sexualising and abusive'
(Independent Second Opinion Panel, 1987) and on the grounds that
children have as much right to be believed when denying that abuse
has not taken place as they have when insisting that it has (Children's
Legal Centre, 1988). There are many ways in which the various components of the system into which children are pulled, owing to the
pressures to gather medical, legal and other forms of evidence, compound the initial abuse. Survivors of sexual abuse need an indefinite
amount of time and space and a secure relationship with non-abusing
care-givers before they can safely relinquish hold on the painful
secrets within. One psychotherapist I interviewed recalled that in a
case she was dealing with it has taken six months from an initial disclosure before the child could name the perpetrator and give details
of the abusive relationship. There is an added dimension to this
problem. The medical and other forms of inquiry are generally
directed toward detecting or revealing an 'event', the moment of
abuse, that leaves in its wake a clear system of signs. As I have
already suggested, however, forms of abuse which are long-term and
incremental in their affects may not be open to contextualisation as
'events' or leave behind them systematic signs. The abusive relationship is a process rather than an assault out of the blue. Children need
time to assemble the meanings of the abusive relationship in a secure
context for themselves, rather as they would assemble a collage:
therapy is the surest context for the inquiry.

The minds and bodies of children can become a battle ground

over which competing professionals struggle for supremacy as each
attempts to establish the 'truth' of the allegations in accordance with
its own particular grids of knowledge. 'Secondary victimisation',
which we have defined elsewhere as abuse by agencies who become
involved with the child (Blagg and Stubbs, 1988), is a serious problem. It is convenient to argue that the solution to this problem lies in
closer liaison between agencies and more joint training to break down
the barriers of mutual hostility and suspicion. This may indeed prove
beneficial for the needs of child victims. Too often, however, the aim
of improving relationships between hostile agencies becomes an end
in itself, irrespective of any improvements in services for client
groups. The research on multi-agency work, referred to in my introduction, revealed many instances in which initiatives in multi-agency
co-operation across a diversity of sites were judged successful simply
because of better relations between professionals (Blagg and Stubbs,
1988; Blagg et al., 1988). In the child sexual abuse field the pressure
to improve liaison in the wake of the Cleveland affair, and subsequent official pronouncements, in which 'working together' has
been identified as a panacea for such tragedies (see Butler-Sloss,
1988) may make for situations in which the co-ordination of agency
practice via the creation of Special Assessment Teams comes to
designate the primary goal, with the important issue of child centredness relegated to a subordinate position. Nowhere is this tendency more
clearly illustrated than in the report on the Bexley experiment. Here
increased multi-agency co-operation was considered to be desirable
on its own terms and the research report considers the 'success' on
this dimension to be sufficient proof of the schemes success as a
whole:

> The continuation of the joint investigative approach has been
> described by a senior manager as a 'self justificatory ought'. This
> feeling has been confirmed by every single respondent, and
> doubts relating to the lack of objective outcome data point to the
> need for detailed research, NOT the failure of the project. *The
> project has clearly succeeded in its aims relating to the improvement of
> communication between agencies, and it cannot be demonstrated that
> it has failed to reduce trauma for the children* (Metropolitan Police
> and Bexley Social Services, 1987, emphasis added).

I am not trying to suggest that good relationships are not a pre-
requisite for better practice, or that the Bexley scheme has not been
successful in improving services for children. What I would suggest
is that we cannot assume that better practice flows, automatically,
from better relationships: the method must not be confused with the
goal. All agencies are capable of making mistakes in the way they
handle and assess children. Breaking down the barriers between
agencies is a waste of time if we do not at the same time break down

the barriers between ourselves and children. Images of good and bad victims circulate in the minds of professionals from all agencies, and each agency has its own particular method of processing and managing children as 'cases', and so 'resolves' the problem in ways that disempower the child. Professionals may see the 'case' resolved upon the successful conclusion of a prosecution, upon the child being taken to a place of 'safety', or upon the clear substantiation of an allegation through medical investigations and successful inter-agency cooperation. It greatly facilitates the success of the agency projects if the child is an ideal victim: the right age, the right gender, with clear medical symptoms and a family that is already 'known' to the police and social services. Moreover the long-term needs of the victim for therapy after the professionals have done their work may have less priority than the initial inquiry. Indeed, many professionals, as Pithers suggests, tend to assume that once they have intervened to stop the abuse the problem somehow disappears (Pithers, 1988).

One can gain a vivid sense of the problem of adult solutions to the crisis by reference to one of the most moving accounts of surviving sexual abuse, Maya Angelou's *I Know Why the Caged Bird Sings*. At eight years old she is raped by the foster-father. When the truth comes out her uncles savagely beat the man to death. The child is left feeling guilty because she has not said no, and must therefore be to blame in some way: should she not be punished too? She also believes herself to be an accomplice in the abuser's murder. Now however the family honour is satisfied and she becomes an embarrassment, her brooding silence reminds them of something they now wish to forget. The adult crisis is now resolved: hers is only just beginning. Maya Angelou concludes that adults find it hard to bear sullen and morose children who refuse to get over things adults have deemed resolved and in the past: eventually she is beaten by her family and she retreats into total silence. Children are capable of remaining silent, 'perpetuating their own loneliness' as Alice Miller puts it (Miller 1987) in order to spare close adults the consequences of what other adults may have perpetrated upon them[4].

All of the issues I have raised in this paper have emerged in some form during counselling and in my interviews with other therapists and counsellors. Survivors recall many negative features of their treatment by professionals: 'help' which leaves them powerless when it ignores their wishes; 'interviews' which become interrogations; 'care' which leaves them isolated and alone; 'therapy' which demands they acknowledge their 'role' in the abusive relationship; 'medical examinations' which feel like rape. Many adult survivors in particular say that they would not have disclosed had they known what was in store for them in the system.

These are difficult lessons for us to assimilate. I do not wish to

suggest that all intervention is abusive or intrinsically punitive, or
that intervention necessarily conforms to some inevitable 'master
pattern' of punishment and control along those lines set out in Stan
Cohen's pessimistic vision (Cohen, 1985). Intervention by concerned
professionals is a necessary step in repairing the damage caused by
abuse but it must be carried out in a child centred way. I would like
to inject a little optimism here and suggest that significant steps are
being made to improve services for victimised children both at the
inquiry stage, with the use of specially trained multi-agency teams
staffed mainly by women, in court where children's testimony is
being taken seriously, and in therapy, with the creation of survivors
groups and other forms of counselling. Other contributions to this
collection amply demonstrate that professionals are learning valuable
lessons and introducing them into practice. More of course needs to
be done. Taking child victimisation seriously requires that we side,
unequivocally and unconditionally, with children and that means
talking to them, listening to them and believing them; it means coming down from the commanding heights of professional power and it
means ridding ourselves of those stereotypes of deserving and
undeserving victims, children must not be held responsible for the
crimes of adults. I leave the last words to Martha Janssen:

it wasn't she who failed at all.
She is the victim
not the criminal.

Footnotes

1 The counselling work was not carried out for research purposes and I never structured this work along the lines of a sociological inquiry. The material I have used as
   the basis for exploring the children's perceptions was not just gained from verbal
   accounts, but has been assembled from a diverse range of sources, from collages,
   'sculpts', paintings, stories, poems and group discussion. I have also interviewed
   therapists running other groups and working on an individual basis with abused
   children and adult survivors.

2 This research was conducted under the ESRC's 1985 Government and Law Initiative and looked at multi-agency work across a number of sites, including child
   sexual abuse.

3 I am not trying to suggest that this is by any means a common practice although
   adopting a family therapy model of treatment, some would suggest, inevitably carries with it an implicit and dangerous tendency to share out blame amongst the
   whole family: how else can it operate? Therapists I have spoken to who use the
   model deny that encouraging mothers and children to 'own' their responsibility
   and look at their own behaviour is the same as blaming them. Mothers and children
   may not be capable of making such subtle distinctions. One psychiatric social
   worker, who uses the model in therapy, went on to say that he considered child
   sexual abuse to be a 'victimless crime'!

4 This story, incidentally, was chosen by the survivors group, as the best illustration
   of the ways adults respond to abuse.

2 Investigating child sexual abuse—a question of relevance

Corinne Wattam

Introduction

A child centred approach to investigating child sexual abuse is *practically* a very difficult matter. Saying so is one thing, identifying the reasons and trying to resolve them, quite another. The Butler-Sloss report gave broad advice on the importance of listening to the child, working together, and recommended changes in the law which would enhance the rights of parents and their children (Butler-Sloss, 1988). These are general prescriptions for some very complex and fundamental problems, although it is not altogether clear just what these problems are. Inquiries are inevitably retrospective; they focus on a result, and because of this, may gloss over some of the components of the process, leaving the problems only partially resolved. Lord Butler-Sloss recommended that the child should be 'listened to'. Professor Olive Stevenson, at a Post-Cleveland Day 13 July 1988, remarked that this was something she was advocating 20 years ago. But, 'listening to', along with all the other components of a child centred approach, are not simply dealt with in such prescriptive terms. If the investigation of child sexual abuse is observed as a social process rather than as a procedural matter, many features become visible which shape the way in which social workers, police officers, doctors, and others involved in an inter-agency response to children who have been sexually abused, work together and with children. It is not that practitioners don't listen; they do, and understand and respond. What cannot be ignored is that these activities are achieved in the context of organisational and procedural requirements, professional cultures and personal understandings that are part and parcel of their day to day work.

In *Working Together* it is stated that; 'Strengthening the common basis of understanding is essential to the task at hand' (DHSS and Welsh Office, 1988). Before it can be strengthened, however, we need to know a great deal more about the ways in which understanding is achieved by members of society, routinely, ordinarily and commonsensically, as a feature of the natural organisation of social interaction. This chapter is about making visible some of the taken-for-granted features of the common basis for understanding that form part of the natural organisation of the investigation of child sexual abuse. To do this I use an observation of a social worker receiving a referral. Whilst this is an account of one occasion, it has a certain familiarity; the assignation of child sexual abuse is uncertain, it is a possible case, there is discussion of the referral between a police officer and a social worker, and between colleagues. But its familiarity stretches further; the parties involved use certain commonsense devices to make sense of the information confronting them. These devices are a shared means of making sense, and as such, features of our commonsense knowledge of society and its workings (Garfinkel, 1967). Such knowledge, though perhaps prosaic in some ways, is, nonetheless, integral to our competence in constructing interactions that constitute our everyday life, and this includes the everyday life of those dealing with child sexual abuse as part of their daily work. Such knowledge includes, for example, knowing the fine grain details of how talk is organised, the recognition and display of social identities, the practical operationalisation of inferential reasoning, and so on, which constitute the practical reasoning through which everyday life is constructed. In short, the devices that are, for the most part taken-for-granted, but which are nevertheless fundamental to talk and interaction between people. Displaying, in the extracts used, some of the details of this series of conversations enables us to show something of the way common understandings are achieved. Whilst individually professionals may differ in their interpretation of the events reported, they must also inevitably share in some of the processes by which this accomplishment comes about. The problems it highlights are those that routinely confront practitioners who must respond to allegations of child sexual abuse.

Listening, understanding and responding are selective processes; that is, organising what is heard, seen, understood, is to do so in terms of what is deemed relevant. In other words, 'the perceptual field', to call it that, is organised in terms of what is accountably relevant for the task at hand. In conducting a child sexual abuse investigation, the colour of a child's socks is noted or attended to if it is relevant to the investigation — whether it be to put the child at ease, or to lend detail to a statement. Investigators search information for relevance, but it is not always clear which parts of the information are relevant for whom. Relevance for the child, social worker, police officer, forensic surgeon, solicitor, teacher, health visitor, magistrate and so on will not always be the same. As Schutz (1972) observed, one important question is 'why these facts and precisely these are selected by thought from the totality of lived experience and regarded as relevant'. This notion of relevance presents a useful device with which to analyse now children are listened and responded to. Given that there will be a number of different frameworks of relevance, it is not hard to see how confusion, and 'cross purposes' develop. But the problem has greater implications. How much does each adult involved in the investigation of a case of child sexual abuse take into account the child's own set of relevances? How far do the people exercising the law, and their set of relevances, determine what happens to the child? In examining the observation below, the focus has been on how relevance is achieved and displayed. What is seen by the parties to it as relevant, and why? Five areas will be considered; the organisational setting, the formulation of versions, motive, use of 'normality', and the context of information.

The observation

1   SW 1   We've got a possible sex abuse.
2   SW 2   Are you on duty?
3   SW 1   No, but everyone else seems tied up today
(SW 1 Made telephone call to police)
4   SW 1   Hello Pat, we've got a possible sex abuse, don't know
5   much, referral came in on Friday. It's not the boy,
6   it's from the babysitter actually, the boy went round
7   to his house and he'd forgotten something so he went
8   back, and when he went in he saw the boy with his
9   trousers down and father kneeling behind him, father
10   jumped up as he walked in the room and that's all
11   we know, he's been holding onto this since Wednesday, so
12   what do you want to do?
(Policewoman indicates she is not coming out, she has another sexual abuse investigation that morning, and is on her own today.)
13   SW 1   Oh, but if we find out something has happened you will
14   have to be involved won't you, to take statements and
15   so on . . . mmm, right . . . bye.
(SW 1 then telephones the school, introduces herself, name and agency, lowers her voice.)

16   SW 1   We have a very sensitive problem, can you tell me if
17   (name of child) goes to your school? He does, in that
18   case can I talk to your head master?'
(SW 1 is put through to head teacher and arranges to see the child in
school later this morning. On returning to the office after interviewing the child, she talked once again to SW 2. She had interviewed the
child with the teacher, with whom he had a good relationship. His
mother left when he was 6.)
19   SW 1   Lovely boy, shock of blonde hair, the teacher
20   suggested he was quite open and direct and would
21   probably appreciate direct questions. It was quite a
22   good interview really, quite informal, I'm sure
23   something has happened. Began by introducing myself
24   and telling him what I did, went on to look at sorts
25   of touching and whether dad did anything to him he
26   doesn't like. Interesting really, he said 'No, I
27   won't let him, I told him I'd tell', I said, 'Well how
28   do you get to say that, that doesn't really come up in
29   normal conversation?' he said something about going for
30   a walk with Dad through the fields, and Dad spent a
31   penny and ran about with his trousers down, and he told
32   him he didn't like it. He also said he didn't like
33   staying in and that he and his sister go out every
34   night, not always together. He's 11 not 13, but that's
35   all really, so we left it at that, well, we said we
36   didn't believe we had got the full story, but we left
37   it that he could come back to the teacher if he had
38   anything else to add.
(There then followed a discussion with another worker about the
family background)
39   SW 2   Why did mum leave?
(She calculates the age of the sister at the time.)
40   She'd be about the right age for telling something
(SW 3 comes in with a referral form just received via another team,
explaining that the duty officer visited the referrer at the weekend.)
(3 days later)
(SW 2 looking at the referral information)
41   SW 2   Didn't tell me about this touching him in the car
42   SW 1   I have no doubts about this man, d'you think I should
43   ring (police)?
(SW 1 looks again at the referral, saying it was a much fuller
account.)
44   SW 1   Mr X was so shocked he just grabbed the cigarettes
45   and went back to the pub, said that whilst Mr Y was
46   not touching (the child) he couldn't understand why he

47   should be kneeling in that position. Mr Y leapt to
48   his feet, apologised and left the house. That's the
49   bit that's pushed me on . . .
50   SW 2   What have you arranged to do now?
51   SW 1   I'm going back to the school next Monday to see the
52   boy. I think I will contact Pat. I did contact her at
53   first, and I got back to them afterwards and said the
54   boy didn't tell us anything.
(Picks up telephone and starts dialling, puts it down again. Looks at
another file on her desk, looks up.)
58   SW 1   Trouble is Pat is up to here with it at the moment,
59   she's about to go on holiday.
(Some minutes later SW 1 dials police and gets through. She restates
the original referral and gives the more recent referral information.)
60   SW 1   I'm not sure what we do now. I'm convinced he's been
61   abused, (pause), it would be (police officer) so you'll
62   tell her all about it, good, (pause) Bye.

1   Organisational relevance

The sequence above begins with 'We've got a possible sex abuse'.
One thing to note about this is the indication of 'ownership' of a common problem that is the proper concern of not 'just anyone' but of
persons who act in an organisational capacity. The talk displays
organisational relevance. A pre-requisite to understanding it is the
knowledge that this is a social worker at work. What is said is said in
an organisational context. Knowing this helps to make sense of the
following remarks regarding 'duty', and everyone 'tied up today'
(lines 2 and 3).

   The referral itself is categorised in terms of its organisational relevance. Any information referred has to be categorised in a way that
makes it relevant to the organisational capacities of the person receiving it. In this way referrals are judged appropriate as 'something this
organisation can deal with', or else referees are advised to seek help
elsewhere. This referral was not diverted, so its appropriateness to
the agency has already been judged. Having accepted it, how else
might information about a boy with his trousers down and his father
kneeling behind him be categorised here (lines 8 and 9)? Other work
that child care social workers properly involve themselves in can fall
into categories such as physical abuse, emotional abuse, neglect, and
so on. Given that this information has been accepted as a referral, and
it does not obviously fit into any other category, it becomes 'a possible sex abuse'. The social worker is not necessarily being loose in
her description; she is justifying her involvement in organisational
terms. In this way the case becomes 'a case of possible sexual abuse,

and action that follows is guided by what such a categorisation implies. The categorisation brings in all the organisationally relevant activities for responding to a possible child sexual abuse case. Hence, after announcing that this is such a case, one of the first things the social worker does is to telephone the police. In a sense, it sets the agenda for what is to follow. This feature can have other repercussions. For example, if the case is not a sexual abuse case, and enquiries are made about the family at a later date, what is known about the ambiguity of information in such cases may allow the 'possible sex abuse' label to stick. It might also prevent sexual abuse being recognised, if the categorisation is, say, physical abuse. For example, some of the children I have interviewed said they told teachers their fathers were hitting them. In the absence of bruises, or evidence, this was not followed up and the children continued to be sexually abused. Children are unlikely to be aware of how information gets categorised, and this might explain why, when some children send out such diverse messages to draw attention to themselves, they cannot understand why no-one asks them about sexual abuse. This is not to apportion blame, but to ask how it can be otherwise, given that we 'naturally' categorise and respond on the grounds of relevance, and that relevance is partly derived from the information or evidence to hand, and the organisational setting?

Furthermore, it is not necessary for the joint interviewing officers to go into detail about what a 'possible sex abuse' is. Implicit in its use here is a measure of shared, if tacit, agreement about its meaning. But, and as with any categorisation, rule or principle, there is a penumbra of tacit understandings concerning, in significant part, how it is to be employed and used, which may not, occasion by occasion, be understood in common. There is, too, the danger of packaging complex experiences and events through such categories such that they are redolent of labelling, so losing sight of the individual within the process. But, in this case, it is not that the social worker seems unaware of such possibilities. Later she describes the case in a different organisational context as a 'very sensitive problem' (line 16). This description is used by a social worker, talking with a staff member of the school (who could, potentially, be anyone in the school who happened to pick up the phone), and is clearly different from the description given to the police officer. It is still the same 'problem', so to speak, but presented in one context as a 'possible sex abuse' and in another as a 'sensitive problem', both descriptions geared towards getting the organisationally relevant response. If, for example, the two had been presented in reverse order the police might, because of their own organisational relevance, wonder what a 'sensitive problem' would be. They are, after all, accustomed to dealing with 'sensitive problems'. In the same way a school secretary may well be taken aback by 'a possible sex abuse' as an initial contact, especially in conjunction with the name of the child, not merely for reasons of delicacy but also because, as with any organisation, the structure of authority within schools also involves a distribution of rights and responsibilities with respect to confidential matters. In short, interorganisational relations involve a set of morally structured understandings to do with the way in which knowledge of and about persons is distributed in terms of rights as to who is to know what about whom.

Brief and ordinary as it is, the example illustrates interagency co-operation in action. It shows how persons shape their responses with regard to the sensitivities of the interpersonal, and fundamental, dimension that 'working together' inevitably involves. It also indicates how easy it might be to get it wrong, since such interaction is based on implicit assumptions about ways of presenting information, which are rarely 'sharable' in an open way but, as said, largely tacit. It also highlights the negotiated character, the 'feeling out' of understanding, through the course of the talk. In this example it might not have helped co-operation between participants if the term 'a possible sex abuse' had been challenged at the outset. A similar note of ambiguity is present in line 14. The statement 'You will have to be involved' could be construed as a social worker telling a police officer how to do her job. I have also witnessed the reverse situation, where social workers have felt they are being instructed to work in a certain way by police officers, or other practitioners. These examples serve to illustrate the very sensitive and negotiated balance of power and responsibilities in inter-agency co-operation, which can, on a very personal level, have repercussions for the way in which investigations proceed.

On a different note, practical matters have effects on organisational relevance. Whilst it is beneficial for social workers and police officers to investigate jointly, this is not always possible. Not only is this known, it is accepted as an ordinary state of affairs. The social worker does not complain that it is unusual that the police cannot jointly interview the child, she accepts the matter and considers the next step. This could be interpreted solely as a matter of resourcing, but the implications are more far reaching, because of the ambiguity involved in child sexual abuse investigations. It is often the case that the first interview with the child is inconclusive, as it was here. This social worker tells us that she did get back to the police, to say the 'boy didn't tell us anything' (lines 52–54). Now it is clear that with reference to the interview with the child, it is not the case that the boy didn't tell her 'anything', but she felt that she had not got the 'full story' (lines 35 and 36); so 'anything' here indicates anything of relevance to a joint investigation.

Whilst initially the machinery for joint interviewing can be set into motion relatively easily, a reading of lines 42–59 indicates that starting up that machinery again, midway, requires a different set of relevances; that is, having already stated this is not a case for joint investigation, has it now become one? The question of how relevant a case is to the police is difficult to answer, given the ambiguity and uncertainty involved in cases of child sexual abuse. There is nothing 'topically' different (about the incident leading to the referral) in that final sequence. It is just that something has indicated to the social worker that this is more than 'a possible case'.

The influence of organisational relevance filters through the whole process of investigating and responding to child sexual abuse but often in ways that are mysterious to the child. At the formal interview, for example, children arrive largely unaware of the organisational relevance to their interviewers. The child will have his/her own set of relevances. In taking statements, interviewers are asking the child to do something very difficult — not just because of the disturbing content of the information the child is asked to impart, but because of the 'un-ordinary' way in which they must present it. Generally, children are unaware of the need to put information into a format that will stand up in court, make a satisfactory statement, give sufficient evidence, and so on. Furthermore, telling children they must do this because this is the way it needs to be done for 'evidential purposes' (however this may be phrased) does not sufficiently explain, again for the child, why information must be given in this way. For example, telling a child that she/he must remember the colour of the socks she/he was wearing because the court needs to know this, does not tell the child why the court needs to know and what the purpose of this could be. If the answer is that it gives weight to the evidence, to illustrate the child is a competent witness, has a good memory of events, and is considered more likely to be telling the truth if such detail is remembered, then it can raise for the child the issue of whether she/he is being believed. From the child's point of view, if what is said is believed, why does she/he need to prove it? Furthermore, the details which may be most upsetting for the child, and arguably the most crucial in terms of therapeutic 'healing', are often not those that are relevant to proving a case. Children, for example, often have to resolve the conflict engendered by absolute secrecy, e.g. sharing an evening meal with someone who abused you last night, and no-one else knowing that. This could be a matter of great importance to the child, but in terms of gathering evidence to make a case it would be the abuse, rather than the conflict that would be most relevant.

Organisational relevance and child centredness are not synonymous, and given the current and impending legal context, this is not likely to change. There remains a need to gather sufficient evidence; that is, evidence that will stand up in court, and/or lead to the prosecution of the perpetrator, so that the child can be offered protection. It is as if the only way of meeting the child's needs involves running a somewhat irrelevant (for the child) obstacle course. Attempts to improve the process are merely attempts to make the obstacles easier to negotiate, to make it less traumatic for the child. Joint interviewing is advocated as one way of doing this, but it is not possible to start with the child and ask what she/he wants. We look at the child, and look at the system and its resources and ask how can the child be protected with these? The unfolding of that answer involves formal and informal interviewing, medical examinations, use of video, all of which raise the question of whether the child is fully able to consent. This is what an organisational (adult) solution to the sexually abused child's predicament looks like. Not surprisingly, many children elect not to go through it. Whilst any measure that improves the investigative process for the child is important, it encourages those who intervene to assume they are acting in a child centred way, when clearly, they are often unable to do so. Matters could be improved, however, if the balance was weighted less in favour of organisational relevance and more in favour of relevance for the child. In child centred terms, information should be gathered in the context of the child's set of relevances, which can be identified, acknowledged and shared.

2 Versions

As Schutz (1971) observed we live in a world of 'multiple realities' and very often for victims and perpetrators of child sexual abuse, social workers and other professionals, these are a source of conflict. Jehu (1987) uses 'cognitive therapy' to confront victims with information that disproves their version of events. When victims feel they are to blame or that they are the only one this has happened to, for example, they are given information to help them see it differently. Perpetrators use versions of events to justify their acts, for example, suggesting they were only being affectionate, or that they were doing no harm because they didn't hurt anyone. These have been described as 'cognitive' distortions and must necessarily be tackled if the abuser is to recognise the full import of his actions (Becket, 1988). 'Distortions' are not far removed from what Pollner has described as 'reality disjunctures' (Pollner, 1975). These appear when people differ in their interpretation of events, such that they dispute and challenge the correctness of another's version. Pollner maintains that the holder of one version will seek to persuade another that theirs is correct. One way of experiencing the world becomes a 'credentialled version' which serves to undermine the other version. For example, the clinician's version of a patient having hallucinations (schizophrenia) undermines the patient's version (this is real). Perpetrators, because of their power, undermine their victims' versions, sometimes so strongly that victims come to believe their version of events counts for little.

A child centred approach would advocate that the child should be listened to and believed. It is the perpetrator's version which ought to be undermined, since the child's version would, by virtue of it being believed, be the 'credentialled version'. This is not always the case, such as when judges claim perpetrators were in any way justified in their actions. Or when, in the investigation, the perpetrator denies the charge, and the child's statement is disregarded on grounds of 'insufficient evidence'. Whilst this does not always mean the child is not believed, it shows that within a legal context the child's version is undermined. Questions about the ability of children, at whatever age, to understand truth and falsehood serve to reinforce that it is adults who ultimately judge whether children can hold a 'credentialled version' or not. Furthermore, it could be argued that children are only allowed to hold a 'credentialled' version if an adult agrees, certainly within the legal context of responding to child sexual abuse.

The way in which this is revealed to children, may serve to reinforce their feelings of powerlessness or subordination. In the case above, the social worker tells the child she doesn't believe she's got the full story. This possibly well-intentioned attempt to give the child opportunity to say more, conveys to the child that the worker holds the 'credentialled' version. In doing so it helps to display the asymmetry of the power relationship between his questioners and himself, reinforcing what he will already know from other components of his experience. The issue of whether the child should be believed or not is an obvious one, but such asymmetry is conveyed in many other minute, and unstated, ways. Once again, this is not to allocate blame, but to raise the question of how it could be otherwise?

During the sequence, the social worker presents at least three 'versions' of the events — 'a possible sex abuse', not the 'full story' and 'I'm convinced he's been abused'. Versions 'summarise' a way of looking at an event, such that an interpretation can be made for practical purposes. The event, in this case, is given in the lines 6–11. The versions held by the social worker develop as the investigation goes on. The first is based on the initial referral, the second on the interview, and the third following another referral of the same event. In addition, as the investigation proceeded, the case was discussed with another social worker in the office. Versions are grounded on what their holders see as relevant. So what is it in this sequence that the social worker saw as relevant, that helped her to arrive at these versions?

3 Motive

One feature which lends authority to the version of 'a possible sex abuse', is the absence of motive on the part of the referrer. To illustrate the importance of motive in child sexual abuse investigation, I want here to introduce a small vignette.

A man telephones a social work agency. He says that he met a woman friend in the pub last night, where she told him that her nine year old daughter was being sexually abused by her father. The woman wants to talk without her husband knowing. The man asks about the investigation process. He is going round to the woman's house later to tell her what to do next. The social worker receiving the call describes what will happen and emphasises the importance of the child's safety. She advises that if the investigation gathers enough evidence to confirm that sexual abuse has occurred, the mother may have to make a choice between her child and her husband. The man replies 'Oh, that's OK she's wanted him out for the last nine months.'

Partly because of that closing remark, among the questions that would be asked at some point in this case will be those aimed at finding out;

a The status of the referrer — is he more than just a friend, a boyfriend for example? (There is organisational reference for this on some referral forms, where the relationship of the referrer to the child is asked for).
b The status of the marriage — the nature of the relationship, type of marital problems, previous attempts at separation and so on.
c Why the mother has decided to do something now.

Each of these, among other things, explores a motive for referral. If any indication was given of a motive, other than wanting to protect the child, the case would be considered with this in mind. Studies of false accusations show that children rarely lie about sexual abuse (Goodwin et al., 1982; Faller, 1984). On the whole this is accepted, and so the case would not cease to be a case on the basis of the presence of other motives for referral. However, the absence of motive, as in the observation above, allows the version of a 'possible sex abuse' to remain intact. This is a third party account, from a person who is not related, and these are features relevant to the credential of the version. In short, why else has he referred?

Absence or presence of motives for making allegations has effect later in the process. For example, when a case gets to court, motives can be used to the advantage of solicitors and defendants, and can serve to undermine the child's case. It is also used to disastrous effect in judging children, especially older children, who may be portrayed in court as having been willing parties, that they were somehow motivated to be abused.

4 Using normality

A second feature is the way in which (in this case) practitioners use their own sense of what is normal to identify what is significant (to achieve relevance). The second version, not the 'full story', is based on the interview with the child. In the account of the interview, the first narration of what the child said is also preceded by 'interesting really'. The social worker saw some significance in this remark (lines 26–29). Arguably, the remark indicates the importance of what the practitioner regards as normal for determining relevance. Relevance, for the interviewer, of the child's answer to a question regarding 'touching', is derived from it being something she would not normally expect, i.e. 'that doesn't really come up in normal conversation'.

The information in the second referral continues to reinforce the social worker's versions. It highlights the way in which ambiguous information derives significance from the interpretation made of it. The person making the first interpretation was 'shocked'. This is not a reaction expected from an observation of 'normal' behaviour. In terms of 'commonsense reasoning' this was probably not 'normal behaviour', even though a father kneeling behind his son, who has his trousers down, could constitute such a thing, for example, where the boy has hurt his leg and the father is looking at it. In addition, it is said that the father apologised and left. 'Normally' speaking, people do not apologise unless they have done something wrong, or perhaps because they are nervous, and what could have been wrong about a father kneeling behind his son, or what could have made him nervous? The social worker says that this was the bit that pushed her on. In the context of 'a possible sex abuse' it is not difficult to see the tenuous 'normatively constructed' string that helps draw the line from 'possible' to 'convinced'. Such practical reasoning is experience in action. Very often in cases of child sexual abuse it is all that practitioners have to go on. This developing sense of something being 'not quite right', may be explained later in the investigation when more information is available (Wattam, 1989).

However, it is important for investigators of child sexual abuse to try to be aware of their own sense of what is 'normal', and to consider how they use this to reach judgements. Expectations about bedtimes, and bedtime behaviour, appropriate touching, sexuality in children, sleeping arrangements and so on are all yardsticks on which cases may be assessed. Little enough is known about 'normal' family life, and while this is being researched by Dr Margaret Groke at Great Ormond Street Hospital (for brief review see Wattam, Hughes and Blagg, forthcoming) it will not prevent practitioners from using their own sense of what is normal in their every day practice. This is largely because judgements have to be made in particular situations, for that occasion. For example, is it normal for a child to spend 20 out of 30 minutes in an interview with her hands down her tights, or for a child to draw pictures of her mother and father with breasts, and so on? A child centred approach could explore the child's sense of what is normal, and the grounds for that normality'. In the observation above, the social worker used her own criteria of normal conversation, whereas a child centred approach might explore what normal conversation, in that context, would consist of for the child.

5   Relevance from context

Already, the importance of context for the interpretation of information has been displayed; the context of the organisational setting, and of interpreting signs given by the child, point to some of this. Elsewhere in the sequence, some relevance is drawn from the fact that mother left and from the age of the children at the time, and also something about 'touching him in the car'. In addition the child says he doesn't like staying in at night. Each of these segments of information would not amount to much on their own in terms of reaching a conclusion about whether sexual abuse has occurred. Contexted as they are in the accounted sequence of events they become significant (Smith, 1979). As such they also contribute to strengthening the case. So, their significance is not only derived from the other information we have, they also contribute something to it. Once again, very often this is the only type of information that practitioners have to go on. It combines to indicate that something is wrong, giving the impetus for further investigation. In later stages, such as the interview with the family, it is possible that other information is contextualised to make a case — for example, mothers can find their behaviour is reinterpreted, in the context of a proven case of child sexual abuse by a father, to implicate them as parties to the abuse, to suggest they were in some way responsible for what happened, when they may have genuinely been unaware of the repercussions of their actions.

   In a child centred approach, the context of the child's information should be considered. During the investigation, information held by the child about the abusive experience can have elements of its context changed from say, 'loving daddy' to 'being abused' or 'getting nice presents' to 'accepting bribes'. There are facets of sexual

experience that are difficult to express. Indeed, it is arguable whether
the whole experience is a 'tellable' thing, the sort of thing that
can be put into words. Once the child is confronted by police officers and social workers it is obvious that what they have been
involved in is 'not a good thing'. Acknowledging that what happened was wrong, and that the perpetrator was wholly to blame,
for example, serves to change the context of all the other details
that went with that experience, details which the child might not
tell anyone about. It is important that investigators are aware of
this. If they are not, the changed context of parts of the experience that cannot be told, might leave the child feeling confused
and having to draw his/her own relevance from the investigation.
This can result in a familiar outcome where children continue
to blame themselves despite being told it was not their fault. It
is not that children do not tell everything that can be the most
damaging, but that in having to look at their experience in a different context they are left to review what has not been told in this
new framework. In a sense, the investigation can result in the
child's jigsaw being taken apart, and she/he may be left to reassemble
the changed pieces, alone.

Attention should be paid to the child's context, and the ways in
which the child may be trying to make sense of what is happening
within the context of a formal interview. In addition consideration
should be given to the assessment made of what the child says or does
in this context. With very young children it is often the case that
judgements are made on whether their behaviour is age appropriate,
in drawings or play, for example. Now, in 'formal' interviews children are put into a very 'un-ordinary' setting, no matter how much
attempt is made to make it friendly or familiar. For example, how
usual is it in a young child's experience to be spoken to/played with
for half an hour, sometimes longer, with an adult other than a care-
giver? How much is this taken into account when judgements are
made about whether the child is displaying 'normal' behaviour? Perhaps more important, how much is this taken into account when
children are seen as unresponsive? What adults say is interpreted,
along with its informative content, as 'something an adult has said'.
There are certain matters relating to talking to adults that are not the
case for talking to other children. Such as 'speak when spoken to',
'don't speak to strangers', 'don't answer back' and so on. Whilst
these are not always adhered to, they represent ways in which children orient themselves to talk with adults, in part because adults have
directed them to do so. The adult world of a child's experience is the
only adult world they know and there will be things that are taken for
granted about that world as things that adults do or know about —
which might include sexual abuse. When such matters are breached

this makes the adult asking seem different, and that difference may evoke mistrust, confusion and silence.

Finally, perhaps the most important point of relevance for the child is his/her position in relation to the abuser. This she/he carries into the interview and keeps with him/her, and there is no guarantee that the position will be any different after the interview. In many cases, she/he will know that the abuser is all-powerful, and this will have been reinforced by the number of times she/he has tried to tell and nothing has been done (Milner and Blythe, 1988). A child centred approach to investigation must take into account before, above and beyond anything else, the context of the abusive relationship for the child concerned.

6 Evidence or inference

The sequence presented earlier shows some of the reasoning involved in grounds for suspicion. An analysis of it shows that grounds for suspicion are founded not just on information, but also in the way it is expressed, and the context in which it is presented. They are also founded on the receiver's set of relevances; organisational, contextual, normative, or otherwise.

In the context of current legislation for child protection it must be shown that the child's development is being impaired or neglected. Impending legislation will require harm suffered, or risk of harm suffered, to be legally accountable and supported. Child sexual abuse does not always result in unambiguous physical signs, so cases become dependent on verbal and circumstantial evidence. Such evidence will be constructed, displayed, and interpreted in a court setting on the same grounds of relevance that have been illustrated above. When talk takes on a 'forensic' status it is subject to the same scrutiny as other types of forensic evidence. For instance, when bruises are scrutinised, questions asked centre on how 'normal' these are, are they bruises which occur in normal circumstances, or in abnormal circumstances as the result of an accident, or are they non-accidental? Of a statement about sexual abuse questions will centre on whether this is something that would arise out of normal circumstances, or in abnormal circumstances as the result of an accident, or does it represent an inflicted abusive experience. The importance of what is 'normal' is far more significant for sexual abuse. Without physical signs, courts must make assessments on the basis of what is known about 'normal' children, such that they can say 'normal' children of a certain age can distinguish between telling the truth and lying, or have sufficient recall to remember certain details accurately, and so on. Much of this is covered by the work on children as witnesses, but here I want to point out that no matter how reliable, or otherwise, we can prove children to be, such normative constructs will remain the criteria for assessing any particular case on singular occasions.

When evidence concerning a non-accidental injury is presented, motive is taken into account in determining what should be done. Was this a deliberate attempt to harm the child, or was this a genuine attempt at discipline that got out of hand? Whilst people have opinions about whether children should be the victims of corporal punishment at all, motive in this context can make a great difference in the outcome for the child. As I have indicated above, motive also features in the assessment of child sexual abuse. There is less acceptance of the more obvious deployment of motive. No motive justifies the sexual abuse of a child. Nor should any motive, such as revenge, undermine what a child has to say. However, the use of motive is more subtle. It is a practical reasoning device (Coulter, 1979) by which, among other matters, verbal and circumstantial evidence can be judged on particular occasions. This does not need to be stated by the person making the judgement for it to happen. For instance, questions such as why the child changed the subject there, or laughed at that point, or wouldn't look at the interviewer when she/ he said that, and so on, are questions relevant to making sense of the type of video material now available to courts but which also lend themselves to variant, and sometimes exotic, interpretations of occasions which are, as said before, 'un-ordinary' for the child.

This points to a fundamental problem. No matter how child centred an approach seeks to be, the court setting can never be child centred. The court must remain sceptical, and assess the evidence. It cannot assume that the child is telling the truth. The court can only make it easier for the child to face its scepticism. In which case, the investigation, and the gathering of evidence for court purposes, cannot be entirely child centred, since ultimately the evidence may be used in a non-child centred setting.

Conclusion

A child centred response to child sexual abuse is difficult to apply in practical terms. Listening, understanding and responding are all activities that are achieved by attending to that which is relevant in the organisational and legal framework of the practitioner, and in terms of practical reasoning.

Organisational relevance determines how information about a child can be categorised, presented and acted upon. It sets the agenda for what is to follow. Inter-agency co-operation is, to some extent, dependent on how much each participant takes account of their own and others organisational relevance, and how this is displayed in the interaction between individuals. Children are largely unaware of organisational relevance. This is important to the issue of whether interviews with the child, and the investigation process itself, can be both legally acceptable and therapeutic. What is relevant to a child may be important 'therapeutically' but not legally; the information may be similar, but the emphasis different. The two need not be exclusive, so long as it is acknowledged that child centred relevance and organisational relevance are not synonymous. Measures which make the process less damaging, such as joint interviewing, do not necessarily become therapeutic unless child centred relevance is established.

A child centred approach would allow the child to hold the 'credentialled' version of events, not only in terms of their experience of the abuse, but also in the way they present other matters of relevance to them. This is not always the case. On the whole adult versions take precedence, and children's versions only achieve authority if they can be dispayed as valid in an adult framework. Versions are grounded on what their holders see as relevant. In addition to organisational matters, relevance is achieved through features used 'ordinarily' to make sense of information.

Such features include motive, a sense of what is normal, and context. Whilst in practice it is agreed that motive should not be assessed as a variable determining the validity of information, it nevertheless remains an ingredient of 'making sense' which, in practical terms, cannot be ignored. Not least because judgements may be made by a court where traditionally motive is a presentable and assessable matter. Responses to children can also be determined by what we would 'normally' expect; in terms of 'normal' children, 'normal' behaviour, and 'normal' talk. Child centredness would require practitioners to try to be aware of such 'normative constructs' and be sensitive to their application. In addition, interaction would start on the basis of what is 'normal' for the child. Finally the importance of context is noted, in terms of how it influences practical reasoning for both practitioner and child. A child centred approach must take into account the context of the child's experience in an abusive relationship, and also the implications of changing the context of information retained by the child.

An awareness of such features is important because child sexual abuse is an inexact construct, and evidence is often ambiguous. It depends on these features, amongst other things, for its interpretation. Verbal and circumstantial evidence takes on a 'forensic' status and are subject to the same scrutiny as medical or physical evidence. Courts must remain sceptical in their assessment, and whilst this is the case the organisational response to child sexual abuse is unlikely to be entirely child centred.

3 Powerplays— considerations in communicating with children

Jeannie Wells

There was once an old sailor my grandfather knew
Who had so many things which he wanted to do
That, whenever he thought it was time to begin
He couldn't because of the state he was in.

A.A. Milne, The Old Sailor

Marietta Higgs, Sue Richardson and Heather Bacon used this poem in a post-Cleveland inquiry account, to help describe the feelings engendered by the dilemma of deciding what must be done first when sexual abuse collides with established thought and practice. The old sailor 'in the end did nothing at all . . . nothing but basking until he was saved'. It is difficult for practitioners to do nothing at all in the face of current political and public pressure. However the degree of pressure and anxiety must result in some paralysis. The politics and pressures thrown up by the Cleveland crisis emphasise the dilemma of the co-ordination of practice with the provisions of service and resources. Despite the disputes and discussion there is general agreement that we need to get better at communicating with children.

To understand why this is not a simple matter, and also to understand how some basic skills can be utilised to improve communication, it is first necessary to look at the way children have been treated in the past. ⌈Adult survivors⌉ of sexual abuse give accounts that demonstrate the difficulties of seeking or obtaining help when they were children. Women, particularly, have done this and documented it, recognising that the struggle to deny their knowledge of suffering in childhood is the cause of their often severe symptoms. Many have been dissuaded from acknowledgement of the abuse by therapies which have been undertaken in the hope of receiving help, many of which can now be construed as constituting a means of denial of their experience, and of child sexual abuse itself. The validation of their experience by the writing of books and speaking out will encourage resistance in the future to such forms of denial, whether disguised in therapy or teaching. ⌉

Meanwhile, new emphasis on the concept of 'communicating with children' is an acknowledgement that the nature of communication must change, from advising, interpreting and controlling, to listening, hearing and validating children's experience. Only then will it be possible to begin to dismantle the continuation of abuse through generations. We have to incorporate this change into our culture and socialisation, which means that instead of losing the child's language and expression, it must be retained as an authentic part of our culture.

Difficulties inherent in the ability to disclose sexual abuse encompass language, where children use words particular to their age, gender, culture and environment, and also access to the right to be heard, which is overwhelmed by a tradition of adult notions of power, status and supremacy. Denial of correct anatomical language to children, for example, combined with the suppression of any power that children may exert over their own bodies, results in private language between children. Most of this is lost in adulthood.

To discover the language of children in isolation from individual work with them, would be a huge and constantly changing task. An exercise, used in training, to reveal practitioner's experience of such language is testament to this. This exercise concentrates on remembering words of childhood associated with acts of masturbation, sexual activity and body parts, especially genitalia. 'Pinky', 'pooky' and 'Mary' are amongst many hundreds of names ascribed to genitals which adults can recall. 'Slit', 'knob', 'crack' and 'shaft' are descriptions, among many of an inherently violent nature, that are used by male adolescents to describe the genitals of both sexes. The development of such language reflects socialisation and culture. Despite the wide variance the words have a commonality; most, except those at the latter end of the adolescent scale, are lost in childhood. Thus the dilemma for practitioners of discovering the language of a child is fraught with hundreds of possible permutations. Practitioners may recognise this very easily in, for example, physical examinations of children. A child's perception of its 'belly' may be its chest, stomach or abdomen!

As part of the repression of childhood experience, adults interpret children's language instead of exploring its meaning. Validation of indicators and language require a depth of investigation and shift of perspective, which must necessarily move away from traditional ways of retrieving information from children. Methods of interrogation, threat or entreaty, with requests to 'tell', reinforced by accommodation to powerful adult needs, mean that a child may only reveal what is expected. This can lead to what D.W. Winnicott (1964) and others have described as the 'reinforcement of the false self'. A healthy life with balanced interactions is not possible with the suppression of early, unmet emotional needs, which can be further denied in investigation of sexual abuse.

To unlock the inner reaches of a child's world, practitioners are increasingly moving away from investigative work, which reflects traditional adult power relationships with the ability to silence, shut down and interpret, to more reflective, open, facilitative work.

Abused children often find communication a very difficult and painful process which often may involve manifestations of behaviour traditionally believed to be delinquent and antisocial 'acting out'. This can take the form of truanting, promiscuity, drug and solvent abuse or other self-abusing and abusive behaviour. The main response to this exhibition of pain has been to respond to symptoms, rather than causes, by containment, removal or suppression. Such reactions reinforce the sense of powerlessness and abandonment.

Adult perception of children's behaviour is reinforced by hundreds of years of cultural and social expectations that in effect and in terms of current thought, invalidate the genuine experience of being a child. Roland Summit (1983) describes an increasingly well-known phenomenon: 'If a respectable, reasonable adult is accused of perverse, assaultive behaviour by an uncertain, emotionally distraught child, most adults who hear the accusation will fault the child. Disbelief and rejection by potential adult care takers increase the helplessness, hopelessness, isolation and self-blame that make up the most damaging aspects of child sexual victimisation.' This denial of the reality of the abusive experience is common to violence against women. The traditional upbringing of males in this society, and in other cultures, has encouraged the denial of emotional needs across a broad spectrum. The notion of the 'stiff upper lip', the unacceptability of public expression of tears or affectionate touching, without sexual connotations, are still evident in the development of male children and their subsequent experience as adults.

Increasing recognition of the extent of abuses of power has provided practitioners with the realisation of their propensity to abuse, by way of 'secondary victimisation' (Blagg and Stubbs, 1988) when working with children. Therapists, such as Alice Miller (1987), assert that theoretical knowledge is not enough in itself to facilitate good communication and understanding. Empathy and understanding of our own childhood journey will create an interaction with children that allows them to release the secrets of their experience. Understanding of traumas involved in this experience will enable practitioners to deal with the increasing revelations of children which extend the 'normal' sense of reality. To understand why acts of overpowering cruelty, terror and manipulation are incommunicable at the time of their occurrence, Summit (1983) has highlighted five categories associated with the child sexual abuse accommodation syndrome. He shows that each category 'reflects a compelling reality' for the victim, and that each category represents a contradiction to the most common assumptions of adults. They are:

1 secrecy;
2 helplessness;
3 entrapment and accommodation;
4 delayed, conflicted and unconvincing disclosure;
5 retraction.

The secrecy combines the source of fear and the promise of safety, 'everything will be alright if you just don't tell'. The child is immediately invaded by the badness and danger associated with the overwhelming secrecy. If the child begins to 'tell', the conspiracy of adults, informed by their own suppressions, will usually deny the experience of the child, 'how dare you talk about such things'. Such combinations of response cause the entrapment and accommodation of the events. Summit concludes: 'Unless the victim can find some permission and power to share the secret and unless there is the possibility of an engaging, non-punitive response to disclosure, the child is likely to spend a lifetime in what comes to be a self-imposed exile from intimacy, trust and self-validation'.

Secondary victimisation can occur from the failure of investigating and validating adults to see the powerlessness of children. The years spent repressing the horror of the powerlessness makes the adults unable to communicate understanding and empathy. Children become used to having their difficulties interpreted by adults. In a culture where children's company is not particularly celebrated, especially in the nuclear family, childhood is peppered with phrases like 'do as you're told' and 'don't tell tales'. Rationalising punishment and coercion for the child's 'own good' is described by Alice Miller (1987) in her work exploring the roots of violence in childrearing. 'A merely intellectual knowledge of the laws of child development does not correspond to our expectations or needs or if — even worse — it should pose a threat to our defence mechanisms'. She cites Freud, and her later disassociation from his 'drive theory' as an example of the consequences of denial and suppression, with the subsequent rationalisation provided by cultivated defence mechanisms.

Freud developed his theories about his patient, known as the Wolf-man, based on the assumption that they were fantasies. This left the Wolf-man bereft of empathy for his feelings and an inablity to integrate those into his experience. Miller asserts that the Freudian ideology made certain that the pain or confusion and helplessness, felt by a child who had been sexually abused, could not be exposed, but that a feeling of power could be gained through the 'illusion' of 'oedipal' guilt. This process ensured that patients still felt responsible for what had happened to them. Suffering himself as a child, and subsequently repressing the experience, enabled Freud to misuse the experience of the Wolf-man to justify the continuing denial of his own experience. Freud's conclusion, which provided an important premise for his 'drive theory' establishes something that he could only have conjectured. It can be established with witnesses that an act has taken place, but no-one can be sure that something did not take place if both parties to the act had an interest in keeping it secret. 'Even the victim cannot bear the truth because of the accompanying feelings and fear, shame and guilt' (Miller, 1987).

By accepting and coming to terms with the trauma of our experiences, overshadowed by centuries of the misuse of children, we may be able to recognise that our importance as communicators with children is not based on the stuff of theory alone. Survivors of abuse who have been able to talk of their experience, and integrate it, see through the deception of theories that deny them the knowledge of their experience. Through the acknowledgement of their trauma they are empowering us as adults and children, so to speak.

Many practitioners at this time feel victimised by the fact of their advocacy and witness for children. There are strong, powerful cultural taboos laden with traditional misconceptions that will continue to deny the pain of reality. Those who have begun the journey of awareness in communicating with children's reality, need the support of others who will not deny the existence of such repeated suffering.

Boxes of anatomically correct dolls, grabbed at the first opportunity when confronted with a child, seem to represent the struggles of adults to bridge the communication gap of language and experience between themselves and children. They have a use but will not work alone. Thus, training courses are filled with practitioners from all disciplines, searching for clues, justifications and rationalisations for child sexual abuse. It is noticeable that many participants are women, perhaps owing to the expectation of an empathic response, which may not be present.

Any one of us can be the person to whom a child may initially speak, either deliberately or accidentally. Whether we hear or not, whether we see, is dependent on our ability to acknowledge the powerplays that exist and our propensity for warmth, interest, sincerity and respect. Some people are naturally, almost intuitively, good at this, others need help to develop it. There are others who do not like children and, hopefully, will not be in a position where contact with children is necessary, especially in this context. These prerequisites, the understanding of power and the need for empathy and respect, are necessary to the development of good communication with any child, in any circumstances.

The biggest fear of many practitioners is of abuse where bruises are not obvious, where there is suspicion without disclosure or physical indication. In a small survey of social workers, conducted in a social services department in 1984, it was clear that social workers were very reluctant to pursue cases of suspected abuse. If there was 'only suspicion' of incest, cases were abandoned without attempts at a process of validation (Wells, 1985). This tendency is still not, in my experience, an uncommon reaction. The justice system requires victims to 'tell all', therefore, by implication, practitioners must 'find out all' as soon as possible. Understandably, they may feel daunted by the task, perhaps turning to 'experts' for help. Anyone who has been cast in the dubious cloak of 'expert' will recognise that the fanatical search for such a body is not an acknowledgement of expertise, but rather that an 'expert' is someone who isn't you, but someone else whose skills you could never possibly attain. In this way the 'incapable' practitioner is excused responsibility both with that particular case and also for improving their ability for handling such cases in future. The notion of 'expert', however, remains a confusing one. Court experience will testify that tribes of 'experts' can be brought in by prosecution and defence, each 'expert' expertly denouncing the other. Perhaps a more honest appraisal of a skilled practitioner, is the acceptance of the assertion that they are confident of their opinion and practice. Practitioners are forming together to consult one another and lay down the defence of their professions to further their expertise. This is a significant step forward in multidisciplinary experience where previous 'professionalism' was associated with *not* communicating with each other. Bernadette Manning, of the Standing Committee on Sexual Abuse of Children, speaks of the commitment to try to help workers to find out what has happened in cases of sexual abuse, instead of 'Oh, my God, I think this child has been sexually abused, get me an expert quick' (Campbell, 1988).

To improve practice, support is needed to contest the cultural pre-conditioning which ignores and dismisses children, particularly if there is not an immediate grasp of what they are trying to say. 'Dad put his too-too in my mouth' could be easily dismissed with admonitions like 'Don't be silly . . . ' or 'Talk properly . . . ' by both practitioner and parents alike. Children must be listened to from a standpoint of believing what they are saying. In other words, they need to be heard. The 'baggage' which we bring with us from our cultural and social heritage makes the idea of children being heard an unnatural and challenging notion. They will be 'spoiled', 'indulged', 'become arrogant' — these are common responses to children gaining this right.

Indifference and lack of compassion towards children was endemic for centuries. Emphasis on the development of children and their 'morality' evolved between the sixteenth and nineteenth centuries to encompass the idea of a child being both good and evil. Religious puritanism, for example, produced attitudes such as those of Susannah Wesley, the wife of John Wesley, who wrote in 1872: 'Break their will betimes; begin this great work before they can run alone, before they can speak plain or perhaps speak at all . . . conquer their stubbornness; break the will, if you would not damn the child . . . Therefore: (1) Let a child, from a year old, be taught to do this. (2) Let him have nothing he cries for, absolutely nothing, great or small; else you undo your own work. (3) At all events from that age, make him do as he is bid, if you whip him ten times running to effect it . . . Break his will now, and his soul will live, and he will probably bless you to all eternity.' (Carver, 1978) In just over a hundred years from that statement, further suppression of children has been enshrined in therapy and teaching. We have manipulated the experience of children and overlaid it with these inherited constraints, no matter what the individual child has presented to us.

This also means there has to be an acknowledgement of the denial of different cultural experiences. Knowledge and understanding of other races, perceptions and rationalisations will extend and service the overview within our dominant white European culture. Such acknowledgement requires much the same pre-requisites of interest, warmth, sincerity and empathy. Practitioners have to be prepared to hear what each child they encounter is saying, and encourage them to speak, recognising that their language is likely to be different from their own. Once children begin to speak it is important to affirm what they are saying and encourage them to tell more of their story. Most children are not aware of adult expressions and concepts and can only describe the feelings of an incident. One child, for example, described penetration of his anus as 'like a brick inside'. It is necessary for the child's healing and the professional validation of a child's experience, that listening and believing are fundamental to the task.

A child needs to know who and what their interviewer is in order to feel that some control and framework can be exercised. A social worker may be described as a worker who talks to children and families about problems they may have, and helps to sort out those problems. Giving a child your name printed on a card helps a child to have tangible evidence of your involvement. Never assume that a child automatically knows who you are by your association with a building, like a hospital or a police station. It helps to say where you come from and what you are called as a professional to enable a child to harness the location and context of your work. It doesn't help to say that you're a friend, that you will solve everything for the child, or that you will not tell anyone else. The latter, particularly, would be a lie and children do not need further betrayal by workers, however unintentional it is.

The anxiety and compassion of practitioners may provoke real difficulties in being honest with children about their role and task, but dishonesty compromises a practitioner professionally as well as betraying the child. It ultimately makes the task of communication much more difficult. Many children are very controlled and watchful in their behaviour and may be ready to say whatever they believe an adult wants them to say. This can produce muddled and ineffective results, unless children are freed to speak in their own way about life and events. A willingness to make a child feel comfortable, and a genuine interest in what they have to say, will help children to talk about their experience. Enabling children also requires attention to the power relationships between adults and children, for example, in the shape of physical size and gender.

Components of interviews with children contain powerful cultural and social features. After the discovery that a six year old boy had been forced to engage in oral sex with a forty year old man, the police officer conducting the first interview was being told about the erect state of the abuser's penis. The officer inhaled noisily, tapped his pen on the table, hard, and left the room. In stunned amazement, the child and I contemplated his exit. He returned some five minutes later to tell us that he thought it inappropriate to proceed, through lack of evidence. 'The child's word against his', he said dismissively. The fact that the child had been speaking explicitly about sexual activity is one unacceptable cultural and social feature. In this case there was also the misguided association of same gender abuse with homosexuality, itself socially and culturally discouraged, which may have invoked the personally repressed experience of this practitioner, which consequently may have produced that result. Sgroi (1982) comments on societal responses to child sexual abuse, that place the child firmly into the 'damaged goods syndrome'. She says, 'The fact of the child's premature inappropriate sexual experience, if acknowledged, becomes a trigger for the conflicts, ambivalence, guilt and fear regarding human sexuality, which are harbored by members of his or her family and community. The youngster. is likely to be viewed with intense curiosity, pity, disgust or hostility, depending on the perceptions and hang-ups of the people who learn about the sexual abuse.' Acknowledgements of such strong inhibitors to good communication are essential in the preparation for talking to children.

Patronising children is a common error of adults. It is a defence mechanism which achieves control over children. Recognising that, as practitioners, we are neither 'aunties', 'uncles', friends or saviours, is an important part of clarifying our role. To imply, or explicitly suggest that we are, creates confusion and betrayal. Social work is often perceived by others as 'befriending'. At its most diminishing this means chatting over cups of tea. The social work skills, which are explored in training to assist 'enabling', sometimes blur vision about the notion of helping. Creating a clear framework for the practitioner's role will help the professional tasks undertaken to be more recognisable and quantifiable. This clarity is necessary when practitioners are subjected to the powerful emotional 'pulls' that sexual abuse creates in all of us.

The recent 'crisis' in relation to the politics and perspectives in child sexual abuse threatens to introduce more opportunity for denial and suppression. Conflict still rages about the diagnosis of sexual abuse. Frameworks exist for validation, but there are still disputes amongst professionals about the *meaning* of children's statements. 'How can we know that people mean what they say, or that they mean what they think they mean?' (Campbell, 1988). For practitioners who have begun the journey as advocate and witness, communication with children is central to their endeavour. To get better at this complex task, made more difficult by our collective historical traditions, practitioners have to enter the vulnerable world where these children have been, where they continue to be, and where adults came from. Professional conflict is inherent and inevitable in the progress towards a resolution of better practice. It should not be a disincentive to furthering skills. Recognition of communication skills which are already possessed by practitioners is a starting point, since many have developed modest but effective aids to the process.

One example is the 'Pin People' method of communication which was developed during times of desperate lack of resources (Wells, 1988). A pre-requisite of using this technique is that a practitioner has a duty to attend to the initial power relationship which inevitably exists between adults and children. The practitioner is required to give an account to the child of their name, title and intent, such as, 'Hello, my name is Jeannie Wells. I work with lots of children, and sometimes with their families. If they have problems, my job is to help them to sort them out to make happier lives for them. Shall we

find out what your life is about? I have a game here which will help us
to know who you are, what you like and what you don't like. We can
start together with this piece of paper . . . would you like to choose a
colour? . . . '

Whilst such a conversation occurs, consideration should be given
to height, voice, gender and environmental power plays. A child
should be at the same level as the practitioner (usually facilitated by
both working on the floor). After a comfortable, quiet, unhurried
and respectful introduction, the practitioner and child will be seated
at the same level with paper and coloured pens to hand. The practitioner may then introduce the exercise, i.e. 'I don't know very much
about you yet. Perhaps this will help me find out, and for you to help
me. If you choose a colour then I will start . . . ' Draw a round shape
thus:

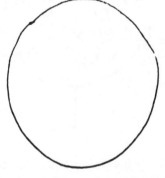

Ask the child: 'What part of you might this be?' If a child cannot
reply at this early stage, the practitioner would indicate that this
could represent the face and head of a child. Colour of hair and shape
is indicated and coloured by the practitioner. Then eyes are added:

The child is asked what these are and the usual response is that the
child is engaged sufficiently to say 'eyes'. The eyes can then be

coloured by the practitioner to be the same as those of the child. Ears
are added similarly and the child may indicate size and shape. Add
the nose and ask the child what this represents. The child will use the
language to describe its body parts that are culturally, socially and
age appropriate. Add the mouth, but ask the child if it is a 'smiling'
mouth or a 'sad' mouth. The child will usually be completely
engaged at this stage of the activity. Add the neck and ask the child to
name this part of itself, thus:

The top of the body is delineated by a straight line for the shoulders,
thus:

The child is asked what this part of the body is called. The arms are
then added, jointed in the middle and extending into fingers, which
can be numbered.

The main part of the body is then addressed by drawing a straight line from the shoulders.

The child is asked to describe the front and back part of this body, above the line of the waist. The practitioner may check which part the child is describing by asking the child to point to the part on its own body. Many children confuse chests, stomachs and abdomens. It is important for the practitioner to know the child's term of reference. The mid-line of the body is indicated thus:

The practitioner has, at no time, invented words or led the child to indicate anything other than spontaneous responses for naming body parts. The next area for identification is below the waist and between the legs, front and back. It is important not to prompt the child but patiently, throughout, await their words. Children are usually relaxed at this stage and their responses easy and uninhibited. At this stage there is no exploration of these areas, but rather a naming process. Thus the figure will be taking shape.

The legs are jointed in the same way as the arms and the toes are numbered. At the completion of this 'pin' shape, there are opportunities for further exploration of the child's experience by using the drawing as a base. Clothes and shoes may be added as an outline, using the child's favourite or most familiar clothing.

The child can be asked which have been the hurting places on this body. These places can be characterised by drawing a small rectangular shape to represent a 'plaster' or a double rectangular shape to represent a 'bandage'. The difference between the two is highlighted by the importance of the hurting place and the degree of hurt. As each 'hurt' part is acknowledged, the child may choose a plaster or a bandage to indicate the degree of 'hurt' to that place. The drawing may build up to indicate the following example at the child's request:

This process validates the child's feelings and self-image. It is directive and unambiguous. It does not lead, intimidate, or patronise the
child. In addition to revealing the child's words for body parts, the
exercise can be extended in a number of ways. For example, to establish the depth of a child's self esteem, the practitioner may draw ear
covers over the ears on the pin drawing. This is done to indicate that
the child in the drawing can no longer 'hear' the comments of others.
The child can then be asked what comments might be made.

Many such methods are being used by practitioners and part of
their continuing development must be to share these skills. The toy
box is an increasingly well known phenomenon for practitioners. As
the contents are likely to be a diverse collection, reflecting the
worker's expanding skills, the box will not suffer the fate of many
anatomically correct dolls, remaining in isolation and little used.

Numerous documents and inquiry reports entreat practitioners to
'see the child'. However, hearing is also a vital component in ensur-
ing the safety of children. Amongst the barrage of instruction, direction and constraint practitioners are heir to, it is important to clarify
some useful, simple, basic elements.

Five things to say to a child
1 I believe you
2 I am glad you came to me
3 I am sorry this has happened
4 It is not your fault
5 We are going to do something together to get help.

Five things to do
1 Listen
2 Believe — be clear; let them know you believe
3 Affirm — whatever feelings the child has
4 Refer — follow up procedures
5 Follow up — support the child

This list was devised by myself and Mary Walsh of the Sexual Abuse
Consultancy Service. It was created as an enabling definition about
'how' we might begin to communicate in a more facilitating way.
During a therapeutic session, a child sat weeping with Mary. The
child was gently reassured of continuing help and acceptance, and
was advised, 'I am here to take the monsters out of your head and put
rainbows in your eyes'.

By 'switching off' adult agendas and entering a child's world, better communication is effected, and healing is possible.

4 Making sense of sexual abuse — charting the shifting sands

Eileen Craig, Marcus Erooga,
Tony Morrison and Eileen Shearer ©

Introduction

Managing sexual abuse is a challenge that is testing the skills, knowledge and resources of all agencies to their limits. It is also testing the personal resources of everyone involved. Being a 'professional' does not provide any emotional immunity from the potent and intensely personal issues that underly many of the professional dilemmas in this area of work. Unless we acknowledge and confront these acute pressures and our own feelings and reactions there is a risk of being overwhelmed by them. In the end, our ability to carry out our responsibilities to sexually abused children and their families may be threatened.

This chapter seeks to provide a framework for practitioners to understand the conflicting pressures which we experience working with sexual abuse. It is a chance to reflect on and analyse where these pressures come from, how they affect our practice, and ways in which effective teamwork can play a vital role in coping with sexual abuse. The chapter ends with an overview of our approach to treatment, focussing in particular on an integrated groupwork programme.

In contrast to most of the contributors to the British literature on sexual abuse (Bentovim et al., 1988; Glaser and frosh, 1988) we are a team of social workers working in an authorised child protection agency. We hope our contribution will go some way to bridge the gap between existing literature and the experience of social workers and others working within the statutory rather than the clinical sector. Our team of five social workers has a responsibility to provide a 24 hour child protection line and investigation service, as well as providing a management service to other agencies in Rochdale. This involves holding the Register, and convening, chairing and minuting child protection case conferences. We also provide an assessment and treatment service, and undertake training.

A secondary issue with regard to the literature is that a large proportion of very influential treatment work and research has been undertaken in North America. Whilst this has much to contribute to our understanding of sexual abuse, it is also limited by some key differences in our respective legal, organisational and inter-agency systems. The dearth of written work therefore from a front-line statutory British perspective is a major deficit. This is particularly so at the time in this country when societal, governmental and professional responses to sexual abuse, and perhaps to child abuse in general are at a watershed.

Our own experience reflects this. Following our work on the assessment and treatment of serious and fatal physical abuse (Dale et al., 1986) we were painfully confronted with the fact that such a model is not easily transferable to sexual abuse. The reasons for this lie in factors of causation and the presentation of sexual abuse which differ from those affecting physical abuse and neglect. Four key differences can be identified. First, most studies suggest that over 90% of those adults who sexually abuse children are men. Second, the diagnosis of sexual abuse relies more heavily than any other form of abuse on what a child can tell us. Third, sexual abuse in families is characterised by extreme pressures on the victim to keep the secret, and not to tell. Finally, many people, including professionals, still find discussion about sexual abuse painful and are liable therefore to minimise or even suppress its reality. Sexual abuse forces us to examine issues of gender, power, the place of children and sexuality to an extent that has not been the case for other forms of child abuse.

This is not to say that those issues do not arise in relation to other forms of abuse and our experience in managing sexual abuse cases may lead us to explore them more deeply. Equally, treatment approaches for other forms of abuse should not be entirely discounted for sexual abuse. For instance our earlier work with physical abuse has confirmed that it is crucial to pay attention to processes both within the family, and within the family-agency system. It has also confirmed the importance of adults taking responsibility for their actions. However the prominence of gender, power, and sexuality in sexual abuse has certainly contributed to the very polarised societal and governmental responses which make the current climate of practice so confusing and undermining for those at the front-line. Understanding the current context in which we are working is vital both for our personal and professional survival.

Levels of context in working with sexual abuse

The concept of 'levels of context' (Adcock, 1988) is useful to clarify the existing maze of conflicting ideologies and exhortations. It is also helpful in examining the effects of this confusion on decision-making and on professional feelings and actions. Although each level of context is separated out for the sake of clarity, obviously these levels inter-relate and intermesh with much more complexity in the wider world.

1   Social/public attitudes

Public views and attitudes about child sexual abuse are strongly held and publicly expressed in the media. The effects of media coverage in Cleveland on social workers and their clients has been profound and criticisms of professionals acting 'too fast, too soon' in this instance contrasts with the equally fervent and often persecutory criticisms in recent child death cases, that action was 'too little and too late'. Contradictory public attitudes can leave workers feeling paralysed and uncertain of what society really wants us to do. As Louis Blom-Cooper, QC expressed it in the Kimberley Carlile Inquiry Report (Greenwich Area Health Authority, 1987)

> Those who undermine the confidence and morale of the people that society is sending out in its name to protect children, should realise that they are unwittingly putting children at risk.

On the one hand sexual abuse is seen as self-evidently wrong and damaging, and media campaigns to raise awareness, such as 'Childwatch' promote this view. On the other hand, lifting the veil of secrecy on sexual abuse meets with resistance in terms of denial and minimisation of the problem.

The 'discovery' of sexual abuse taps deeply into individual doubts and fears about sexuality and importantly (more than in other forms of child abuse) challenges the abuse of male power in families in relation to both women and children. Ray Wyre found extensive examples in the popular press of stories which perpetrators were able to use to justify their actions as 'normal' (Wyre, 1988).

Thus the notion that sexual abuse may be prevalent is a deep threat to a society which clings to the view that the family is the best and safest way of meeting children's needs.

It would seem that child abuse is wrong — but only if taking action does not involve any redistribution of power within the traditional structure of the family life. Clearly then, social/public attitudes are contradictory and polarized. As Alice Miller's work has shown, the roots of this contradiction lie in the value (or lack of it) society places on children. She writes:

> We are still barely conscious of how harmful it is to treat children in a degrading manner. Treating them with respect and recognizing the consequences of their being humiliated, are by no means intellectual matters, otherwise their importance would have long since been generally realized. To empathise with what a child is feeling when she or he is defenceless, hurt or humiliated is like suddenly seeing in a mirror the suffering of one's own childhood, something many people must ward off out of fear . . . We must ward it off with the aid of illusion, such as for example, believing that children were mistreated in previous centuries, or are so in distant countries or cultures (Miller, 1985).

The effects of these ambivalent and often strongly polarized social views about sexual abuse on social workers' practice can leave them feeling extremely unclear about their mandate, producing either a sense of helplessness or the adoption of a rigidly polarized view based on cherished personal belief systems. The needs of the child are unlikely to stay in clear focus when we are struggling to resolve these conflicts in ourselves.

2 The governmental/political context

Government procedures, policy and resource allocation are influenced, therefore, by a society which takes an ambivalent view of child protection and the value of children, and by expert opinion which cannot be said to have achieved consensus — medical or psychological. Sexual abuse is generally not life-threatening and the energy to reform generated by the Cleveland crisis was fuelled not by concern to prevent sexual abuse or protect children, but to protect 'families' (i.e. adults), from over-zealous professional action. This impetus for change is reinforced by organisations such as PAIN and the Family Rights Group. In Cleveland for the first time, alleged perpetrators have fought back with all the considerable power and articulation at their command, thus shifting the focus of concern from children to parents.

The Report of the Inquiry into Cleveland (Butler-Sloss, 1988) has undoubtedly made a very important contribution to the debate about how to deal with child sexual abuse in Britain. There are, however, certain key issues raised by the Report which are of concern. The Cleveland Report does not make clear any standard of child protection as a baseline and exhorts social workers to find a 'middle ground' between parents and children in child sexual abuse cases. This notion of 'middle ground' is a comforting myth which creates the illusion that there is a way for social workers dealing with sexual abuse to be even handed and 'fair' to all parties. Attractive as this idea may be, it does not adequately recognise that child sexual abuse is, by definition, about the inappropriate use of power by an adult abuser who is also often a member of the family. Our intervention must positively discriminate in favour of children if we are to redress the imbalance of power which is the root of their abuse. But, *such positive discrimination in favour of children must not lead to neglecting the treatment needs of parents. What is required, initially at least, is a differential response to the different needs of individual members of the family*, both for protection and support.

In sharp contrast, the Jasmine Beckford (Brent Area Health Authority, 1985) and Kimberley Carlile (Greenwich Area Health Authority, 1987) Inquiry Reports urged social workers to act more strongly to protect children. The recent DHSS Guidance, *Working Together* (DHSS and Welsh Office, 1988) is an uncomfortable attempt to reconcile the themes of protecting children and minimising the intrusion of officialdom into family life. This is nowhere better displayed than in *Working Together*'s recommendation on parental participation at case conferences, where no principles of practice are offered on how such a policy can be carried out. Official guidance seems to have tacked on the notion of parents' rights achieving greater importance without any attempt having been made to unravel the argument put forward by the parents' rights lobby. There does not seem to be any recognition that, in practice, some of the argument is diametrically opposed to a philosophy which places children first. This would seem to imply that official-dom lacks a coherent philosophy which can encompass the need for positive discrimination towards children alongside effective treatment for parents. Perhaps a reactive approach to child abuse policy is unsurprising in a political climate which is individualistic, anti-state intervention, committed to reducing public expenditure and local government services, and wedded to a philosophy of 'consumer as king'. Children, needless to say, are not powerful consumers in their own right.

The pendulum swings of media/public opinion, expert recommendations by inquiries and the consequent ill-thought-through changes in official guidance based on individual cases which have gone wrong leave social workers confused and ambivalent. These are compounded by significant gaps in our knowledge about sexual abuse, as well as a failure to use existing information and research, particularly in relation to perpetrators. In the Cleveland Inquiry report the lack of expert evidence on the subject of perpetrators appears to underpin the contradiction in the report about concern for the child on the one hand, and the need to protect 'innocent' parents on the other. This is most acutely reflected in the suggestion that resources earmarked for children (Section One: Money) might be used to keep perpetrators out of families.

Ultimately the double message conveyed by official guidance to social workers is 'do more, do it better and do it with fewer resources'.

3 The legal context

The law provides social workers with society's mandate to protect children and intervene in family life. Recent reforms reflect political ambivalence about protecting children. It has long been agreed that child protection legislation is confused and confusing, and long-standing pleas for a Family Court have not been heeded in the drafting of the Children's Bill. This seems to be more concerned with limiting professionals' legal powers and increasing parental rights, than with improving services for children and families, thus continuing a process which has already been apparent in other child care legislation changes. The effect of Cleveland on recent legal changes is clearly visible; that of Beckford and Carlile is less clear. The proposed use of Place of Safety Orders only in cases of immediate danger to the child seems unhelpful in cases of suspected sexual abuse, and there is an assumption, presumably based on Cleveland, that Place of Safety Orders have been over-used in the past. This view was not of course supported by Dingwall, Eekelaar and Murray's study (1983) which though some years old now nevertheless describes a process of 'sifting' by professionals, so that only the most glaring and severe cases actually reach legal proceedings, and illustrates that professionals in fact prefer to intervene in the least coercive way possible.

In the arena of Care Proceedings the diagnosis of abuse has become increasingly a matter for court sanction. Despite Cleveland's focus on medical diagnosis, sexual abuse is much less reliant on the existence of physical signs for its detection than is physical abuse. Children, and especially boys, are reluctant to tell the secret. Some of us perceive a shift from diagnosis of physical abuse by (generally) high status male doctors to diagnosis of what is seen as the less concrete evidence of what the child says and does, often by a lower status female social worker. This has implications for the position of the social worker in increasingly complex and contentious child protection court hearings, which can become the arena in which the conflicting views of adults and professionals are fought out with the aid of more and more lawyers and expert witnesses. The social worker is *not* seen as an expert witness, and may well mirror the child's experience in criminal proceedings of being a powerless but central witness who is not listened to, and open to attack by the opposing lawyers. In response to the increasingly adversarial conduct of Care Proceedings, and faced with 'experts' at war with each other, another polarization occurs between the 'professional' and a 'common sense' view, the latter often being the reaction of lay magistrates under such extreme pressures. In practice 'common sense' views reflect the perspective of bemused adults rather than the experience of abused children.

In terms of criminal proceedings in sexual abuse cases, there are a number of issues surrounding the prosecution of alleged perpetrators and the relative weight given to the children's evidence in court. A preponderantly male judiciary operates a system which struggles to provide children with justice at present. The current initiatives to offer child witnesses more protection in such proceedings are clearly to be welcomed, as are changes in the laws relating to corroboration. However, if courts really want to hear the voice and experience of children, it is imperative that video-testimony is introduced so that abused children can talk at a time, and in a setting, which is more truly child-centred.

Finally as writers such as Parton and Martin (1989) have pointed out, social work, particularly in the field of child protection, has become increasingly defined by lawyers in terms of its roles and responsibilities. Parton and Martin describe this as a trend towards 'legalism' in social work as reflected, for instance, in the chairing of child death inquiries by lawyers. It is interesting to note that the Cleveland Inquiry did not examine the role of lawyers, magistrates or judges despite the crucial part they played. The question arises as to why we have allowed lawyers to define our work in this way. Perhaps it is yet further evidence that social workers have lost some of their identity as professionals: a process of invalidation that may mirror some of the experiences of abused children.

4 Professional context — ideology and philosophy

That professionals do not agree about a whole variety of issues in relation to sexual abuse was clearly demonstrated during the Cleveland crisis. The medical debates apart, there is also disagreement about theories of causation. Different actions follow from different viewpoints and these disagreements are being aired increasingly in public and legal arenas. It is worth noting, too, that the theories of sexual abuse which do exist (with the exception of Alice Miller's work) are theories written from an adult point of view, rather than based on children's own experience.

On the one hand, family therapists have seen sexual abuse as a consequence of poor marital relationships, poor communication and weak generational boundaries in families. Mothers who do not fulfil their role as 'emotional housekeepers' for the family are (covertly) held responsible by the therapists for their partners' sexual abuse of children. The Cleveland Report failed to distinguish between the perpetrator and the non-abusing caretaker, preferring to talk rather of 'parents' abusing children, and making no distinction. This dangerously confuses the boundaries of responsibility.

On the other hand, research on and treatment accounts of perpetators lean towards the view that sexual abuse is an addictive and deviant behaviour that is supported by deviant fantasy and masturbation (Finkelhor, 1984; Wolf, 1984). This behaviour is planned and sexual abuse affects children at a very young age and of both sexes. The research also indicates that the vast majority of perpetrators are male, and offend both inside and outside their immediate family (Abel et al., 1986). This information actively undermines family dysfunction theories which generally see incest as a matter of a father turning to an adolescent daughter when his needs are not met by his partner. The Cleveland Report quotes Professor Sir Martin Roth, paragraph 28 'in many cases mothers play a role in the genesis of the sexual abuse of their daughters . . . Mothers elect the eldest or one of the eldest daughters to the role of the child-mother . . . '.

Feminists have rightly objected to the view that women can be held responsible for their partners' acts, and point to the greater power of men both in society and within the family. They would argue persuasively that the issue of relative power within the family between men and women is not effectively addressed in theories of family dysfunction. This clash of theories leads to dispute and confusion over the role of the mother and professionals' perceptions of this. There are, however, limitations to those 'feminist' positions which see all women as blameless victims. It is our experience that some mothers simply do not believe their children when they disclose sexual abuse, and others have either failed to protect their children or failed to offer them adequate care in the past. It is also a fact that mothers form a sizeable percentage of adults who physically abuse or neglect their children.

Some feminists have made efforts to equate women's rights with child protection, but this is not a tenable position, just as the parents' rights group have attempted to equate family rights with children's rights — equally untenable and misleading. Women do have needs, and the right to have them met, but their needs cannot be assumed to coincide with those of their children, who are developmentally immature and have even less power than women to defend themselves. Hence a *coherent position on the role and responsibility of mothers is critical to effective management of child sexual abuse cases, especially because the mother's response is so vital to the children's subsequent recovery from abuse* (Shearer, 1988).

The effects of the increasingly public conflicts among the experts resonate powerfully within the multi-disciplinary network as well as in individual social workers, with similar consequences. Rigid conflicting belief systems clash within and between agencies, a conflict which closely mirrors power struggles within abusing families. This is compounded by unresolved gender issues and a skills gap reported by some female social workers which has developed between female front-line workers and their mainly male supervisors and managers. The painful results of these unresolved processes surface most acutely in case conferences and supervision. A final and sometimes devastating factor of course may be that the professionals recall their own forgotten abuse. Is this yet another facet of sexual abuse we find hard to face?

The consequences for decision making and the performance of staff are self-evidently harmful to children, parents and workers alike.

5 Consumer and client context

There is a lack of public confidence in our ability as social workers to investigate and protect children, in what are increasingly under-resourced services for children who come into care. This has fuelled a new and powerful parents' lobby demanding full partnership and power-sharing within the professional arena. At present this viewpoint appears to occupy the high moral ground because professionals are so sensitive to the deficiencies in their practice and services. This is compounded by an awareness of the deficiencies of the alternative care system. Treatment for all family members is not available when scarce resources are used in ever larger numbers of investigations. *Often the choice appears to lie between protecting and treating one member of the family at the expense of others. This is unacceptable and forces social workers and courts to seek impossible solutions or unsafe compromises.* Investigating sexual abuse can only be effective if it represents the beginning of treatment, and only if treatment is the outcome of the investigation will our mandate to protect children remain secure.

It is not surprising that deficits in service have led to a consumer (that is parents') outcry which is most strongly reflected in the demand for parental participation at case conferences. The Cleveland Report has made it plain that we must become clearer about our duties and responsibilities towards parents when we are obliged to invade family life on behalf of children. However, notions of 'child-centredness' should not stand in stark opposition to parental rights; our *primary responsibility to children inextricably involves us in a commitment to offer effective services to their families.* We need to make such a commitment to parents, while remaining clear that the real consumer is the child and that parental rights are not absolute rights, but duty rights, which are to be exercised in the interests of children.

The constellation of factors described above inevitably make a practitioner's responsibility to protect children and service families a minefield. The current climate represents a crisis in our attitude towards the protection of children. Meanwhile social workers continue to carry the burden of having to protect children whilst respecting the rights of parents. In the next section of this chapter we describe our efforts to create a working environment that enables us to carry out this difficult task.

Surviving sexual abuse — the importance of teamwork

The creation and maintenance of a healthy team is fundamental to the professional/personal survival, support, and development of workers involved in child protection work generally. An effective team is particularly necessary in sexual abuse. Our work in this area has affected us both as a team and as individuals. These effects vary according to factors such as gender, personal history, current personal circumstances, and past professional experiences. Some of the more acute stresses derive from situations in which we feel helpless, stuck, or very angry. Some examples have included experiences in court, involvement with professionals who minimise sexual abuse, working with mothers who do not believe their children, or simply coming to terms with the sheer extent of sexual abuse. The team is our starting point in enabling and empowering us to understand and share how working with sexual abuse affects us. It is also the source of our energy to undertake this work.

Effective teams do not happen by accident however, and team care is not a luxury (Morrison, 1986). It requires a specific commitment and constant nurturing by each team member. Unless team processes are tackled openly and honestly, there is a risk of mirroring the abusive dynamics of the families we work with. Equally, if we do not meet our legitimate needs for support and the expression of our feelings within the team, we are more likely to look to our families, or even our clients, to meet them, and thus be unable to effectively carry out professional responsibilities.

The foundations of the team lie in a clear mandate about our role and a shared value system, both in terms of a philosophy of practice, and personal/team integrity. This recognises that many personal and professional issues interact in this work. The roots of our value system include a commitment by individuals to growth and to taking responsibility for their feelings, wishes and needs. A safe environment is essential to pursue these aims, so that feelings, needs and vulnerabilities can be shared, and feedback given and received.

The core of team maintenance is the weekly team meeting which deals with business and team processes. Each meeting gives space for individuals to share how they are. We have been constantly surprised that the simple permission to share strong feelings can be so immediately healing and refreshing. Team meetings also provide peer evaluation and feedback: the key to maintaining the team's practice value and standards. Team days are used to deal with both long term planning and the more difficult or stuck team processes, and usually involve an outside consultant helper. Healthy teams do not ignore or deny differences between individuals, but use them both as signposts of conflicts within the team, and as an opportunity to develop together by valuing and respecting the differences between members.

The various problems we have resolved and continue to resolve in the team as a whole can only be worked through a setting where power is openly and clearly defined (otherwise covert abuse of power can come to mirror the dynamics of the abusive family), and in which attitudes of respect, acceptance and sensitivity are a group expectation. In the past few years issues of gender linked to power have become more important, both during the transition from an all male team, and increasingly with our involvement in working with sexual abuse. We continue to grapple with this as an issue. For example, it is important that the role of male workers in sexual abuse cases is validated by the whole team.

Team meetings and team support are not a substitute, however, for individual supervision which is crucial to the maintenance of professional standards, and to our self care and development. It is also important that an individual's struggle with the effects of sexual abuse on ourselves can be explored in supervision.

We have also become aware that even as a strong cohesive team which is able to solve problems effectively, we can't 'go it alone' in sexual abuse. We have, therefore, developed a network of colleagues within our own agency, and with workers from other agencies and disciplines, who 'feed' us intellectually and emotionally, help us to feel less isolated and crucially prevent us from feeling like victims in this work, by their validation and encouragement.

Many colleagues will recognise the stresses described here and have similar needs for personal and team support. However, organisational structures and cultures vary greatly, not only within the social work profession, but even more widely in other helping professions, including the police. Notions of team work and supervision may not at first sight seem easily assimilated. Nevertheless, workers from all agencies need both permission and a safe forum in which to deal with the issues and feelings we have described. At a simple level it is important for colleagues to meet to share feelings and to develop networks to do this. There are clear implications here for the training of managers in all agencies dealing with sexual abuse.

Strong healthy teams and individuals are not without problems or conflicts; what they do have is a recognised way of dealing with feeling, needs, conflicts and change, based on clarity, trust and honesty. Unless we pay attention to our professional relationships, we cannot be available to our clients.

Treatment work

We have earlier described the need for treatment services to respond differentially to the different needs of family members. The following sections provide an overview of work with different parts of the family. Establishing an integrated treatment programme is not easy and we are conscious of a need to do more work on this. What is described, therefore, are the key components and lessons from our experience of this work so far. The gaps reflect the fact that we are in many ways only at the beginnings of treatment; there is much to learn and to evaluate.

Work with children

The treatment needs of sexually abused children and ways of meeting them are explored in other chapters of this book and we therefore simply summarise here the main points of our learning from working with children. Treatment issues and goals which we have found helpful are outlined by Sgroi (1982) and complemented by Kee McFarlane et al. (1986), who provide detailed and accessible frameworks for both group and individual work with children.

A combination of individual and group work has been provided for almost all the sexually abused children referred to us. Whilst groupwork has been useful it is essential that this is not used *instead* of individual work. It is an old adage, but 'groups' are not a panacea for lack of resources for individual work. Many children have needed a lengthy period of one-to-one work supported by at least one group experience. The importance of children having a trusted protective ally outside the family, cannot be over-emphasised, especially where the mother does not believe the child. Changes of worker, disrupted visiting patterns and premature closing of cases all undermine the changes of the vital relationship forming.

In summary then, these are lessons drawn from our work with children:

1 Children cannot be regarded or treated in isolation from all the other social systems in which they exist. Other members of the family must be involved in treatment, although where they are unwilling, treatment for the child alone must of course continue. It is also essential that foster parents, schools and other members of the multi-disciplinary network are committed to, and support the treatment programme.

2 Each child requires an assessment of her/his individual needs at the start of any treatment. Sexually abused children often have multiple needs and it is important that the focus is not solely on the abuse, but rather on the needs of the whole child. Many children have developed emotional, behavioural and attachment problems which must be assessed for treatment.

3 Children who are not obviously symptomatic at the time of disclosure invariably have treatment needs which require careful assessment. Thus, initial over-adaptation to the trauma of abuse will, in the longer term, make recovery all the more difficult. Lack of treatment initially can leave children vulnerable to dramatic deterioration later, such as attempts at self-mutilation and/or suicide attempts.

4 It can sometimes take many months to create a safe-enough environment for children to disclose the full extent of the abuse and to communicate their needs openly. Hence the importance of a long-term stable relationship with a social worker, through which the child can share the depths of the trauma and acknowledge their own needs (Dawson and Johnston, 1989).

5 Children in group treatment programmes may need to silently and privately rehearse the work they need to do by almost 'sitting out' and observing other group members, whilst learning skills and words to help them actively participate later or in a subsequent group.

constantly with child victims can lead to victim-like feel-
le worker and persecutory or angry feelings towards per-
s. Our experience of individual workers doing work both
.ctims and with perpetrators has demonstrated that this can
be a means of reducing this polarity and empowering the worker.
7 Direct work with child victims involves detailed exploration of
intimate and distressing issues around sexuality. For example,
the acting-out through sexualised behaviour, which affects many
sexually abused children, can be directed at the social worker.
Dealing with this sensitively is not easy and it is imperative that
workers, both female and male, can talk out the very personal
effects on them within the setting of a safe team and in supervision.

Work with mothers

It is our contention that learning to work effectively with mothers
who do not, or cannot, believe that their children have been sexually
abused, is the biggest and most critical challenge facing workers. Our
experience is that such mothers can induce in us strong feelings
of helplessness, despair and frustration, and yet the responses of
mothers at the point of disclosure are central to decisions about protection and thereafter to the prognosis for the child's recovery.

Moreover, given the deficiencies of the care system, and the vulnerability of sexually abused children within it, even when children
are not believed inside their families, it is increasingly necessary to
look first at the alliance of mother and child and to mobilise the
means of facilitating the mother's continued support of the child.
However, this must be prefaced by an assessment of why the mother
is unable to believe her child has been abused and whether it is safe to
keep mother and child together.

In our assessment of, and work with mothers of abused children,
we are clear that it is not they but the perpetrators of the abusive acts
who are responsible for what has happened to their children. The
issue to address, therefore, is not so much one of 'failing to protect'
but one of establishing the expectations of mothers as responsible
parents. In this, problematic gaps in parenting can comprise behaviours such as not believing children who try to tell what is happening
to them, being unable or unwilling to act in the child's best interests,
or exposing a child to further risk.

Most of the literature, and our own experience, suggest that it is
not a lottery as to which mothers will believe their children when they
disclose sexual abuse. Many workers report that where children are
the victims of sexual abuse, problematic relationships are often
observed between these children and their mothers (for example,
Nelson, 1987; Walker, Bonner and Kauffman, 1988). Specifically it

is regularly reported that there is emotional or physical distance and a lack of what are viewed as maternal protective behaviours which 'contributes to the difficulty that children have in breaking out of the abusive bind' (Glaser and Frosh, 1988). In our experience where these problems are most active, and where there remains a strong emotional tie to the perpetrator, a mother has the most difficulty in believing and coming to terms with, the abuse of her children.

Giving mothers a therapeutic opportunity to deal with their feelings about what has happened is necessary, both for their emotional survival and growth and so that they can provide parenting for their children. The position of mothers of sexually abused children may be likened to the grieving process. Those mothers who are unable to believe their children can be seen as being in a state of arrested grief. They are stuck in denial. In the same way that a bereaved person needs to move through the various stages of mourning, mothers of sexually abused children need to be enabled to move through their grieving if they are not to stay stuck in the denial stage.

Additionally, issues of the mother's own sexual victimisation may surface during treatment and these also need to be addressed in some depth if the mother is to make progress in supporting her own child. It is therefore vital that treatment services for mothers attend to both their sense of loss, helplessness and guilt, as well as to the problems in the relationships with their children. In providing this, groupwork can be a very helpful approach. (Erooga and Masson, 1989). As Glaser and Frosh (1988) observe, 'Groups offer particularly suitable settings for helping sexually abused children, their parents and even abusers. This is in large part due to the central defining characteristics of the group, the *collective* aspect, which offers an alternative experience to the isolation, secretiveness and shame that is central to child sexual abuse.' However, it remains a problem that mothers who most vehemently deny the possibility of sexual abuse to their children, also deny their eligibility to join such a group. Sponsors in the form of other mothers who have 'survived' similar experiences can often provide essential crisis support for those mothers isolated by their decision to believe and support the adult perpetrator, rather than the child. The considerable support and treatment services necessary for these mothers requires a partnership between professionals and lay input, something which has largely been missing from our approach to physical abuse and neglect.

However, where formal treatment offers are not taken up there is clearly a need to mobilize community resources for mothers in these situations and the 'live-in sponsor' which is being tried in some parts of this country is worthy of further exploration. The provision of crisis support, especially from other mothers who have been through the process of arrested grief and thence been able to believe and

support the child, may hold out the best hope, if matched by treatment services, of gaining movement with mothers who are stuck in
shock, disbelief and isolation. If we accept that mothers are crucial to
the recovery of children from sexual abuse, then progress in this area
could reduce the need to remove so many children into care and
increase the prospects for their healing.

Work with perpetrators

It is vital that a response to child sexual abuse includes work with
perpetrators, for treating them is a major contribution to the prevention of child sexual abuse. Research indicates that men who abuse
children, either within or outside their family, abuse large numbers
of children throughout their lives. Therefore both control and treatment are essential elements of any response to perpetrators. Some
workers involved with children are resistant to this idea, either
because they identify with their client, the child, and feel angry at the
prospect of the men being 'helped' rather than punished, or because
they do not think that treatment can be effective. However, as Judith
Becker (1988) observes, the original impetus for developing work
with perpetrators came from those working with victims, who saw
treating perpetrators as the only way to break the chain of treating
the consequence of abuse, the victims, rather than the abuser.

In Rochdale we have, with the local probation service, run a 12
month group with men who have sexually abused children, (Morrison et al., 1989) and are currently running a second group. The basic
premise of these groups, and of our other work with perpetrators, is a
view of child sexual abuse as an addictive cycle of deviant and com-
pulsive behaviour. Because of the addictive component, the risk of
re-offending is very high, and treatment is aimed at controlling, rather
than curing, behaviour with the risk of recidivism being life-long.

Assessment

A lack of information about the extent of individual perpetrator's
activity and the addictive nature of sexual abuse has led both social
work professionals and the criminal justice system to underestimate
the level of risk presented by perpetrators, and to make inappropriate decisions in case conference and sentencing respectively. As
well as a need for treatment, therefore, is the need for assessment of
risk in individual cases, to provide the necessary information on
which to base decisions which can assist in the protection of children.
Our initial experiences have shown that such assessments, undertaken over a relatively short period of time, possibly two or three
interviews, are usually sufficient to identify the individual cycle of

abusive behaviour, in itself indicative of the level of risk presented, and the extent to which the man is able to take responsibility for his behaviour, usually low at the outset, and his motivation to undertake a treatment programme. These brief structured assessments are carried out jointly with colleagues from the local probation service.

Multi-disciplinary context

Child sexual abuse is often characterised by secrecy and with this, as with all areas of child abuse, comes the danger of professional relationships mirroring those of the clients with whom they are working. Thus, a 'worst case' example would be of professionals working with perpetrators, but mirroring the position of their clients by being both isolated and invoking a veil of secrecy over the work they are undertaking. To prevent mirroring, and to ensure co-ordination to maximise children's protection, multidisciplinary co-operation in this field is particularly important. The primary agency for working with child sexual abuse perpetrators, because of their unique role in working with offenders, is the probation service, though we would suggest that to maintain perspective it is also important to involve one or more of the child protection agencies in work being undertaken. It is similarly important to include those professionals involved with other family members when embarking on a selection of contracting process with individual perpetrators, both to empower the individual workers and also to ensure that other family members' views and needs are taken into account. It is also important for representatives from the probation service to either attend, or have access to, minutes from child sexual abuse case conferences where they are likely to be preparing a social inquiry report, so that they can have accurate information about the nature of the abuse which has occurred, rather than solely relying on the man's own description. All of these steps ensure that *working with perpetrators starts from the victim's perspective.*

Because of the power and control elements of sexual abuse, and the high level of denial and minimisation which takes place, in both assessments and group work there is a need for structure with a high degree of therapeutic control. For many professionals this can initially be an uncomfortable style of work, but one in which it is important to gain skills, whilst avoiding the pitfall of becoming punitive, if the chances of successful intervention are to be maximised.

In terms of the content of therapeutic work, it is essential from the outset to establish that deviant sexual arousal is a major focus of the work, and that acknowledgement of the sexual element of the abuse is essential if work is to proceed. Key issues would usually include confronting denial and acknowledging responsibility, the denial usually following through a process of minimisation and rationalisation; an in-depth examination of the offences themselves, the preparation for and subsequent fantasies about the abuse; the exercise of control and power during the abuse and ultimately personal responsibility for the abuse all require attention. Issues which are also crucial concern the use and abuse of power, individual men's own deviancy cycle, developing an awareness about their victims and attitudes to women in general. Work on feelings and communication is an important element, as for many men the expression of personal feeling is something in which they have poor skills.

The amount of work which is necessary for individual men to significantly diminish the risk they present to children is becoming increasingly clear. Most American programmes entail at least a two year commitment and provide open invitations to return for treatment at any point. Neither 'persecuting' nor supporting perpetrators changes them, but treatment may do so. One thing about which we can be sure, however, is that offering perpetrators no treatment maintains the removal of abused victims, rather than the abusers, as the first line of protection, a position that only inflicts further trauma on already traumatised children.

Family work

There has been much debate about the place of family work in the treatment of sexual abuse, particularly its relationship to individual and group work. This debate needs to continue. At present our experience of perpetrators suggests strongly that they should not be part of the whole family sessions until, and unless, a number of preconditions have been satisfied. These start with the informed agreement of the victim, and of the non-abusing parent and children in the family. In parallel, the perpetrator must have made substantial progress in his own therapeutic work towards identifying and intervening in his own cycle of abuse, completely accepting his responsibility for the abuse and understanding the damage to the victim.

The premature use of whole family sessions risks repeating the abusive dynamics of control, power and secrecy. It also distracts the perpetrator from looking at the sexual component of the abuse, which cannot be tackled in front of the victim.

Family sessions do have a role in treatment, but more as a prelude to reconstructing the family rather than the starting point for treatment. Sadly it is our experience that few perpetrators can be safely reintegrated with their families.

Conclusion

We have attempted to provide some understanding of the climate in which we are currently dealing with child sexual abuse, from the perspective of a child protection team, dealing with investigation, assessment and treatment. At times progress appears to be made, whilst at others it feels more like a process of surviving the storms. We are acutely conscious of how much more there is to be done, but remain pessimistic as to whether society really wants to provide either the resources or the mandate to do the job properly. 'Protect the children without changing society' appears to be the message.

Perhaps such thoughts are overly pessimistic and maybe they are not the reality. What is real is that working with child sexual abuse carries with it the constant threat that we could become another group of victims. It is only by working as a team, with a shared belief system and support for each other, that we preserve our determination that we will not become victims of this work, both because of the personal cost if we do so, and because powerless professionals cannot protect children.

5 Healing action— action methods with children who have been sexually abused

Anne Bannister

Jean runs a Centre for children and families who are experiencing some kind of crisis. She told me about Jamie, a four year old who had lived with his grandmother for most of his life. Now grandmother had died and each day, at the Centre, Jamie continually re-enacted her illness and death using a doll to represent grandma. Sometimes he played a doctor, sometimes he was himself, but a young nursery nurse was worried that Jamie continued to do this each day. She thought it was morbid and he should be encouraged to play other games. Jean, who has years of experience in working with young children, advised her colleague to encourage the game for as long as Jamie needed it and she asked me what I thought of this advice. I agreed wholeheartedly and added that the nurse could offer to join in the game, if Jamie would allow it, and perhaps Jamie could then be allowed to reverse roles with his grandmother and the nurse could play Jamie. Jamie (played by the nurse) could then tell grandma (played by Jamie) how much he missed her and ask for advice on what to do. Grandma might be able to provide some comforting advice and roles could then be reversed again so that Jamie actually received the comforting advice from the nurse playing grandma. Since the suggestions came from the child in the first place this would be far more powerful than any kind of reassurance that the nursery nurse might have given alone.

This 'role reversal' is a basic principle of psychodrama and is used in many action techniques such as drama therapy, play therapy and simple role-playing. Jean understood that a child needs to replay the traumas in life in order to understand them, to express feelings about them, and to integrate them into everyday life. As counsellors we may be well aware that bereaved adults need to talk about the person who has died. Children, too, need this but often talking is insufficient and since play is a child's normal means of communication then 'playing' or 'enacting' is the natural way for a child to begin the process of healing.

Children who have been sexually abused have suffered a trauma which may be similar to bereavement in some respects, with some important differences. There is likely to be extreme anxiety and maybe depression, although sometimes the child appears more angry than depressed. There will be the same sense of loss and of guilt and tremendous feelings of betrayal. One difference is that the abused child will probably be eroticised and this may show in sexualised behaviour. Another difference is that the abused child may have been moulded into a victim role which will not be easy to overcome in other areas of life. Conversely, the child may have become rigidly controlling of others. This is an adaptive mechanism where a child seeks to gain at least some control in a situation which feels beyond control.

Adam and Alice Blatner (Blatner and Blatner, 1988) remind us that it is a well-known principle of play therapy that children need to triumph over persecuting others, whether real or fantasy. Only when the child experiences a sense of mastery can he admit and feel his vulnerability. Most of us who have worked with children for many years are familiar with the child's eagerness to instigate 'monster play'. The abused child nearly always seeks to play the monster first of all since it is the monster who is powerful. After he is allowed to express this power by 'zapping' the other players, whether they are dolls, puppets or the therapist, then the child may be ready to play the victim himself, and to talk about the experience of abuse.

The expression 'act-hunger' is one used by Dr J.L. Moreno, the creator of psychodrama and sociometry. It means the intense need that lies within us to act out our life problems. Freud does not actually use this expression but describes similarly how people often rearrange their lives, after a traumatic event, in a way which ensures that the event will be repeated. It is as if we say to ourselves, 'just let me play it again, this time I'll get it right'. Family therapists are familiar with patterns of behaviour which repeat through generations of families. Perhaps this is an unconscious inter-generational 'act-hunger', where we repeat the mistakes made by our parents though we may consciously have been striving to do just the opposite.

If this re-enactment can be addressed in therapy and if the child can be offered choices about future behaviour, then it is possible to break this self-defeating cycle. To be admitted into a child's world, to join in his creativity, to share his own power and pain, is a privilege that we cannot take for granted. Alice Miller (Miller, 1987) suggests that if a sexually abused child is to survive without personality damage then a trusting relationship with an adult is essential. It does not matter whether the adult is a relative, social worker, teacher, doctor or nurse, but if that person can enable the child to express feelings and to feel valued then the seeds of healing will be sown.

This relationship must have many facets though if it is to be truly therapeutic. Imparting knowledge may be a part of the relationship but it is not sufficient just to be a teacher; the child may have many things to teach the worker. Making sure the child is protected is vital if there is to be healing; but the child protector needs to allow the child space to learn how to protect himself in future. Like the doctor/patient relationship the child must have confidence that the adult has the skills to help in the healing process; the worker must follow the child's agenda, however, and not seek to impose a method, or 'cure', which the child finds unacceptable.

Lucy Berliner, in an address to a conference in Glasgow in June 1988, suggested that the therapeutic relationship can enable a child to see that people exist who will not betray her when she reveals her vulnerability. Of course, the experience of group therapy can also be an important factor in helping children cope with feelings of betrayal. Berliner also stresses that therapy with children who have been sexually abused should be directive. This may come as a shock to those who feel therapy should always be non-directive. Action techniques may be very directive in that they use the material the client offers and then deliberately channel it so that a specific problem can be addressed. Carl Rogers' client centred therapy can also be used in this way. The therapist (perhaps by role reversal) feels what it is like to be the client. The client corrects the assumptions and so is able to fully express her own feelings.

Children can understand this well. 'You be me', they often say, 'and I'll be the monster'. 'I'm frightened', I say, (as the child) 'I'm going to tell mummy'. 'No you're not', says the child. 'Mummy will be cross, you're feeling mad'. If we are using puppets in our enactment the child may then attack my puppet. Because the child has told me that I'm 'feeling mad', I respond to the monster's attack with gusto and a battle (which did not happen in the real abusive situation) ensues. My child puppet may eventually lose the battle for this is the element of realism. But next time we play the game the child may want to play herself and actually express some of her anger that she could not do at the time of the abuse.

The relationship then, between child and worker, must be fully trusting; it must give sufficient control to the child and yet it must contain clear limits and boundaries. Many sexually abused children have become eroticised or have not learned appropriate sexual boundaries. Children who expose their genitals or try to touch the therapist's private parts should be gently but firmly told that such behaviour is not allowed. This can be used positively in the session if we go on to explain that our body is our own and that 'it's OK to say no'.

Sometimes a child may express feelings of love towards the offender, especially if he is a close family member. The therapist must listen to this, perhaps repeating what the child says. 'You sometimes feel love for your dad'. The child nods, not sure whether she 'ought' to feel this. 'Let's look at some of the loving things he did', suggests the therapist, going on to explore the relationship more fully. The child may be worried about physiological responses to sexual activity, and this may be guilt-inducing. 'I enjoyed some of it so it must have been my fault'. These can be explained in a matter-of-fact way in an effort to reduce guilt.

Telling a child 'It's not your fault', is something nearly always advocated to those working with sexual abuse. It is important that this is done, and that the child is fully confident that the therapist is not judgemental. A child full of guilt will very easily feel judged unless the worker makes her own stance very clear. Simply stating 'it's not your fault', is, of course, not enough for a therapeutic relationship. This is the 'instructive' part of the relationship which then must move on to explore the guilt. It is necessary to discover exactly what areas the child feels guilty about and to look carefully together at whether any of the guilt may be justified. Unless we are prepared to do this, the child may not tell us if she has gone on to abuse others for instance. It is vital to know this but a child may feel too intimidated to tell if the worker is too insistent on complete innocence. The child feels 'If I tell she won't like me and I need her to like me'.

In fact total acceptance of the child is an obvious part of the therapeutic relationship although we do not have to accept behaviour which is violent or damaging to others. This all-embracing acceptance will be challenged frequently by the child, of course. In any adult/child relationship the child tests out limits and boundaries and the responsible adult places these neither too close and restricting nor too far away and loose. An abused child may challenge acceptance even more strongly. If guilt and anger are high on the child's list of feelings he may already have been labelled 'naughty child' and have come to believe it himself. Alternatively some children are so anxious to please that they are almost paralysed in case they should do anything which would be unacceptable.

Both these extremes of behaviour, the excessive desire to please and the 'I don't care about anyone' attitude are symptoms of the damage that is done to children by abusers. A child who is abused has her feelings negated constantly. 'Don't do that' she says to the abuser 'It's OK' replies the abuser, 'That's yucky' she says, 'No, it's nice' responds the abuser, 'It hurts' she cries, he denies it. Every time she has a feeling, the abuser, who is a powerful 'grown up', tells her she is wrong. No wonder adults abused as children say that they don't know who they are or what they feel. The task of the therapist is to allow the feelings to surface again and to confirm that it is all right to feel fear, pain, anger or tears.

Moreno (Moreno, 1987) commented that children play out psychodramatic roles as a means of preparing for social roles. We can see this happening in school playgrounds, in nurseries and even in youth clubs as adolescents test out different roles according to their group preference. Young children will admit adults to this role playing game quite easily. Usually they are delighted that a 'grown up' will play their game and they eagerly instruct the worker on the 'rules'. Naivety is an important aspect of the therapist's demeanour. An abused child takes control as she places the worker in a role. Older children (8–12) are more inhibited and need permission for active play. Once this is understood they will initiate quite complicated games, often using story-book characters. Adolescents may react differently according to the mechanism they have adopted to cope with their abuse. Many older children, especially girls, take on a 'victim' role and so will seldom initiate but will agree with the therapist's suggestions. This should be handled with care since it is important that the child does not feel further victimised. Other children, often boys but also some girls, take a rigid controlling stance and are determined to reject any suggestions the worker might make. In both cases it is important to try to follow the child's agenda. Suggesting drawing or writing instead of just talking may facilitate this. Then we might talk about how we express anger — through the mouth (shouting or singing), through our arms (throwing things or hitting), or through our feet (running, walking or kicking). This can lead to demonstrations and body language in general can be discussed. The teenager is often an expert at understanding the meaning of bodily signals such as 'hair over the face', 'mask-like make-up', 'punk clothes', and so on.

Role playing can be introduced with older children by being open to images that form for the therapist whilst the child speaks. An adolescent girl was talking to me about her abuse. I said that it felt as if the abuser was a great bear who could sometimes give friendly hugs but had the potential for squeezing and smothering to death. The child was responsive to this image so we acted it out. At first there were tears and pain as the feelings overwhelmed the girl but gradually, through role reversal, she was able to make the bear dance to her tune and so gain control. In addition, by playing the bear herself the girl showed great power. Feeling this power is an essential part of therapy. This 'role-relief' is also a rehearsal for assuming a more powerful role in future with an abuser or potential abuser.

For older children straight role-reversal with the abusing parent or a non-abusing parent can be very helpful. The child may learn to forgive herself as she recognises the parents' power. Sometimes, too, she may be able to forgive the parents as she understands their motivation.

Many children, though, prefer to keep a symbolic distance from real life roles. Those experienced in child care will be familiar with a child who projects its own experience onto another child. 'It wasn't me, it was him', is the most common expression but other children have an imaginary friend who takes the blame for all misdemeanours. Abused children often prefer to describe the abuse in the third person. 'It happened to the little boy', 'It was the little girl's grandad', and so on.

The Cleveland Report (Butler-Sloss, 1988) expressed unease at the interpretation of what it calls 'fantasy play' in doing disclosure work with children. It recognises, however, the value of this work from a therapeutic viewpoint. I would prefer the expression 'symbolic play' since fantasy play implies something that is completely divorced from reality. Of course children do indulge in fantasy play (so do adults) but in a therapeutic session, where feelings are being encouraged and expression is facilitated, the play is almost certain to be symbolic. With experience, it is fairly easy to judge from a child's level of feeling whether the play contains elements of symbolism. I would agree with Justice Butler-Sloss that an interpretation of this cannot be used in an 'diagnosis' of sexual abuse, but it is often a very important precursor to disclosure. As I have commented earlier in this chapter, the child needs to express power before admitting his own vulnerability.

Marguerite Parish (Parish, 1953) describes how she used the story of Hansel and Gretel for two children who were leaving treatment. Peter Rowan in a psychodrama session in Washington DC in which I took part, successfully used the story of the Ugly Duckling to help a girl who had problems with body images. This might easily be used in child abuse work since many sexually abused children have problems with body image and self-esteem. I was introduced by an 11 year old to a story about a naughty witch who broke her broomstick and was attacked by the wicked witch but consoled by the good witch. Through this I was able to resolve some distance that had arisen between this abused child and her mother and also to sort out some problems between the child and her sister who had also been abused.

It is important when using symbolism always to follow the child's agenda, and this principle, of course, stands throughout the work. The experience I have described above arose when I asked the child what she liked doing with her mother. She replied 'Having her read me a story'. So I asked her which was her favourite and the action led on from there. A child could be asked to bring a favourite book or to draw a favourite story but there must be no attempt to impose a story which the worker feels is symbolic. The symbolism can only come from the child. The therapist's interpretation may be incorrect or irrelevant. It is not necessary to discuss the symbolism with a child. What is important is that the child has expressed feeling and, maybe, found a resolution. Violet Oaklander (Oaklander, 1978) points to the dangers of interpreting children's drawings. She uses Gestalt techniques to encourage the child to talk about the drawing and to say how he feels about what he has drawn. The therapist's interpretation of a drawing may be correct but if this is given to the child it may prevent the child from giving his own interpretation. Oaklander asks children to do abstract drawings of their world and then encourages them to experience what it is like to be each part of the drawing. Since abused children often aim to please it would be unproductive to suggest to a child what the drawing represented.

A 6 year old made many drawings with me during a year of therapy. She first came to me in October when her class at school had been discussing Halloween. She drew herself sombre, in black, in her house (see figure 5.1). In the garden was something she described as 'a black witch in a black hole'. She drew a similar black hole next to the figure of herself and 'a black hole under my knickers' between her legs. I asked her what the witch felt like in the hole and she said 'Lonely, and frightened'. The girl at this time had been removed from her home where her father had been sexually abusing her for some time. There is no need for interpretation here, it seems fairly obvious, but the picture helped the child to say how she was feeling and to start talking about her feelings of being wicked and bad. (Her father had told her she was 'possessed by evil spirits'.)

Later she drew her family, omitting herself from the drawing but including a sad mother, a wickedly smiling father and two smiling little brothers who were protected by a quilt drawn in bright colours (see Figure 5.2). I asked her about the quilt, 'It takes care of the boys' she said, 'No-one will hurt them because they are boys. But I'm a girl'. I asked who took care of her, 'No-one' she said, surprised that I had asked. It was many months later when she was able to express anger against her mother. On that occasion she took a green 'monster' doll that was in the playroom and stood it high on a shelf whilst lecturing it on its lack of responsibility. Afterwards she hid it amongst other toys, saying it was in the 'dungeons'.

Figure 5.1

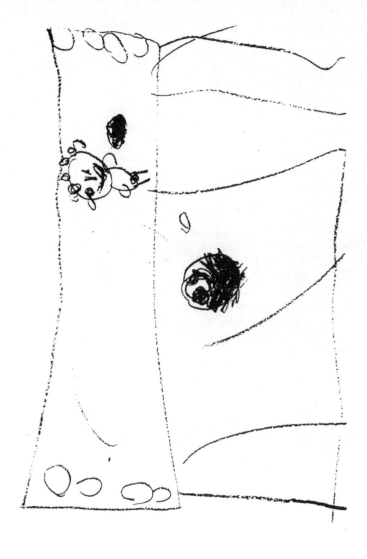

Figure 5.2

Figure 5.3

Figure 5.4

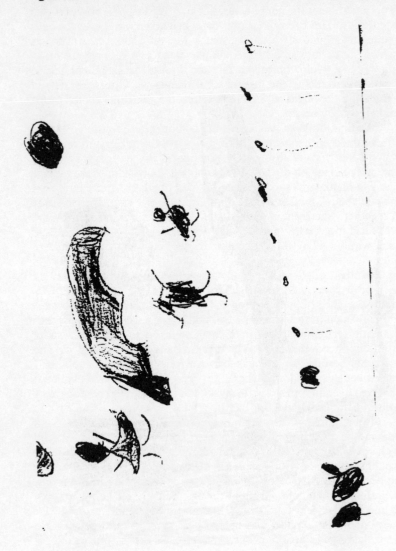

The next drawing, soon after the family picture, was a colourful representation of the house where she had lived with her parents (see Figure 5.3). Her bedroom window was blacked out and over the bedrooms and around the house was much angry red scribble. Anger was starting to surface at last. She had presented as a very angelic looking, 'pretty' child, but given to violent tantrums in school and at home when she would use obscene language. Once she started expressing the anger in therapy sessions the tantrums cooled down and eventually ceased.

The final drawing was also quite colourful (see figure 5.4). The sun beamed on her picture of 'a lovely holiday'. Her future foster parents (not yet a reality) were vague figures in the center of the picture with herself on the left. Flowers filled the bottom of the picture and two blank circles in the sky were described as 'some clouds that are still about'. A large red arc dominated the drawing. We looked at it together. She seemed pleased and satisfied. I was puzzled by the arc. I had to ask what it was. 'That's the bridge I have to go over' she said, without a trace of self-consciousness. She was then seven years old.

Dorothy Langley (Langley, 1984) writes that metaphor is used by each of us every day, mostly unconsciously as we make statements about ourselves. Like me, Dorothy is a dramatherapist and psychodramatist and in this article she reminds us of a well-known psychodramatic technique. The protagonist is asked to describe a room from childhood and to become a significant object within it. The metaphor becomes apparent as the protagonist becomes that object. I remember a psychodrama where the protagonist became an old 'hope chest' or 'wedding chest' with a crack in its lid. She was working on a split in her own marriage at the time.

With children we can use metaphor in very practical ways. An 8 year old boy had been seriously abused both physically and sexually by his father. Fear seemed to sit in the room with us as we played. He would start to play with one toy then move quickly to another before he became involved. He was suspicious of everything in the room, including me. He told me about the children's home he was staying in and how he went round with the staff in the evening making sure every door and window was locked, 'So my dad can't get in'. He drew the blinds carefully in our playroom, 'So that no-one will know I'm here'. Fear was his chief emotion and so we stuck with it, talking about things that made him frightened. I shared some of the things that scare me too. He wandered off to a pile of puppets in the corner and selected a black capped and robed figure and proceeded to menace me with it, swooping down on me with the puppet in his hand, but never coming too close. I showed my fear and ran away, to get help in the form of a friendly dog puppet.

The black robed puppet was sent to prison from which he escaped. By this time the boy was playing himself and the dog and the fearsome person in turn, on his own initiative. The fearsome one suffered several 'deaths' from which he miraculously recovered. The play went on for a long time and we were both exhausted. Eventually the fearsome puppet ended up under a sand-bag. 'A big heavy rock' was how the boy described it. Not yet brave enough to sit on the rock himself, he asked me to do so. Trust was beginning to form and perhaps a belief in my power. Suspicion had been dispelled. The session proceeded with the boy talking graphically and painfully about his experiences of abuse. Fear had been 'squashed' by our joint efforts. The metaphor was clear.

Claudia Jewett (Jewett, 1982) also uses children's symbolic play. She suggests that if a child plays repeatedly in a particular way and the meaning is not clear then the child should be asked about feelings. For instance, if a child is enacting a meal with parents and children, perhaps in the doll's house, the child could be asked how the mummy feels or what one of the children is thinking. Jewett also recommends giving a child a 'fable' such as 'Here is a little boy who is very afraid; what is he afraid of?' This is similar to the techniques in the Anti-Colouring Book (Striker and Kimmel, 1978) which has unfinished drawings for children to complete. One drawing suggests the child should draw 'the worst nightmare', for example.

Sometimes the worker can collude with the child to keep 'secrets' either about the abuse or about feelings. The worker may recognise the symbolism of a child's play but may never try to bring it towards reality 'in case the child is upset'. I often think that workers are protecting their own feelings rather than the child's. One little boy repeatedly placed a boy doll in a cradle and then attacked it with 'a daddy doll'. The child looked tearful whenever he started the attack and so the worker picked up the 'baby' and said she would protect it. The boy immediately stopped the action and moved on to play with something else. It was suggested to the worker that next time she should allow the attack to continue but express sympathy with the baby. 'Poor little boy, he must be feeling very frightened and lonely' she said as the 'daddy doll' attacked the baby again. The boy began to cry, as he had not done before. He seemed to experience relief from his pain and was able to start to share his feelings with the worker.

Sometimes it is important to be quite direct with a child. Drawings of faces, sad, smiling, angry, etc., can be shown to a child who is asked 'Which face shows what you are feeling now?' Symbolic play can be brought to reality by asking, 'Has anything like that ever happened to you?' But care should be taken not to ask this too soon. Sexual abuse is always part of a secret and it is important that the child knows that it can be talked about. Just sharing with the child that I have talked to many children who have had similar experiences is a start to breaking the net of secrecy.

The order of therapy can often be extremely important. The child who could not express his fear and pain was not facilitated by the worker who rushed to protect him. Similarly, a child should not be encouraged to consider forgiveness of the offender until she has expressed her own anger and until she is clear that the responsibility for the abuse is with him. Forgiveness is usually a two-way process, part of a relationship. Children are sometimes eager to re-establish a relationship with the offender often because they feel that they need forgiveness for 'having told the secret'. Some children may also be under pressure to forgive from the non-abusing parent.

This underlines the necessity for working at the child's pace. This does not mean that all confrontation is avoided or that the worker never initiates action. Creativity is the root of all therapy. The child's own creativity must be allowed expression and must be encouraged. The worker may contribute her own ideas, indeed these may be vital if the child is blocked by fear, anger or pain, but bringing a child too quickly from the symbolic to the concrete is unlikely to be helpful.

The frequency and length of therapy sessions will vary for each child but young children need to be seen once or even twice a week at first. Although a child's attention span may be less than twenty minutes such a short session does not give space for the necessary therapeutic structure, so sessions lasting one hour are more productive. During the hour children will automatically take 'time out' for short periods of rest or free play and this is, of course, allowed and encouraged. Most sessions will have a three part structure of reassurance, re-enactment and rehearsal. The reassurance phase helps to build the therapeutic relationship, the re-enactment of trauma is the actively therapeutic part of the session and the rehearsal is preparation for future behaviour, including the sample closing rituals that children may use to finish a session and to ensure that they can come again. The number of sessions will depend on how traumatised the child is by the abuse, what kind of adaptive mechanisms she has used to protect herself and how supported she is by close family and friends.

As I have illustrated, Post Traumatic Stress Disorder (Horowitz, 1976) can manifest itself in many ways. Acute anxiety and depression is common and may lead to further victimisation. Other children avoid discussion of the abuse and may be resistant to therapy, sometimes adolescents seek relief in substance abuse instead. A smaller number of children may show disorganised and psychotic behaviour and a few can become aggressive, exploiting others and exhibiting delinquent behaviour (Hartman and Burgess, 1988).

Many children will respond well after five or six sessions. Anxiety and depression can be relieved, 'acting-out' or aggressive behaviour is reduced and confidence is increased. For the improvement to continue however there must be constant support and monitoring and, at times of further stress, therapeutic input may be increased. It is most helpful, therefore, if the child's mother or carer can be introduced into the sessions eventually so that she can understand the kind of support she needs to give. A non-abusing parent whose partner is the abuser, may have many therapeutic needs of her own and it is important that these are addressed, if possible before she is asked to assist her child. For many children the kind of support that she can give is vital for their continuing improvement. On the other hand a non-abusing parent who has many unmet needs of her own may tip the precarious balance unfavourably and prevent a child from receiving help. A simple illustration of this occurred when a 7 year old boy was heavily avoiding all discussion or re-enactment of the abuse and he was even denying that it had happened although he had previously made a full statement to police and social workers about abuse by a babysitter. After two unproductive sessions the therapist asked the social worker to work more deeply with the mother to discover her feelings. It was discovered that mother was still shocked and full of guilt. She had not been able to discuss this with anyone since her husband had mistakenly tried to 'protect' her from it and had himself conducted all the previous discussions with police, social workers and therapist. After the mother shared her feelings with the worker she was able to talk a little to her son who then came into the third session showing relief and looking more relaxed. The next two sessions were most productive and the mother then had a joint session with the therapist prior to continuing the work herself.

Case example

The following case illustrates many of the techniques and attitudes of the therapeutic model which I have evolved and which I have attempted to describe in this chapter. Like all the examples given, names, details of the abuse and abuser and sometimes the age or sex of the child have been changed in order to protect those children who have come to the NSPCC for help in the past ten years.

Michelle was 7 years old when she was referred to the Sexual Abuse Unit. Her elder sister, Tracey, aged 12, had disclosed that she had been abused by an uncle, father's brother, for the past five or six years. A medical examination had confirmed that intercourse had taken place. Tracey and Michelle were already in care when Tracey told her foster mother what had happened. This was a voluntary placement because the children's father had died recently and their mother was in hospital with a terminal illness.

Michelle had also been medically examined and the anal dilatation test was positive indicating that she may have been anally abused. She had not disclosed anything however, and Tracey felt that her sister had not been abused. Michelle's behaviour in school had been causing some problems. She had been showing her genitals to other children in the class and, on one occasion, alarmed a male teacher by rubbing herself against the front of his trousers.

In the first therapy session Michelle seemed disorganised and confused. She soon noticed a baby's feeding bottle full of orange juice and asked what it was for. 'For children to have a drink', I said. She poured orange juice out of a toy teapot into a cup and looked at it thoughtfully. 'Only for little kids?' she asked. 'No, any kids' I replied. She politely offered me some orange juice from a cup. Within five minutes she was drinking from the bottle and she carried it around for the session.

Again and again she took the toy ambulance to the doll's house and put 'the poorly man' inside it and took him to hospital. 'The little girl' remained in the house 'all alone and sad'. The 'poorly man' died and 'the little girl and her sister' cried.

Michelle re-enacted her father's death several times in the following sessions and she regressed by sucking the bottle. Mother did not figure largely in the re-enactment. There seemed to be no protective figure except Tracey. Michelle's act-hunger seemed to be directed at the death of father and her need to return to babyhood when, perhaps, she had felt protected by him. Soon she was able to express her anger. Using puppets she instigated a game where she became very powerful, deciding who should live and who should die amongst her friends and members of her family. Only Tracey and some new friends survived the holocaust each time. Father sometimes lived and sometimes received the death sentence. She thoroughly enjoyed this game and insisted upon it in each session but at other times she would revert to her more familiar 'victim' role. Once she made a baby 'called Michelle' from modelling clay and placed it in a cradle and hung it from a tree. She sang 'Rock a Bye Baby' softly and sadly. Baby Michelle fell from the clay cradle and out of the clay tree as she sang 'When the bough breaks, the cradle will fall'. 'No-one can help the baby' she said.

She introduced a ritual into the sessions, counting the posters on the walls before she left. She drew several drawings of a man with a large penis between his legs and carefully cut up the drawing and dropped it into a 'secrets box' in the therapy room. Eventually, she began to talk about her father's abuse of her and also about how he had been the main carer because of her mother's illness.

She saw an episode of *The Lion, the Witch and the Wardrobe* (Lewis, 1981) on television and asked to act it out, taking the part, at first, of one of the children who rescues the Lion. Then she insisted on playing the Witch, a very powerful person who had control over everyone. Eventually, having experienced the power of the Witch she was able to play the character with whom she really identified — the Lion. In Michelle's enactment the Lion was strong and brave and able to help others. The Lion suffered when the Witch tied him up (disempowered him) but his friends helped to rescue him and they thanked him for allowing himself to be caught because this protected them. With puppets we held a closing ceremony. All the friends admired Michelle's strength and power and also her kindness. The Witch was dead so the Lion dug a hole and buried her. Michelle's healing had begun.

Conclusion

Action methods are a way of harnessing the natural techniques children use to heal themselves. The method can pre-empt or overcome certain defenses which may turn out to be harmful to the child in the long term. Because the method is child/client centred it is unlikely that there will be any negative repercussions over a period. It is true that the child's behaviour is sometimes regressive for a short period while the work is proceeding. In my experience this behaviour usually disappears as the work progresses. Most children very much enjoy the sessions and try to prolong them. The self-control and self-expression which the method offers is of specific help to anyone who has been abused. It avoids the trap of therapist imposed interpretation which is often bitterly resented by abused children as they grow older. The methods described in this chapter have referred mainly to 'one-to-one' work but, of course, most dramatherapy and psychodrama is conducted in group sessions. I have successfully used the methods with abused adolescents and adults in group settings.

6 Developing anti-racist practice—problems and possibilities

Paul Stubbs

As debates about the sexual abuse of children reach an hitherto unknown intensity in Britain, and the academic literature grows at an ever increasing pace, one silence remains. From reading many of the key texts and articles on the subject, one could be forgiven for forgetting that Britain is, and long has been, a multi-ethnic society. In many texts, the issue of the sexual abuse of black children is ignored completely. In others the issue rates a token mention, only to be filed away to be returned to on another, unspecified, occasion by other, unspecified, writers. My suggestion in this chapter is that this silence is significant and not a simple problem of omission which can be remedied by merely adding 'race' on to existing analyses. Rather, the issue of services for black children, families and communities raises, in a particularly acute form, general issues about the kinds of frameworks necessary to develop a sophisticated, child centred, approach to the sexual abuse of children.

It must be stated at the outset this chapter is not an attempt to arm social workers with a tried and tested formula with which to produce effective, measurable, improvements in practice. Rather, in raising some of the complexities and dilemmas which face social workers in this difficult and contentious area, I hope to open up a number of issues for discussion and debate. Unfortunately, in this as in so many other issues in social work, uncertainty is all there is. This is a message which does not fit easily into a managerial culture interested only in solutions to problems.

For myself, this chapter is framed in terms of two guiding principles without which I do not feel it is possible to discuss these issues adequately. The first of these principles is the necessity of framing discussion in terms of a recognition that Britain is not merely a multi-ethnic society but also a profoundly racist one in which black people daily face a systematic oppression which severely limits their life chances and opportunities. In addition, we must address the realities of racism within those agencies charged with intervening in the sexual abuse arena.

Secondly, and following on from this, we must strive constantly to develop anti-racist practices in our work. Again, this cannot be a once-and-for-all achievement but, rather, must be an ongoing process opening up social work and social workers to a previously unheard of accountability to black people and communities which may, in fact, be profoundly threatening to their professional identities. This, in essence is the argument which Lena Dominelli develops in her book *Anti-racist Social Work* (Dominelli, 1988), and which I propound in my recently completed PhD thesis on *The Reproduction of Racism in State Social Work* (Stubbs, 1988a).

My doctoral research, which included a study of child care policy and practice in two inner London social services departments, did not directly address the issue of the sexual abuse of children. This is a fundamental omission which can, perhaps, be partly explained, although not excused, by the fact that, at the time of the primary fieldwork in late 1983, there was little discussion of sexual abuse within social services departments. Nevertheless, elements of the thesis relating to models of the black family, to general concerns regarding racism and child abuse, and to the difficulties in developing anti-racist practice, are relevant to this chapter.

A second source of material for this chapter comes from ESRC-funded research on 'the multi-agency approach' together with work which I undertook as a consultant evaluating a scheme of joint working in Rochdale (cf inter alia Blagg and Stubbs, 1988; Stubbs, 1989).

There is a third element which is, I feel, worthy of mention here, even though it is a good deal vaguer and more amorphous than the research experiences I have just discussed. Crudely stated, I could not begin to write this chapter without having undergone a lengthy process of making sense of my own personal and professional experiences as a white man practising and writing about social work in the field of both sexual abuse and services for black families. Being a man writing about the former and being a white person writing about the latter each in their turn produce considerable dilemmas and doubts. These are compounded when one is a white man seeking to address the issue of racism and sexual abuse.

Later in this chapter I will address practice issues concerning both the 'race' and 'gender' of the workers involved in this area. Here, I want to claim that I *can* write about these issues as a white man. I have arrived at this point through a realisation, I think, that there is, at the present time, an important movement in and around social work and social work education which my own work, here and elsewhere, seeks to be a part of. This movement is seeking to define and develop a critical social work practice, the purpose of which is to challenge oppressive social relations based on 'race', gender, class, age, sexuality, and disability. Whilst I do not wish to develop a lengthy discourse outlining a theory of oppression (anyone interested would do well to start with Brittan and Maynard, 1984), some points can be made.

Firstly, the concept of oppression connects the personal with the political whilst avoiding what I term pessimistic reductionism which takes one of two forms. The first, pitched at the political level, suggests that nothing can be done to challenge oppression — that racism, patriarchy, and so on, are 'built in to the system', and that state agencies such as social work exist to perpetuate such oppression. The second, pitched at the personal level, suggests that all white people are racist, and all men are sexist, and that they cannot, and will not, change. My own approach suggests that the politics of oppression are extraordinarily complex. Whilst acknowledging that, as a white man, I may perpetuate racism and sexism in my daily encounters, and certainly enjoy many privileges within a racist and sexist society, I believe that I can develop a framework in which these issues can be discussed and which begins to challenge racism and sexism within social work practice.

Secondly, an understanding of sexual abuse must discuss power relationships, both within families and in terms of the ways in which powerful agencies detect, investigate and deal with sexual abuse in particular kinds of families. Only in this way can we avoid a disconnecting, or delinking, of the issue of sexual abuse from fundamental questions about our society, about male power, and about family life.

Thirdly, a framework which discusses sexual abuse in terms of the politics of oppression, allows us to contextualise the current crisis of sexual abuse in Britain. In my view, debates about sexual abuse occur in the context of a current ideological offensive seeking to shore up a definition of the 'normal family', seen as increasingly under threat. The reality is that the supposedly 'normal' family is, statistically speaking, somewhat deviant, and may, indeed, be the kind of place where the sexual abuse of children takes place on a massive scale. Elements of a composite picture of the 'normal' family include having two parents, being patriarchal, with a male breadwinner and female housewife, being respectable (working or middle class), being heterosexual (hence Section 28 defining homosexuality

as a 'pretended' family relationship), and being white. In developing
an anti-racist perspective on sexual abuse, we must look at definitions of 'the black family' found in and around social work.

The myth of black family pathology

Elsewhere (Stubbs, 1988a, b) I show that racist stereotypes of the
black family are not confined to the popular commonsense of the tab-
loid press. Rather, they have a dominant place in sociological and
social work texts produced in the last twenty years in Britain. These
frameworks have skewed the kinds of research questions which have
been addressed in the field of 'race relations' and, I suggest, have
influenced the frameworks utilised by social workers in making sense
of their practice with black families. Little has changed since Daniel
Moynihan's infamous report on the 'Negro' family in the United
States (Moynihan, 1965), which defined the black family as inherently weak, unstable and, literally, diseased, i.e. as pathological.
Accounts have continued to focus on the problems within black families in a way which is, at best, partial and, at worst, such a distortion
of reality as to be mythological.

Whilst space precludes a thorough discussion, it is important to
deal briefly with the components of models of the Afro-Caribbean
(or, as most of the literature would have it, 'West Indian'), and
'Asian' family structures, found in the social work and sociological
literatures. Following Moynihan's framework, the Afro-Caribbean
family tends to be seen as deficient, disorganised, and inherently dis-
integrating. The main concern is seen to be the absence of a stable
father figure, so that families tend to be female dominated or to be
marked by a degree of instability in marital or common law unions.
Problems of illegitimacy and of identity are said to arise from this
instability. There are also hints within the literature of an excessive
use of discipline and of a repressive morality in the exercising of
parental authority, each of which mitigates against the healthy development of Afro-Caribbean children.

In contrast, 'Asian' families are seen to be problematic precisely
because their family structure is too tight. It is argued that 'Asian'
families tend to be insular in terms of preserving religious and cultural traditions and extended family networks. All of this is said to
pose acute problems for women and girls forced to lead a narrow life
in a repressive domestic environment. Young people, particularly
young women, are said to be 'torn between two cultures', unable to
tolerate strict rules, particularly arranged marriages, and ill-equipped
to integrate into 'British society'. Examples of these constructions
can be found in many textbooks, in which phrases abound such as
that 'Asian' families are 'distant, withdrawn and isolated' and 'unused

to discussing personal and family problems' (Cheetham, 1972) and, even in the suggestion that Asian sexuality is 'heavily repressive' (Triseliotis, 1972). These frameworks continue to be present in more recent texts (e.g. Coombe and Little, 1986) and, of course, to be used to legitimate racist immigration legislation (cf Cohen, 1981).

Despite some later recognition of the strengths of black family structures, most of the literature continues to emphasise cultural pathology as an explanation for the problems of black families. Any exclusive concern with culture must serve, in my view, to disconnect discussion from the issue of how racism affects black families and, also, leads to a crude generalisation whereby the problems faced by black individuals and families can always be traced back, in some way, to inherent cultural pathology.

These frameworks have a definite relevance for a discussion of racism and sexual abuse, posing a number of problems for the development of an anti-racist perspective. There are real dangers, I think, in the development of research which extends pathology models of black family functioning into the relatively uncharted territories of sexuality and the sexual abuse of children. We must be wary of a search for 'hard facts' concerning the prevalence of sexual abuse within black families, tracing its incidence to a number of 'precipitating factors'. Such research studies would not, of course, provide objective evidence, but would raise all of the general problems of what is to count as a definition of sexual abuse, present in existing research studies, compounded by the racist pedigree of the research traditions which would be utilised.

In addition, the pull of cultural explanations leaves us in a very difficult position. There is a tendency, at the moment, to read off from individual cases of sexual abuse of black children, a confirmation of pathology models of black family functioning. We must be clear that 'culture' can never explain the sexual abuse of black children; to invoke it is yet another example of muddled thinking which fails to challenge racist stereotypes. We face great problems in beginning a debate about the relationship between the sexual abuse of black children and particular black cultural and family forms in a racist society, and in a child protection arena where the dominant literature in its silence about 'race' and racism, actually upholds white middle-class values against which black families are seen as deviant. Indeed, the concepts of 'children' and 'childhood' utilised within the orthodox frameworks present in a taken-for-granted way constructions which are, in many senses, a product of a particular historical time and place — modern Western middle-class society.

However, it cannot serve the interests of developing an anti-racist perspective, nor can it be in the interests of black children, to deny that black children suffer sexual abuse. In many ways this remains the position held implicitly by many. It is a position which is being challenged by the development, in the United States and in Britain, of a tradition of black feminism. It is not a coincidence that some of the most important treatments of the sexual abuse of black children can be found in books such as Alice Walker's *The Colour Purple* (1983) and Maya Angelou's *I Know Why The Caged Bird Sings* (1984). The issue is also being addressed by a number of black women writers in Britain. One of the most harrowing accounts can be found in Joan Riley's important novel *The Unbelonging* (1985), whose central character Hyacinth is brutally raped by her father, and subsequently faces the racism endemic within the white care system.

Whilst it is impossible to deal with the arguments of black feminism here (cf White, 1984 and Lorde, 1984 for valuable introductions), its challenges to white racism and black sexism, and its engagement with the problems of white feminism, provides an insight into how an anti-racist perspective can be developed. In breaking the silence around the sexual abuse of black children, this literature must be taken seriously by those working in and around social work. Most importantly, it allows us to see the issue of sexism within pathology models of both the Afro-Caribbean and 'Asian' family.

In terms of the Afro-Caribbean family, we must ask why is it, exactly, even if we take it to be a proven fact, that the relative absence of male father figures is, in itself, problematic. How can we reconcile a construction of the necessity of a father figure for family stability with a recognition that fathers are, often, perpetrators of sexual abuse against their children? In addition, there are real dangers of the mother-blaming which is already rife in the orthodox literature on sexual abuse, being directed against Afro-Caribbean women with a particular intensity, as they are accused of forming 'unstable' relationships.

In terms of 'Asian' family functioning, it allows us to be extremely sceptical of an orthodox literature which professes concern for the fate of women and girls through invoking the sexism supposedly inherent in Asian culture. This literature, of course, more usually neglects sexism completely. In the process, a picture is constructed which seeks to render Asian women and girls as essentially dependent, passive victims needing state help to be saved. In contrast to this, black feminists inside and outside statutory social work agencies are leading the way in the development of an anti-racist practice — a point which I return to in my conclusions to this chapter.

In addition, black feminism makes a major contribution to anti-racist theory. We must replace pathology models of the black family with a more nuanced approach. There is, clearly, not one black family wholly good or wholly bad. What there are, are different 'sex/

gender systems' (a term used to describe patterns of familial and sexual relations), in which patterns of male dominance take different forms. To address this adequately we would need to look at diversity within and between black families, discussing religion, regional trends in Britain and in Britain's colonies, and so on. We would also, I think, hold on to some notion of the black family as a key site of resistance to state racism, and as a source of strength and dignity for black people facing oppression. Building on a recognition of racism, we must replace mythological constructions of 'the black family' with a concern with real black families in which the sexual abuse of children is neither endemic, a cultural norm, nor completely absent. Black children may be sexually abused by black men who are their fathers or father substitutes, or they may be sexually abused by white men who are their father or father substitutes. These real events should not, however, be used to form crude generalisations about black families. In addition, starting with racism directs attention to the problems of the response of official agencies in this field.

Racism and agency responses

It is important to recognise that, for black children, the effects of the interventions of powerful agencies may be distinctly different, and in many cases worse, than the effects of interventions for white children. Addressing the varied and complex ways in which agency responses may be structured by racism is a necessary step in the questining of certain taken-for-granted assumptions of a child protection orthodoxy in Britain. Research and practice discussions must pay less attention to the problems of black families and more attention to the problems of agency responses. From my own research, and from accounts by other practitioners, academics, and so on, a number of worrying patterns emerge. Agency responses may be either over-controlling, abusive and punitive on the one hand or, conversely, there may be a failure to intervene to protect black children on the other hand. Both responses are structured by racism, or indeed, by a paralysis induced by fear of being labelled as racist. In addition, even if black children are protected, we must look at the possibility that subsequent responses may themselves constitute abuse.

All of this must lead to a questioning of an essentially benevolent view of agency interventions in the arena of sexual abuse. The orthodox approach tends to suggest that policy and practice in the management of sexual abuse may be flawed at the present time, but that this is remediable through the development of better inter-agency co-operation. This is an essentially technical response to a political problem of a kind all too familiar within social work. In sexual abuse this notion of benevolence has problematic consequences for all children, but its effects are particularly pernicious for black children. As Harry Blagg and I have suggested (Blagg and Stubbs, 1988) closer links between statutory agencies in the sexual abuse arena may well lead to an increased likelihood of sexual abuse being suspected in those families with whom they routinely come into contact.

If, and I suggest this is the case, social workers and, particularly, the police, tend to treat black families with a degree of suspicion — as undeserving, deviant, even criminal — then the racism within each agency is likely to be compounded within a multi-agency approach based on closer links between the two agencies. Some schemes have begun to develop a framework for child centred practice although, even here, the issue of 'race' and racism has been left off the agenda. Indeed, in some cases, social workers who hold an anti-racist perspective have not challenged police racism because they do not want to rock the boat, undermine all the effort which has been put into developing a better relationship with the police in the interests of most children, and wreck what is, essentially, a good scheme. Those who are aware of the problems of police racism often feel powerless in terms of how best to challenge this. Whilst recognising the difficulties, my suggestion is that issues of race and racism must be in the forefront of people's minds at the start of negotiations with the police concerning sexual abuse.

Whilst it is all too easy to play the fashionable game of knocking the police, and whilst I recognise that some police forces and individual officers are making great progress in the area of sexual abuse work, it must be recognised, I think, that black communities tend to have somewhat negative experiences of policing. Two kinds of examples from research and from discussions with practitioners will suffice to indicate the kinds of problems which may arise. Even if these anecdotes were isolated examples, and I suspect they are not, they are important precisely because they quickly gain currency within black communities and may inhibit black children from disclosing sexual abuse.

In one case, police responded to social services' concerns over the possible sexual abuse of a black child by storming into a black household in riot gear and harassing all members of the family before arresting the man concerned. This was justified because the family lived on a 'problem estate' and there was concern about the safety of police officers.

In our own research in the North of England, two incidents involving allegations of sexual abuse against 'Asian' children have a striking similarity to each other. In both cases, the police action was premised on the assumption that 'Asian' families and the community as a whole would 'stick together and protect its own'. Consequently, since the perpetrator was not known in either case, the police harassed and arrested a large number of men within the extended family and in wider friendship networks. In one case, the child was removed from home at great speed and taken some distance to an all-white environment. This action appeared to be premised on an assumption that 'Asian' children are not merely hostages within their own family but within the community as a whole.

In these anecdotes, a worrying picture emerges of sexual abuse being used as little more than a pretext for coercive intervention against a community already defined in negative terms. The problem is, of course, that interventions in the sexual abuse arena do not take place in a vacuum. In the current climate of relations between the police and black communities, it is hard to persuade black children and/or their non-abusing relatives that the police will offer protection and a sympathetic response.

Similar issues arise in terms of the response of social services. Again, this is a complex area with very little concrete research evidence. However, it is clear that Afro-Caribbean communities remain, rightly, concerned about the large numbers of black children received into local authority care, and also concerned about the quality of that care, much of which takes place in predominantly white residential establishments, or in white foster and adoptive homes.

Issues about the dangers of social workers intervening on the basis of stereotyped assumptions about black families, or being forced to act because of the prejudices of other agencies such as education, the police or the courts, are as relevant to the issue of sexual abuse as to the more general areas of child care and child abuse. In addition, concern about the failure to encourage a positive black identity amongst black children in care, has a particular importance in terms of black children who have been sexually abused, who may well develop a picture of blackness as equated with badness. Social workers may also face problems in assessing and supporting non-abusing carers because of a failure to challenge racist stereotypes.

Another problem area concerns the development of a so-called 'rule of optimism' amongst social workers through which they fail to intervene in cases of alleged abuse within black families. This is a very complex issue and is often invoked by those who wish to be part of a backlash against the development of anti-racist policies and practices. Nevertheless, the case of Tyra Henry, as discussed in an excellent enquiry report (Lambeth, 1987), alerts us to some issues here. There must be a concern when social workers force a non-abusing black grandmother to return her grandchild to a situation of danger because they failed to respond to her need for material assistance to avoid the threat of fuel disconnection. Apparently, one factor in the decision of social workers was the belief that the older black women were strong, self-reliant and capable of coping with all manner of adversity.

In my own, and others' research (Stubbs, 1988a, b; Rodney, 1987) a picture emerges of black communities tending to figure primarily in the social control functions of social work and to receive much less in the way of tangible social services. This was very much in the minds of 'Asian' community groups in one Northern town where we researched issues of inter-agency relationships. Without going into great detail, it was not surprising that 'Asian' leaders did not attend a discussion at the invitation of social services chiefs to discuss a series of alleged beatings of children in the Mosques which were seen as child abuse. The leaders felt that they had been summoned to social services about this issue in sharp contrast to a singular lack of concern about many of their demands for the provision of social services including 'Asian' home helps and appropriate meals on wheels services.

In my view, these examples show how the issue of racism reveals even greater strains in the already tense relationship between child protection and child centred practice. I have a great scepticism about the existing child protection orthodoxy in Britain which appears to consist of a set of professional certainties and, interestingly, is marked by an eerie silence on the issues of 'race' and racism. This is, perhaps, unsurprising when one realises that the orthodoxy tends to treat parenting in a vacuum in which issues of material poverty and structural oppression are systematically excluded.

The focus is on the interpretation of individual events and incidents following which quick decisions, often involving the separation of children from their parents, are made. Within this, the space for autonomy and discretion, or even time to think, much less to be creative, on the part of individual social workers is severely constrained. These tendencies go beyond an imperative to protect children from abuse, which necessitates painful decisions to be made quickly, and seems, in addition, to involve a renewed emphasis on professional confidence and expertness which is not, in my view, in the interests of individual parents of children. Indeed, the whole child protection apparatus appears to be built on a bedrock of a certainty about what constitutes a normal, good, family which the issue of sexual abuse must lead us to question.

Stated crudely, my worry is that when there are concerns about abuse of black children, the context of how responses of parents may differ within a racist society, cannot be addressed. In the example above, what would have happened had the concerns been about the sexual abuse of 'Asian' children in the Mosque? One possibility is that because of a lack of understanding, social services would have been paralysed into doing nothing. More likely, however, a sexual abuse investigation would have begun with arrests and a number of repercussions being set up within the community. In the context of this, parents may well have been asked to believe their child and protect them, in a way which made things very difficult for them.

In a way, these issues need debating before they happen rather than wait for individual events to occur. They also illustrate, I think, the importance of starting with 'disclosure' rather than 'detection' in the arena of sexual abuse. We must be prepared to listen to, and really hear, black children when they describe what has happened to them. In addition, we must avoid the 'secondary victimisation' produced by insensitive questioning and subsequent placements in white environments which fail to stress the importance of a positive black identity. There are worries that black children, particularly older black children, fail to attain the status of 'a deserving victim' and are subjected to all manner of abuse by those charged with investigating their concerns or with their subsequent care. We must address, I think, the danger that the challenging behaviour of young black children in care who have been sexually abused, actually leads to more punitive outcomes in terms of being propelled into secure units and such like. Indeed, widening a definition of sexual abuse, we need to look at the reality of abuse by white men in positions of power and trust in black children's lives. In short, we are faced, at the moment, I think, with a sorry picture that what is bad for all children within the existing system is, in all probability, worse for black children.

It's alright for you to talk: towards anti-racism?

Thus far, I risk a number of criticisms from practitioners, many of whom are struggling to develop anti-racist practice in very difficult workplace situations. I may be seen to have dealt in crude generalisations in order to produce a very pessimistic picture. I may be accused of offering nothing for the beleaguered practitioner, in terms of discussing the detailed complexities of individual cases, or, indeed, of giving any idea of how good practice may be developed. This section attempts to address some of these issues whilst continuing, unfortunately, to sound warning bells rather than to offer quick and easy answers. One clear message of this chapter is that we cannot build an anti-racist practice in sexual abuse in isolation, disconnected from broader issues concerning child care and social work practice for black children, families and communities. In addition, we must address specifically the issue of services for black women.

Following on from this, we must reject a simplistic suggestion that black social workers can solve all of the problems. As my own research shows (Stubbs, 1985), black social workers face problems of isolation, marginalisation and exploitation within social services departments. In the sexual abuse arena, black workers may be asked to advise on the 'cultural' aspects of cases, whilst being offered no opportunity to challenge the fundamentals of case management. Another possibility is that black workers will be allocated difficult cases involving black children with little adequate supervision or support and, of course, no necessary access to additional resources over and above those available to white workers. Any perceived inadequacies by black workers in their handling of such cases tend all too often, to be generalised to the inadequacies of black workers as a whole. In addition, black workers may be consulted on, or allocated, particular cases regardless of their interests, experiences, skills, commitments, identities, politics, and so on. Above all, as Lena Dominelli (1988) suggests, this process seeks to absolve white workers and management from any responsibility in pursuing anti-racist practice themselves.

In my view, the cause of anti-racist practice is much more likely to be advanced by initiatives from black workers themselves, especially through some form of collective organisation such as black workers groups. These groups challenge a pernicious individualism at the heart of the current organisation of social work, which tends to force black workers into conforming to a model of 'the good black social worker'. Collective organisation by black workers can offer a formidable challenge to existing policy and practice in a way which is more accountable to the black communities they serve and avoids the dangers of co-option and the creation of yet another new group of 'experts'. Within this, there remains a role for white workers committed to anti-racist practice, in supporting black colleagues and debating these issues in all-white and mixed settings.

All of this helps us to address the key question as to how important it is for black workers to do the direct, face-to-face work with both black children who have disclosed sexual abuse or who are suspected of having been sexually abused, and with their families. Whilst advocating that initial disclosure work with sexually abused children should be done by women (Blagg and Stubbs, 1988), issues of 'race' seem more complex. Some of this complexity is noted in the discussion on anti-racist practice from an important feminist conference on sexual abuse which suggested:

> Black children who have been abused, particularly those in care, need good role models in order to counterbalance their feelings that they have been abused because they are black. For many black children, disclosing to a white person may feel like betraying their community; although for many other children there may be greater shame attached to disclosing to someone from their own community (MacLeod and Saraga, 1988).

Without a good deal more evidence and concrete accounts of practice, it would seem to be wrong to make a clear pronouncement on this issue. Children need to be empowered to make real choices in this area and, I would suggest, it is vital for whichever workers do the face-to-face work to have a commitment to anti-sexist and anti-racist practice. Even more importantly, workers need to begin a dialogue with each other and with those abused children and non-abusing caregivers on the receiving end of their services, so that these issues can be debated in a way which goes beyond the playing out of professional certainties.

Whilst we clearly need much more discussion about casework practice, we also need to look at the development of policies in the sexual abuse arena which address the needs of black communities. At the moment, I would suggest that very few policies do this. One exception is Islington social services which specifically sought to include black groups within the policy, and to look at the importance of black family and community networks as a source of support and protection (MacLeod and Saraga, 1988).

Beyond this, we need to look at the process through which social services policies and practice are arrived at. Elsewhere (Stubbs, 1989) I have suggested that these issues can never merely be internal professional and statutory concerns, but that we must strive to build community-based, preventative approaches to the sexual abuse of children. This has a general relevance, but some very specific points can be made with reference to the development of anti-racist practice. Social services departments must enter into a dialogue with black community groups, particularly with black women's groups, in order to develop policies which address their experiences. In addition, departments must support and, if appropriate, fund black projects, or projects which specifically put forward an anti-racist and black perspective in the sexual abuse arena.

The whole issue of dialogue with the black community is fraught with problems which usually result in departments engaging in the process in a very half-hearted way and with the black community once again being pathologised, this time for failing to agree amongst itself. From my own research and practice in the North of England, I believe there is a real danger that the dialogue tends to take place with male dominated groups. In one case, the involvement of a black feminist refuge was opposed by white male managers and black male social workers with equal vehemence. Issues of gender and race, yet again, appear to be inextricably linked.

Finally, a community-based, preventative approach is absolutely vital in creating a climate in which black children can be protected from abuse. Only by listening to black children and black survivors of sexual abuse, can we expect to derive any improvements in practice.

An unreconstructed child protection orthodoxy cannot be taken to black groups with the expectation that it will be wholeheartedly embraced. We must listen to Marlene Bogle, writing about her experiences at Brixton Black Women's Centre:

> We feel that statutory bodies use us at their convenience and when it suits them. They refer to us cases which they cannot manage, and they come to us for advice on specific cases. But they do not open themselves to the criticism, advice and help we could offer them to develop a more appropriate service to black children and adult incest survivors. We see ourselves as women who have the experience and expertise to make a valuable contribution to policy and practice within statutory organisations, as well as working alongside them . . . This state of affairs leaves us feeling exploited and taken for granted. Our help is desperately needed and we cannot give up on the women and young people coming to us for help (MacLeod and Saraga, 1988, paper by Bogle).

Conclusions

In this chapter I hope to have begun a much needed debate about service provision for black children, families and communities. We clearly need much more research, accounts of practice, and accounts from survivors. My only proviso is that this material must be framed in the context of an understanding of racism to have any value. The issue of racism is central to the current operation of child care, child abuse, and sexual abuse services. This is so much the case that I would suggest that improvements in services for black children are likely to have important consequences for all children. The corollary does not hold, however, so that improvements in services for white children, in tending to neglect the issue of racism, seem likely, once more, to leave black children in a disadvantaged, oppressed position.

Finally, whilst I have concentrated on Afro-Caribbean and 'Asian' populations within this chapter, since they face many of the processes I have discussed with a particular intensity, many of the arguments of this chapter hold for other groups who suffer from racism directed against them. We need similar accounts to this one charting the experiences of other black groups, and groups such as travellers and the Irish (Irish Women's Group discussion in MacLeod and Saraga, 1988) in ways which focus on oppressive social relations rather than on the 'cultures' of these groups which diverge from a model of 'the English way of life'.

7 A police response — devising a code of practice

Anthony Kilkerr

For any organisation to look at itself and its performance in a specific field of given activity, with the intention of changing its purpose and application, is, in my opinion, much the same as the signal to stop a super tanker; you must understand that it will succeed, provided that you give it sufficient time and distance in which to do so. To review the response of the Metropolitan Police to the methods and proposals for the investigation of child sexual abuse is very much like that loaded super tanker, running silent, creating an enthusiastic bow wave and a turbulent wake, which is churning up issues which must be addressed before calm and clear policy can be seen.

What I would like to do in this chapter is review some of the experiences of the Metropolitan Police in rethinking their methods and procedures with the intention of effecting some enduring means of serving the needs of abused children. A significant consideration which any organisation has to address is the formulation of the purpose for introducing changes in practices, or more crucially, recognising the need for a social problem to be dealt with in some effective way and, for this, obtaining an agreed and implemented policy.

The police have to take notice of child sexual abuse, review their policy and implement appropriate changes. Equally important in such measures is taking account of the necessary changes that have to be made in the attitude of police officers, if they are to meet the needs of the society in which they live and work. Awareness of these issues has affected the Metropolitan Police response to rape, domestic violence, racial tension and child abuse. I would like to review the development of our response to child abuse, reflect on the adjustments made, and the steps taken, in the hope that further development may ensue.

Having listened to pressure groups, tested the research and observed practice in other countries, particularly in the United States, the Metropolitan Police introduced a policy for dealing with rape victims. This policy placed its emphasis on the ability of the victim to sustain her allegation throughout prosecution of the case at court. With hindsight, it has to be agreed that this well-intentioned policy was not, however, serving the needs of the victims whom we realised were in a state of trauma far and beyond the confusions and shock experienced by many of the victims of other types of crimes. 'Rape trauma syndrome' clearly outlined the effects upon rape victims, the lasting effects on social and personal relationships, and crystallised the need to understand that rape was a crime of violence not 'merely' a 'sex' crime.

A programme of training for investigating officers who would interview the victim, as well as being friend and counsellor in those first moments of reporting, brought about the first steps towards change. This change was supported by improvements in interviewing techniques and in the provision of specific facilities. My own view is that it was from this bold change that our move into a review of sexual abuse policy took shape. Another aspect for consideration was that the police investigation of rape did little to support the victim post-reporting. Nevertheless, the formation of support schemes for crime did bring the police into contact with those professionals who were able to suggest ways ahead. Victim support schemes saw the need for the new dimension of special help for rape victims and, in so doing, also made us realise that the children and families of victims were also in need of support.

Police officers in London had, since the death of Maria Colwell and the 1974 enquiry (Metropolitan Police and Bexley Social Services, 1987), taken part in case conferences. It must be admitted that many of them found the process quite alien to begin with, but the police eventually settled down to the system, forming professional working arrangements with social services and other agencies. Indeed there were, and still are, many sound working relationships between the police and other agencies, struck and sustained throughout the investigation of sexual abuse, predominantly in those cases of non-accidental injury.

An observation here, which will take on significance later, is that the detective going to case conferences at this time, in the late seventies, did so to help determine the next most likely step for police investigation. It is this point which is the key to joint investigation.

When our officers went to case conferences there was every likelihood that the other agencies had gone as far as they could go, and the consideration of a prosecution was the main item on the agenda. From the police perspective, the need to conduct the enquiry was urgent, in many cases pre-empted by the previous investigators pursuing their own enquiries. This often left the detective with a feeling that they were reporting back confirmation of conclusions already reached, often unable to state that there was sufficient evidence to charge an accused with an offence.

Another emerging trend was the weight placed upon the decision of the case conference. If, for example, the police felt a charge could be brought, often the case conference would suggest that in the interests of the child, or the family, there should not be a criminal case. Police exercised discretion by accepting the judgement of the conference, based upon social need and the provision of assistance, which might in these circumstances see the child's name go on the (Child Protection) Register, only to return to the next conference to find the subject victim of further abuse, or worse. The need for a constant policy review was becoming an important message, and each Police District in London was being made aware of this through supervision and instruction.

The way in which children who have been sexually abused are dealt with still reflects a distinction from neglected and violently assaulted children which, in my view, sets limits on the police response. Yet, I must also accept that the next stages in the development of future police policy have benefited greatly from this distinction in the interpretation and in the investigation of abuse.

Most professionals are now familiar with the model for joint investigation tested in the London Borough of Bexley, but, nonetheless, it is helpful to consider the objectives which they set out to achieve, after negotiation and agreement (Metropolitan Police and Bexley Social Services, 1987). The final report states:

> The primary aim of the project, which has its foundation in the two principles of joint investigation and video recorded victim interview, was to bring together the differing skills of social workers and police officers to improve the quality of investigation work to victims of child sexual abuse and their families by
>
> a enhancing co-ordination, co-operation and communication between the police and social services;
> b providing specialist training for investigators;
> c increasing awareness of
>   (i) child sexual abuse,
>   (ii) professional roles and responsibilities;
> d reducing interview repetition;

e reducing medical examination repetition;
f providing improved interview and medical examination facilities;
g introducing interview techniques with enhanced communication to aid disclosure of abuse;
h providing:
     (i) protection for victims, and
    (ii) child and family care at all stages of the investigation;
i providing effective material for use when interviewing suspects; and
j improving decision making.

Each one of these objectives creates a clear and well-defined
intention, which must, and did, create sufficient response to cause
concern, and compel each professional to focus their attention not
only on their ability to apply them, but also on the irritation which
working to them would cause. The ramifications of a, b and c
demanded more than lip service to the concepts and well-intentioned
statements of objectives. Each participating agency had to consider
where it placed the plight of the sexually abused child on its agenda
of priorities for the allocation of resources. All of this, of course, had
to be attended to within a climate of intense activities from various
pressure groups and trying to avoid the charge of being merely moral
entrepreneurs.

Innovation demands both evaluation and the ability to adjust and
be flexible about developing policy. An observation worth recalling
here is the discomfort of many practitioners in Bexley when, coming
to the end of the project, their work was described as an experiment.
Indeed, the valuable work done gave many opportunities to test,
develop and adjust theories which are now being presented as one
important model for the future (Metropolitan Police and Bexley
Social Services, 1987). However, working with sexually abused
children in Bexley was very real for those involved, and their success
was the experience they could pass on to those others equally concerned about child abuse.

Of course, the ten objectives had to be viewed in the context of
work being done by others. Objects d, e and f demanded that, if
there were to be effective changes in procedures, the questions which
could take police and social services joint investigation forward could
only be put by drawing in medical, and subsequently legal, professionals who would be involved in meeting the intention which the
statement of objectives promulgated.

The work of Doctor Arnom Bentovim and his colleague, Doctor
Eileen Vizard (Bentovim et al, 1988) was a source of invaluable
encouragement to the development of the objectives of reducing the

number of interviews and medical examinations. Their work with both victims and their families pointed to the value of practitioners being willing to listen to the experience of others, particularly those who have to rehabilitate children and their families after they have been through investigation. I am not suggesting that the police were a cause of the need to rehabilitate, but suggest that, as in the case of adult rape victims, we needed to think more about the police response. Bexley gave us the chance to formulate a model. Their work took almost three years to report and their conclusions are worth considering. Three significant developments in the investigation of child sexual abuse were established;

> 1 a practical, working model for joint investigation of sexual abuse which can be adapted for use in other areas, and provide a basis for the joint investigation of other forms of child abuse;
> 2 a greater degree of skill and expertise among officers of the Police and Social Services Departments in the investigation of sexual abuse, based upon a broader range of techniques;
> 3 a complementary and satisfactory working relationship between two agencies which reflects differing responsibilities but a common objective in securing the protection and welfare of sexually abused children.

It is, I believe, significant that the Bexley report preceded the Cleveland report, and was referred to by Dame Elizabeth Butler-Sloss (Butler-Sloss, 1988). The views and recommendations seek to give advice on issues to those who sought to address similar matters, all of which are touched on in the Cleveland report, and some of which are still being addressed or seeking development.

These views are levelled at policy and management issues, seeking to draw attention to the need for a clear direction on a policy arrived at mutually for application within the agencies involved in joint investigation. In many respects, these revisions had far-reaching implications for the philosophy and training of the police, the role of medical examinations and examiners, and for the nature of criminal proceedings. We had to ask whether the model could be replicated in other boroughs and, if so, how this could be done?

During 1986/7 the Metropolitan Police had set up a further working party to review its policy on non-accidental injury and also consider the findings of other public inquiries into the deaths of abused children. The terms of reference drawn up were:

1 To review the findings of the Beckford and Koseda inquiry reports together with the Tyra Henry case and their implications for this force, together with the implications of the DHSS review.
2 To review the current force response to the issue of sexual abuse

having regard to the draft DHSS guidelines and taking into consideration pilot schemes and initiatives presently functioning in
this area.

3   Taking into account 1 and 2, to adjust the structure of the force
response to child abuse, consider the training and other resource
implications and make recommendations on a revised force structure.

The need for acting quickly, before either Bexley or the Working
Party had reported, was reinforced by the death of Kimberley Carlile. The DHSS proposals were drafted and the need for policy was
felt both within the London Boroughs and the country in general.
While any conclusions would only apply to London, the Metropolitan Police Working Group felt the pressure for a policy which could
accommodate any future national policy on the subject. The consideration was, therefore, to anticipate national proposals through constant contact with other voluntary and statutory organisations, take
note of their research and developments in approach.

The working party agreed that the policy had to be founded in a
code of practice based upon sound principles. When the principles
were formed and put to the area level policy committee, it was agreed
that the way forward would be based upon them, and that the code of
practice would be the source document for the next stage. It was,
therefore, stated that the Metropolitan Police would base its policy
upon these four principles;

1   To pursue a policy reflecting an intention to protect and care for
the victim, rehabilitate the family and deal with the offender.
2   To maintain the impetus of the multi-agency approach as laid
down in force strategy.
3   To provide a force response to child abuse which ensures the most
effective use of resources in conjunction with local authority
social services departments.
4   Continuously to develop investigative techniques to deal with
offenders and to enable officers to overcome perceived or real
constraints upon investigation and prosecution.

The work is only beginning. The terms of reference directed us
towards the prediction of training and other resource implications
and make recommendation on a revised force structure. The hard
facts were that hopes and dreams are very often difficult to implement, and the plan had to be well argued, thoroughly thought
through and difficult problems faced up to not only as far as child
abuse was concerned but also those to do with the nature of police
organisations. To form the code there were many aspects which
would demand, not just changes in procedure, but the more difficult

changes in culture and attitudes and shifts in philosophy which any effective implementation of the code would need. Questions about responsibility and resources are obvious, but the deeper, and sometimes more intractable, issues to do with professional pride, established and comfortable posts, and of status both within and outside the organisation would also have to be reviewed. Such matters, of course, did not only affect the police. It was necessary, too, to face up to the risk that professionalism could also be used by the various agencies involved simply to preserve the status quo.

A multi-disciplinary workshop was arranged for July 1987 which would get as many of the professionals as possible together to share their thoughts on given areas of policy in a three phased progression;

1   What is the situation now?
2   How would I like it to be?
3   How can it be done?

Because these meetings were to assist in the formulation of police policy, it was felt that we must ensure balance. To do this we appointed independent chairs in each group so that the police representatives, like any other group, could contribute without the feeling that they were working to a rank. The chairs were assisted by two facilitators who would keep the schedule and steer the meetings to a conclusion.

I do not intend to go into detail about the investment of their time by many concerned and dedicated people, other than to refer you to the code itself, to see the range of topics which it covers and the directives and suggestions which it gives, as an illustration of the value of such group work. The progression worked, the timetable was adhered to and the final recommendations were agreed. The next step was to write up and produce it in a final form for the force (Metropolitan Police, 1989).

The item I recall most was the debate on *guardian ad litem*. I recall it because it illustrates importance in all these policy making ventures to both understand the objective and to understand the interpretation of it. On this point, the notion of being able to share information with the guardian was seen by some as being not only difficult but dangerous. In a ten hour session we finally got agreement and an understanding of our commitment to the four principles, particularly the protection of the child. The *guardian ad litem* being the 'representative' of the child and, therefore, acting in the best interests of the child, must be regarded as a 'safe and secure' member of the network with whom the discussion and sharing of information must be undertaken. The failure to do so may deprive the child of sound advice and help.

The role and the contribution which each individual professional makes cannot be seen in isolation from the contributions of others. Indeed, this conclusion was reinforced by Dame Elizabeth Butler-Sloss when she stated that the development of inter-agency co-operation acknowledges that 'No single agency — Health, Social Services, Police or voluntary organisation has the pre-eminent responsibility in the assessment of child abuse generally and sexual abuse particularly. Each agency has a prime responsibility for a particular aspect of the problem. Neither children's nor parents' needs and rights can be adequately met or protected unless agencies agree a framework for their interaction' (Butler-Sloss, 1988).

The obvious doubt is trusting our ability to see that issue and, of course, understand the point at which the next step is best achieved by the 'other' or 'next' agency. The police, by tradition, have had to stand alone, indeed, our training is based upon that ability to act alone. The fact which comes up time and again, and figures in the code of practice as well as the Bexley and Cleveland reports, is the benefit of, and need for, inter-agency training. This concept must be accepted for us to develop policy further.

The code introduced practice directions which need to be thought about, not just in police terms, but in the ramifications for other agencies. The police in London considered the introduction of teams made up of Detective Officers and Youth and Community Officers, in groups of six or nine. The problem this presented social services with was the concept of specialists in a generalist or generic working group. The variation of training backgrounds, skills and career structures, all present difficulties in the development process.

A further problem is highlighted by those cases where the child has been moved out of the family home to 'second phase' situations. The police are used to dealing with cases allocated in the areas where the offence occurred, or allegation made. And so where the child is removed, as is more likely to happen in child sexual abuse cases than in other kinds of offence, and coming under a different division, can present organisational problems. The social services could adjust to this, but the police at first could not. However, coming to understand the needs of the child helped to take that concept forward. Nevertheless, getting the full support at administrative and supervisory levels demanded, and continues to cry out for, a middle and higher management understanding of, and involvement in, the developing policy. This has been felt at each stage of the project's development, and in all the agencies trying to take it forward.

Having drawn up a code of practice, the next point of development involves its acceptance as a basis for policy and its practical implementation. Replicating Bexley could be considered a relatively simple task, but the many and various boundaries allocated to the Health, Social Service, Borough and Police authorities look much like a web made by a drunken spider; an outrageous metaphor, perhaps, but an apt one. From the Metropolitan Police London Borough structure alone, we found that there were only five police divisions coinciding with their London Borough. The fact that there were seventy-five divisions in eight policy areas, superimposed upon the web of thirty-two London Boroughs, with eighty county Boroughs, may give some impression of the problem presented.

Boundaries are one impediment to implementation. Another is whether a policy, despite being drawn up in consultation with a multi-agency group, is one that everyone will be willing to accept and implement. Quite obviously we hoped so, but we also had to be realistic. Not everyone accepted it, nor did some approve of being left off the professions consulted, and some considered further emendations must be included before they would accept it. This was and is not an easy task. A policy put to the Commissioner and his policy committee for their direction must sustain itself then, and throughout implementation and evaluation. We did, however, adjust it to ensure that it met changes in the law and the ever developing knowledge about child sexual abuse which had yet to hear of Cleveland.

The issues raised by Bexley continue to contribute to the debate on training, joint interviewing, medical examinations and criminal proceedings. The shift which has brought meaning to these issues most is reflected in the way in which the first police response has helped focus the actions of other practitioners, yet still finds it difficult to extend itself beyond that first step. The underlying need to provide resources to address both implementation, and the ability to sustain it, compounds the already existing difficulties.

From a police point of view, technical resources can be provided once the need is established, but, with multi-discipline and multi-agency responsibilities there must also be shared costs. Funding has to be clearly defined in any negotiations between police and the other agencies. Implementation is taking the police negotiators into new areas, not seeking funds necessarily, but seeking evidence of an intention to meet costs jointly. In so doing we postulated the notion of barter to a cost effective end. If the Borough provided video equipment, for example, the police should find the accommodation, or vice versa. Though this presented a number of problems, their resolution had to be based on some understanding of the need to help abused children without having to worry about where it would be done and how much it would cost. The main responsibility for this lay at Area Child Protection Committee level. The police representative, it was felt, should therefore have a greater participative role in that forum, not just attend or send a deputy to register attendance. Like others on that committee, the individual contributions and considerations of ideas and developments would ensure that they could return to their area or divisional management groups to see through, propose or direct any implications for practice arising from the deliberations of the Area Child Protection Committee.

In the early days, when the extension of the project in London was moving forward through a structured programme of training, the relations with the Boroughs reflected a tremendous will to do something. The need for negotiations at all stages was reflected in the way in which the various students for training were selected. Some were put through a board, others were brought in to be added to the Boroughs' resources, or were sent along to make an evaluation of what the training would be like. Some police officers were shaken by the training. Some Boroughs did not think it was necessary, or that the core subjects were inappropriate, or were incomplete. All the emotional and organisational problems with which we are familiar in our day-to-day experience were visible. It is worth considering, therefore, that, as we progress in the field of multi-disciplinary training, proposed developments come down from the top in the social services, health, educational and police structures, and where better to ensure that this is so than in the Area Child Protection Committee?

In her recommendations to the Home Office subcommittee considering advice to Chief Constables, Doctor Eileen Vizard states that the purpose of joint training is:

i   To enable police and social workers to develop an understanding of each other's function — the role of the police in investigating criminal offences and that of social workers in child care;

ii to provide a forum for consideration of the criminal and civil law in relation to child sexual abuse, in particular the evidential problems of taking statements from children;

iii to develop interviewing skills and an understanding of the child's behaviour and response to the experience of interview;

iv to address the personal issues for investigators which may surface in work with sexually abused children and their families.

When these points are considered, in conjunction with the Bexley objectives and recommendations, the principles of the code of practice and the spirit of 'working together' and the Cleveland report, there is little doubt that this whole issue is more than just a 'passing phase'. I am sure the police, like other agencies, recognise the possibility that all of this activity is just another 'flavour of the month', soon to be replaced by the next 'fad'. But, I believe that if we are simply responding in this way, just doing enough to be seen to be doing something, then another public inquiry will have to be undertaken to show that these policy changes are serious efforts to address a problem which has ruined, disturbed and disrupted thousands of lives.

In considering policy, however, we must also consider the selection of those who must implement it. It has been suggested that it is role and competence rather than rank that may produce the right people. Those, that is, who would have the skills and abilities to undertake and sustain a commitment to doing the work. In an effort to assist Chief Constables, it was felt that those people involved in training police officers, social services and other agencies, should consider qualities and methods of selection. Among the qualities which have been found valuable by those currently performing a training role are:

i   experience of working with children, awareness of their development and needs, with experience or training in the investigation of child abuse;

ii   commitment to the principle of joint investigation of child abuse, and the ability to sell the idea of training in joint investigation to a wide range of individuals and agencies;

iii   teaching skills;

iv   the ability to organise training programmes and to develop training packages acceptable to local conditions and the varying levels of knowledge and expertise;

v   personal management skills and an ability to work with professionals of both sexes and from different agencies;

vi   credibility within their own organisation, that is, probably a minimum rank or grade such as a team leader in social services departments or a detective inspector in the police force. Possession of the appropriate skills is ultimately more important than seniority, however;

vii   sufficient self-confidence and personal maturity to conduct difficult and often embarrassing discussions about violence and sexuality;

viii   the ability to identify those on a training course who are unsuitable for conducting joint interviews, and to tell them.

Sometimes assumptions are made about a person's ability. Their working relationships may present an apparent breadth of skills yet, when tested, there is a doubt in the specific area for which they were thought suitable. This is no fault of the individual, but simply something which that person just cannot do. In the police there are precedents for the selection of individuals for specific types of work, be it advanced driving, promotion or firearms, and officers do have to meet a job or task profile, so why not for child abuse? Officers being considered for Child Protection Teams should be carefully chosen, a process involving other agencies. The discomfort the police may feel at an 'outsider' being involved should be set against the weight of the responsibility in joint investigations.

If we consider the effort to achieve the Bexley objectives regarding the reduction of the number of interviews and medical examinations, which it was suggested could be of such a quality as to preclude the need for others to put the child through the circumstances again, then those who undertake the first interview will have to be able to function to a given standard. That standard may be realisable in the qualifications gained through training for the task. Police officers so involved may, therefore, have to be qualified just as are their social worker colleagues, in much the same manner as police/civilian fingerprint or scientific examination officers are, and make such a declaraton in presentation of their evidence to court. While this is not the case yet, the investment by the police in training those who will be involved should create wider and justifiable expectations of the quality of service to be provided by them.

As I said at the beginning, the police response to problems is like that super tanker, the reaction to Bexley, along with the need to take stock of what was recommended by Dame Elizabeth Butler-Sloss, as well as all the difficulties involved in changing large organisations and their traditions of working, suggests that change will take time. The latter report (Butler-Sloss, 1988) states:

a The police should examine their organisation to ensure there is an adequate communication network to acheive the recognition and identification of problems at operational level and a system to develop remedies.
b The police should develop, monitor and maintain communication and consultation with the other agencies concerned with child protection.
c The police should develop and practise inter-agency working, including joint planning and interviews of children in investigation of sexual abuse within the family or caring agency.
d Police should recognise and develop their responsibility for the protection of the child as extending beyond the collection of evidence for court proceedings. This should include their attendance at case conferences and assistance to the other child protection agencies.

There is no doubt that the police have responded to all of the above. There is, however, a considerable way still to travel before we can claim any achievement, other than the provision of a model which has had impact. There remain further issues which need to be resolved, including joint funding and provision, joint training to a core syllabus, joint interview qualifications. There is a need for changes in the law regarding the child as a witness, consideration of the rights of children, and a balance in the rights of an accused. As video recording takes on a more significant role in the developing response, we foresee that systems and their supporting systems and their supporting regulations will need to be changed. All these, and I feel sure many more, such as the extension of the power and ability of Area Child Protection Committees, and the training of middle and senior management, will all help ensure that the police will be both able and willing to sustain the momentum of all the efforts to do something for the abused child.

Joint investigation means everyone is responsible. The super tanker is still moving forward, but each one of us from whichever organisation, can only respond as part of a network designed to help the abused child. The ethos of the police response must be communication and mutual trust in the intentions of joint working for the benefit of children and their families.

8 The child witness in court

Rhona Flin and Julian Boon

Each year, a surprising number of children will find themselves in the role of witness for a criminal trial: the majority of these children will be bystander witnesses rather than victims. For a child who has watched a road accident or an assault, the thought of giving evidence in court can be a daunting prospect and the trial itself may prove to be a formidable experience. But in the case of a child victim of sexual abuse, who may be facing many other social and emotional difficulties, the appearance in court and the interrogation by lawyers in an open forum can be highly stressful and potentially damaging. The obvious distress of child sexual abuse victims in criminal courts has been well documented by both the media and by professionals who have described the ordeal as 'a revictimisation' or 'a second rape'. In Britain, such concern has recently prompted legal review and consequently some minor revision of the procedures and rules governing the hearing of children's evidence. In this chapter we examine the status of the child witness in criminal trials and present an overview of current psychological research into children's experiences as witnesses.

As psychologists conducting research in this area, we appreciate the difficulties confronting fellow professionals who must rapidly familiarise themselves with the intricacies of criminal law in order to give expert evidence or to prepare a child for court. Therefore in the first section we have presented a simplified description of the legal systems in England and Scotland and the particular rules that relate to children's evidence.

We then examine, in the second section, the typical legal procedures which a child will encounter during a criminal trial and discuss

recent innovative practices. Frequently child abuse victims will also
be involved in civil cases regarding care, custody or wardship. While
aspects of these proceedings may be experientially similar for the
child, the objectives and legal ground rules can be very different and
any comparison of the two systems is outwith the scope of this chapter (see Martin, this volume or Jones et al., 1987 for further details).
   From the research which we have conducted in Aberdeen (Flin,
Davies and Tarrant, 1988) and our current work in Glasgow (with
Ray Bull and Anne Knox) we consider, in the third section of this
chapter, the question of whether children find attending court to be
stressful and what effects this might have on the child's psychological
well-being or on the quality of their evidence. Our remit is to study
child witnesses in criminal prosecutions and so the findings discussed
below relate to a comprehensive sample of children and not just to
victims of sexual abuse. Finally, in the fourth section we summarise
the practical measures which can be employed by social workers to
minimise any unnecessary stress for child witnesses who have to give
evidence in criminal trials.

Criminal courts and the child's evidence

The basic legal machinery

   In England, all prosecutions start in the magistrates' courts.
Offences are graded into three legal categories according to their
seriousness. The least serious must be tried by the magistrates 'summarily'. For offences in the most serious category the magistrates
must conduct a preliminary hearing, known as 'committal proceedings', and 'commit the case for trial' at the Crown Court. Offences of
medium gravity fall into a third category known as 'either way'
offences; on principle these are also tried in the Crown Court following committal proceedings, but they may also be tried summarily in
the magistates' court if the magistrates think a summary trial would
be suitable and the defendant consents. Where a case is tried in the
Crown Court a child victim may have to appear first in a magistrates'
court for committal proceedings (which determine whether the
accused should be committed for a trial on indictment) and then subsequently at the Crown Court for the trial itself. In the magistrates'
courts, trials are heard by lay magistrates (at least two but more
typically three), who are advised by a legally trained clerk. The prosecution is usually conducted by a lawyer from the Crown Prosecution Service. In the Crown Court, there will be a judge and a jury of
12 persons. The prosecution is conducted by a barrister who will
have been instructed by the Crown Prosecution service.
   In Scotland, the criminal courts are structured into three tiers.

The district courts deal with the least serious cases which are usually tried by lay magistrates (justices of the peace), advised by a legal clerk. A lawyer called a procurator fiscal (a public prosecutor) conducts the prosecution. The sheriff courts are presided over by judges, who sit alone or with a jury of 15 persons when the crime is of a more serious nature. The sheriff court trials are also prosecuted by a procurator fiscal. The most serious cases are tried in the High Court where a senior judge will sit with a jury, and the prosecution is conducted by a barrister, known as an advocate depute.

Child witnesses in criminal trials

Criminal proceedings in England, Wales and Scotland are founded in the same adversarial tradition. This in essence means that the trial represents a contest between two opposing parties, each of which presents their case and the court decides between them. In many other countries an inquisitorial system is used where the court itself conducts an official enquiry. Some British lawyers believe that the latter system might be a more useful approach when child witnesses are involved. McEwan (1988) argued 'Where children are caught up in the gladiatorial contest between parties which is our adversarial method of trial, they are bound to suffer'.

Scottish law differs in several important respects from English law, accordingly the particular rules governing children's evidence are described separately for each jurisdiction.

ENGLAND AND WALES

The position of child witnesses has recently been altered and updated with respect to the Criminal Justice Act of 1988. There is no longer any legal distinction between child witnesses who give evidence under oath and those (generally younger) children who give unsworn evidence. (Prior to this Act, unsworn evidence had to be corroborated, that is, supported by additional evidence.) A child of 10 years and older will probably be asked to take the oath in the same fashion as an adult witness. When a younger child is called to give evidence, he or she must first be shown to be a competent witness. The oath is not generally administered to a child under the age of 10 years, but in order for a child to be allowed to give unsworn evidence, the judge must be satisfied that the child 'understands the duty of speaking the truth'. Whether the child gives evidence on oath, unsworn or not at all, is determined by asking the child questions on their understanding of concepts such as truth, promise, God and the Bible. There is no standard test of competence and in practice such assessments will vary across courts and among individual judges and magistrates. Children under the age of 6 years are generally deemed (by case law), too young to give evidence at all. This is rather unfortunate because they are not too young to be victims of sexual abuse and may well be able to give a coherent account of the events in question.

In the eyes of English law, unsworn and sworn evidence are now of equal status and a defendant can be convicted on the strength of the child's evidence alone. This represents an important improvement to the law because in many child abuse cases no corroborating evidence can be found. Frequently there are no medical signs or these disappear very quickly (Heger, 1989). Child sexual abuse, by its very nature, rarely takes place in front of other witnesses. As an American prosecutor put it, 'These offences do not take place on the 25 yard line of a football game' (*BBC Panorama*, 6 September 1986). However, in sexual cases, the judge is usually required to warn the jury of the dangers of convicting on the basis of uncorroborated evidence. Such warnings may significantly weaken the credibility of the child's evidence in the minds of the jury.

Within the English legal system, there is at present a climate of review and revision. The Home Office commissioned a survey of the psychological research on the reliability of children's evidence which concluded that 'children need not be debarred from giving evidence simply on the basis of age' (Hedderman, 1987). This finding was obviously instrumental in the removal of the corroboration requirement for unsworn evidence. Sadly, attempts to change the competency ruling within the Criminal Justice Act to enable younger children's evidence to be heard were less successful. However, in response to an increasingly vocal lobby, who protested that children were frequently unable to cope with the demands of an open courtroom, provision was passed for the introduction of closed-circuit television (video-link), for child victims of sex and violence offences, in twelve Crown Courts, on an experimental basis from January 1989. This enables the child to remain in a small room outwith the courtroom while they give their evidence via the TV system. A team of research psychologists have been funded by the Home Office to evaluate the operation and impact of this new system. Unfortunately, there is no provision for the video link to be introduced into magistrates' courts and as explained above, child victims may have to give evidence in these courts at an earlier stage of the proceedings.

Many professionals who work with child victims would still argue that the present system, even with a video-link, remains quite unsatisfactory. There are a number of stress factors (e.g. waiting for the trial date, waiting in the unfamiliar surroundings of the court buildings, being interviewed by strangers) which will not be alleviated by the video-link. We believe that the child's evidence should be recorded on videotape during the initial stages of an investigation. Even if the child is still required to appear in court, such a system would confer three major benefits. First, the evidence would be recorded soon after the incident and would be less prone to contamination from decay or interference. Witnesses can wait many months for cases to come to trial and the quality of memory deteriorates over time — in adults as well as children. Second, a video-taped record as opposed to a written police statement demonstrates the full complement of non-verbal communication. Non-verbal behaviours signal attitudes and emotional states and this is a very powerful communication channel, especially in young children. Moreover, the video-tape would also preserve a complete record of the manner and content of the interviewer's questioning. Third, if the necessary legal examination of the child could be conducted outwith the court and recorded on the video (a video-deposition), this might avoid the necessity of the child attending court that child witnesses may find stressful which are unrelated to the giving of evidence.

The question of video-taped evidence is contentious and that procedure is not without legal and procedural difficulties. In civil cases, where the burden of proof required is less stringent (on a 'balance of probability'), and the rules of evidence are less restrictive, such video-recordings are currently admissible as evidence. However, in criminal cases, where the prosecution must establish the defendant's guilt to the more onerous standards of 'beyond reasonable doubt', the potential role of video-taped interviews is much more limited. Principally, out-of-court testimony on any general basis is held to be alien to the traditions of English justice. More specifically, objections to the showing of video-taped recordings have been raised on the grounds that they: a) constitute hearsay evidence which is not admissible; and b) that they allow no opportunity for defence cross-examination. Attempts to make provision for the introduction of video-recorded evidence in the recent Criminal Justice Act were met with strong and successful resistance from the Government. Although no changes were made to permit videotapes, they did, due to growing parliamentary and public pressure, establish a Commission of Enquiry chaired by His Honour Judge Pigot, QC, to examine the question of videotaped evidence and we await their findings with great interest.

SCOTLAND

In Scotland, there is no fixed age limit below which a child is not permitted to give evidence. Children as young as three years of age have given evidence in criminal trials; a situation that would be unthinkable south of the border. As in England, the child must be shown to be a competent witness which means that they can under-stand the difference between right and wrong and that they can give intelligible evidence. The judge undertakes this assessment, although it appears that in practice children are often presumed to be competent witnesses unless there is good reason (on the basis of preliminary conversations with the child) to assume otherwise. Young children (less than 12 years) do not normally give evidence on oath but older children (over 14 years) are usually sworn.

Another important difference between English and Scots law is, that in Scotland, the evidence of any witness, whether a child or an adult, must be corroborated by other material evidence before any-one can be convicted of an offence. In general, hearsay evidence (and video-taped interviews come into this category) is not admissible. The Scottish Law Commission has been examining the whole issue of children's evidence and is currently studying invited submissions to its recent Discussion paper (1988) which considered a number of innovative approaches, including closed-circuit television and video-recorded evidence.

For a more detailed description of the legal rules governing child-ren's evidence and the relevant psychological research into children's eyewitness memory, see Spencer and Flin (1989).

What happens during the trial

Before the child enters the courtroom

Any child who has been cited as a witness in a criminal prosecu-tion is obliged to attend court on the day of the trial unless instructed to the contrary. In practice, many children who attend court are not in fact called to give evidence. In our first study of 110 child wit-nesses based in Aberdeen, we found that of those children cited, only 23% actually gave evidence, a further 43% were waiting in court but were not required to enter the witness box. The latter group did not give evidence typically because of late guilty pleas, (a very significant number of accused persons change their plea at the last possible moment). In other cases when the child was not called, the case was dropped or the trial was postponed. The remaining 34% of witnesses simply did not turn up at the courtroom or were advised that they were not required for that day. Thus in some instances where the defence gives an early indication that the accused intends to plead guilty, it is technically possible for the prosecution to countermand its cited witnesses and prevent the need for them coming to court at all, although in very busy offices this may not always be feasible.

Preliminary findings from our Glasgow project (a much larger sample) show a similar pattern but indicate that these countermanded cases are very much in the minority. Our figures suggest that 45% of cases are subject to late guilty pleas which are entered on the day of the trial, and again, the children involved attended court although they were ultimately not required to give evidence. In addition a further 40% of child witnesses had to attend court but did not give evidence for a variety of reasons, such as adjournments owing to the accused or essential witnesses not turning up, the case being dropped by the prosecution, or simply that it transpires as the case unfolds that the child's evidence is not required. In cases where the trial date is delayed, the witnesses are placed in a position of continued uncertainty. This is especially true where the accused has absconded and it is not possible to schedule another trial date until he or she has been arrested.

Interviews which we conducted with children and their parents who were waiting in court to give evidence indicated that this very long wait for trials to take place can be stressful. In the Aberdeen sample children waited an average of six months between the time of the incident and the date of the trial. This is not untypical of English courts and some witnesses may experience significantly longer delays. The other major stress factor before the trial is fear of the unknown. Child witnesses and their parents (probably like many other adults) frequently have little or no knowledge of criminal court procedures and understandably this increases their anxiety before the trial. One way of reducing such nervousness is to prepare child witnesses (and their parents) for their day in court. In North America there are a wide range of materials available to prepare children for court (leaflets, books, video-tapes and even 'court schools', see Flin and Tarrant, 1989 for details). In Britain suitable leaflets have until recently been non-existent although this appears to be improving. For example, West Yorkshire police have an illustrated pamphlet for children, the Victim Support Scheme have designed a leaflet for adults (National Association of Victim Support Schemes, 1988), the prosecutors in Glasgow now send a useful information sheet to child witnesses with citations and a little book for child witnesses, written by a social worker, is due to be published later this year (Bray, 1989).

Another possible technique which is clearly helpful is for someone familiar with the courts to show the child round beforehand so that they are not plunged into a totally alien environment on the day of the trial. In our experience this now happens in a number of courts, although due to time pressures, this may be carried out on an *ad hoc* basis and usually only for more serious cases. An additional difficulty for those attempting to prepare children in this way is that it is often difficult to predict before the day of the trial, which courtroom will be used and which judge will hear the case. Courtrooms vary in size, appearance and formality, as do judges!

If any special procedures are to be used for hearing the child's evidence, this decision will normally be taken before he/she goes into the courtroom. These measures are usually introduced in cases where a child witness is particularly young and/or where a case concerns serious charges especially of a sexual or violent nature. Most commonly these measures are designed to make the court's atmosphere less strange and intimidating. They include the removal of gowns and/or wigs, allowing the child to give testimony from the lawyer's table in the well of the court or the child sitting with the judge on the bench, or the judge sitting at the table in the well of the court. Many witnesses benefit by being given a microphone, which avoids repeated requests to 'speak up, so that the jury can hear you'. Sexual abuse victims are understandably reluctant to shout the details of a sexual assault across a packed courtroom. Other measures include the use of screens to block the child's view of the accused, the presence of a supporting adult (e.g. parent, police officer, social worker) and clearing the court of members of the public. Unfortunately, the effectiveness of such measures is limited by the basic requirements of the adversarial system and current legal procedures. For example, even when a screen is used, the child may still have to identify the accused in the courtroom. In a jury trial, when the court is cleared, there may be 20 or more unfamiliar adults still present when the child gives evidence. The worth of allowing a supporter in court is diminished if, each time the child looks for the support she expected, she is immediately told 'don't look round because your mummy can't help you here'. If the parent or social worker is a witness in the case they will not be allowed in court until they have given evidence. Sometimes judges will agree to hear evidence in a rescheduled order so that, for example, the parent may give evidence before the child (while another trusted adult waits with the child in the waiting room), and then the parent can sit near the child in the court room. Parents are sometimes very surprised and shocked to find out that they will not automatically be allowed to sit with their child while she is giving evidence.

At any rate, whether any or all of these measures are adopted is entirely at the discretion of the judge and, in our experience, there is wide variation in practice and requests for special procedures are not always granted. This is not to say that social workers involved with child witnesses should not ask the prosecutor dealing with a particular case to at least attempt to persuade the judge to allow a reduction in formality or to permit the presence of a supporting adult.

The child in the courtroom

Once admitted to the court the child will either be asked to take the oath or will be tested for competence to check that they are capable of giving unsworn evidence. There are no special rules for the assessment of competence and, as mentioned earlier, the child is usually asked by the judge a series of questions to establish that the child understands the importance of telling the truth and can give a coherent account of events. Typically, the judge will attempt to talk informally with the child and will ask some general questions such as 'What age are you?', 'Where do you go to school?', and then some more specific questions of a moral or religious nature 'What does it mean to tell a lie?' 'Why is it important to tell the truth?', 'Do you know what the Bible is?'

Once a child is admitted as a witness, there is a common framework for taking evidence from both children and adults alike. Initially, this takes the form of an 'examination-in-chief' in which the prosecuting lawyer attempts to get the witness to tell the court about matters relating to the alleged crime. In English Crown Court trials (and sometimes in Scottish trials) the child will not normally have met the prosecuting counsel before the trial. This means that the person who is attempting to lead the child's evidence to prove the case, is a total stranger to the child. One does not have to be a psychologist to realise that this is unlikely to maximise rapport between the examiner and the child.

Following the examination-in-chief, the defence lawyer has the opportunity to 'cross-examine' the witness on what was said in response to the questions of the prosecution and in their original statements to the police. The principal aim of the defence at this stage is to cast reasonable doubt on the incriminating elements of the witness' evidence by calling into question the credibility of what has been said. (As it stands the law permits the defendant to conduct his own cross-examination of the witnesses, should he so desire, although fortunately this rarely happens.) Finally, there is an opportunity for the prosecution to conduct a re-examination. In this the prosecuting lawyer aims to consolidate the prosecution case by highlighting the incriminating facts, and clarifying any areas which might have muddied the Crown's position as a result of the defence cross-examination. In cases where there are multiple accused, and where during the examination-in-chief, a witness has given evidence incriminating each of them, it is likely that each defendant's lawyer would require to cross-examine the witness. In Glasgow, for example, we have seen cases where a child has been cross-examined eight times by different lawyers — ten examinations in total including two from the prosecution.

In one of the most publicised trials this decade, former *Coronation Street* actor Peter Adamson was acquitted of indecently assaulting two little girls in a swimming pool. Reporting on the trial with the headline, 'Ordeal by witness box', *The Times* (29 March 1983) asked, 'Do the ends of justice really require that a child of eight should be grilled to the point of tears in the intimidating surroundings of a packed courtroom?' This question referred to an incident during the child's cross-examination where she burst into tears and had to be given a glass of water before she was able to continue.

Brennan and Brennan (1988) argue 'Cross-examination is that part of court proceedings where the interests of the child are most likely to be ignored and sacrificed'. The defence cross-examination is sometimes characterised as the key culprit if the child becomes distressed while in the witness box. To our knowledge this has never been scientifically demonstrated and in our experience the situation is much more complex. There are a host of influences which can affect the style of examination used to interview the child. Where, for instance, a child may be reluctant to restate in open court what had been previously said in a police statement, the need for a prosecuting lawyer to apply pressure to extract the information may be at least as great as that of a defence lawyer. Within the last few years, there have been reports of sexual abuse trials in the Old Bailey where the child victims were unable to give any evidence at all during direct examination because of their anxiety and distress.

Undoubtedly, there are aspects of cross-examination that witnesses can find traumatic, particularly the repeated attempts to discredit their evidence, such as 'I put it to you that you are not telling the truth'. It should be said, however, that many defence lawyers argue that it is not in their interest to upset small children in the witness box, as this is likely to have a profound effect on the jury and to weaken the defence case. A number of factors appear to influence the manner and quality of the child's examination. These include: the personalities of all the individuals concerned, the circumstances of the case, and the degree to which the examining lawyer perceives the witness to be hostile or co-operative to the line of questioning. While the project in Glasgow is currently looking at the impact of these factors on the style of questioning used in court, the complexity of the relevant variables and their potentially interactive nature would suggest that any generalisations made concerning the effects of defence cross-examinations would be likely to be simplistic and premature.

In communicating with each other and with the Judge in court, the lawyers as a matter of course use a significant amount of legal terminology (e.g. 'your lordship', 'objection', 'learned friend', 'recess' and 'adjourn'). This has the effect of accentuating the formality of the atmosphere and the proceedings. In addition to the use of such archaic terms, it has been suggested that some lawyers may deliberately use difficult phraseology (e.g. double negatives — 'Did you not say no?') to confuse the child witness, with the aim of calling into question the credibility of their testimony (Brennan and Brennan, 1988). In the Brennans' study of the language used to cross-examine child victims in Australian courts, they report an illuminating catalogue of language constructions designed to make life difficult for children in the witness box. One notable example merits repetition:

> Now he is suggesting some other things to you that might I suppose remind you that might have happened now I suppose it is hard to understand why he says these things to you when you say it didn't happen, that's hard to understand isn't it, but he is allowed to do these things and if you say it didn't happen, all you have to do is say no, okay or if it did say yes, now do you follow that? (Brennan and Brennan, 1988, p.42).

However, children can become easily wrong-footed, even *unintentionally*, by phrases with which they are not familiar. We have seen children misunderstand or become confused by questions such as: 'What is your position in relation to . . . '; 'What happened subsequent/prior to . . . '; 'Did he appear to take offence?'; 'Did he try to resist?'; 'After the transfer [of a weapon from one to another] what, if anything, happened?'

In a related vein, the normal procedure for taking evidence from witnesses is to ask a series of closed questions. Typically these require short answers (often yes/no) rather than an extended recollection or exposition. Frequently this means that the lawyer, in order to retain tight control of the examination will interrupt a witness's natural flow to obtain specific answers to specific questions. This tendency towards a very closed and detailed questioning style is often accompanied by repeated requests to amplify the answers, rather than allowing the child to describe the events in what he or she remembers as the natural order. Despite the fact that lawyers may tell the witness that such questioning is done to avoid confusion, children sometimes complain, while giving evidence, that it has the effect of making them more 'mixed up'. Highly articulate lawyers who are steeped in the traditions and legal jargon of the courts may, understandably, experience difficulty in accommodating to the linguistic requirements of the child and they are unlikely to have received specialist training in child interviewing techniques.

After the child has given evidence they are usually allowed to leave the court building and to go home. Children are not permitted to remain in the courtroom, even in the public benches, to hear the rest of the trial. Whether or not they are formally advised of the outcome of the case may depend on their role in the proceedings or the efficiency of the relevant agency. Sometimes victims complain that they were not officially notified or given any explanation for the verdict and this may cause additional distress (National Association of Victim Support Schemes, 1988).

The psychological effect on the child

Do children suffer from stress when called to court to give evidence? There is very little published evidence which can be used to establish whether children are affected by their experience. However, 'very little evidence of stress' in this context means that the necessary research has not been conducted rather than a proven absence of distress. Anecdotal accounts, media reports and professional opinion all agree that attending court and giving evidence can be highly stressful. Criminal courts are not the most suitable environment for conducting sensitive interviews with child victims. Most people who work with child victims think that this is all so obvious that it is hardly worthy of scientific investigation. However, in reality this is an important issue which does require to be researched because not all members of the legal profession are convinced of the need for change.

If we consider the relevant research which has been carried out with adult witnesses, there does seem to be sufficient reason to believe that many witnesses find that giving evidence is at best a nerve-wracking and at worst a highly traumatic experience. Even expert witnesses report that this can be an ordeal and studies of occupational stress in police officers identify 'giving evidence' as a principal stress factor.

If we therefore assume that some child witnesses will find attending court to be very stressful, then we need to look for possible causes. If sensible changes are to be made to the law, then this kind of research is of prime importance. What aspects of court are stressful for children?

One valuable source of information is the accumulated wisdom of those who must deal with child witnesses as part of their professional duties. We surveyed about 90 individuals (social workers, police, prosecutors and judges) who had experience of working with child witnesses in criminal courts and asked them what were causes of stress for children. Several important problems were described: confronting the defendant; giving evidence, especially being cross-examined; the legal terminology; the formality of the courtroom and waiting facilities. They specifically listed a number of factors relating to the formal layout of the courtroom: isolation of the witness box; proximity to the accused; the poor acoustics; the elevation of the judge; size of the chairs; dimensions of the room and distance between participants (lawyers are skilled at projecting their voices and may stand quite far from the witness during the examination).

These findings are endorsed by similar studies of American professionals (Whitcomb et al., 1985).

What was slightly different about our work is that we were also
interviewing child witnesses before their trials, observing them in
court if they gave evidence, and interviewing them after the trial.
Hardly any research exists, and there is no British work, on what
children think and feel about going to court. For obvious reasons we
did not ask children anything about the case, but we asked them how
they had felt that morning about coming to court. The majority of
children said that they were nervous or worried and we asked them
why they felt this way. Their responses indicated that they were concerned about the following: having to answer the questions and to
speak out in the courtroom; being in the witness box; not knowing
what they would be expected to do; remembering the incident; confronting the accused and fear of retribution. Not all children could or
would say what was making them feel anxious.

It should be noted that this was a very small sample of children
(46), the majority of whom were bystanders rather than victims.
Another possible source of bias is that these children had been
regarded as sufficiently capable to cite as prosecution witnesses and
they may not be typical of the total population of children who
witness or are victims of crime. How many child witnesses are not
thought capable of handling a trial, thus preventing the case from
coming to court? How many parents do not contact the police
because they do not wish their child to have to stand up in the witness
box? These questions are important but cannot be answered. The
lack of relevant statistics on such matters may be concealing significant problems of non-reporting.

Effects of stress on the quality of the child's evidence

This is extremely difficult to assess as it is not possible to gather
any independent measure (e.g. physiological) as to the degree of
stress being experienced or how the witness would behave in a different situation. Although in cases where witnesses cry, refuse to talk or
faint (we have seen all of these) then it seems a valid assumption that
the witnesses are less than relaxed and certainly these reactions are
unlikely to enhance the quality of their evidence. Recently, an adult
rape victim was jailed in England because she was too frightened to
give evidence in court. Courts are deliberately designed to be formal and intimidating to impress the masses and to frighten criminals
and associated witnesses into telling the truth. Whether anxious,
innocent witnesses are more or less likely to accurately recall events
in this situation is clearly a matter which most psychologists would
be prepared to debate. All the psychological research on interviewing

children (particularly victims) would argue that the best quality of evidence is likely to be gathered when the child is relaxed, when the child trusts the interviewer and when the interviewer is well trained in appropriate questioning techniques. We would venture to suggest that this is not the situation experienced by child witnesses in court.

Long term psychological effects on the child

Are child witnesses psychologically harmed by giving evidence? It can and has been argued that children are not affected or (to quote a senior Scottish Judge) that any distress caused to children was 'of a temporary nature and what one would expect of a witness before a court'. Some psychiatrists have stated that children can be helped or empowered by giving evidence. The answer seems to be that again we have very little evidence to support or refute particular viewpoints.

There are several studies which suggest that child victims are negatively affected by having to attend court. Unfortunately most of these have methodological flaws, but David Jones has been researching this question with Gail Goodman in Denver and their preliminary findings on a small subsample of their cases indicated that child sex abuse victims did show some subsequent behavioural disturbance compared to matched victims who did not testify (Goodman and Jones, 1988).

In our own project we are trying to assess long term effects by the use of follow-up questionnaires, a method that is likely to be beset with all the difficulties inherent in this method of data collection. One of the problems in attempting to measure the psychological effects of being cited as a witness and of giving evidence is that, for abuse victims, it is very difficult to disentangle the reaction from post-traumatic stress effects. We can, however, begin to separate these causal factors by assessing stress effects, or the lack of them in bystander witnesses as well as victims. Our experience to date suggests that whether or not the child experiences stress or any subsequent reaction will be the result of a multiplicity of factors, relating to the personality of the child, the parental reaction, the circumstances of the offence, the investigation, the conduct of the trial and the verdict. Whether or not a child victim finds the experience of giving testimony empowering is likely to rest principally on whether the accused was convicted or acquitted.

Helping child witnesses

Before the trial

If a child you are working with will have to attend court to give

evidence then it is important that they have at least some knowledge
of what is expected of them and of what will take place in the courtroom. Research has shown that children being admitted to hospital
cope better when they have been prepared for their experience and
this would seem to be true for child witnesses facing the prospect of a
trial. Parents, too, can be very anxious and careful preparation may
help both parties. The use of leaflets and tours of the courtroom were
discussed earlier. Anyone attempting to advise witnesses will
obviously require a sound knowledge of courtroom procedures and if
you are unfamiliar it would be a good idea to talk to others with
experience and to visit a court beforehand. Members of the public
may sit and watch trials and court officials will be helpful if you
explain the purpose of your visit. On a first visit, criminal courts
seem to be populated with hundreds of very purposeful people who
all know their way around and witnesses need to be told where to go,
who to speak to, where to wait, etc., in order to feel reasonably confident about their visit.

If you are not sure about the meaning of basic legal terms, then
most legal tomes would be the worst place to start. Reference books,
such as the *Readers Digest* guide to the law (*Reaers Digest*, 1985) can
provide a basic introduction. It is important to remember that children are not only ignorant of the law but they frequently misunderstand words which they claim that they know (adults probably do the
same).

In a study we conducted with non-witnesses (Flin et al., 1989),
we found that children under the age of ten years have a limited com-
prehension of legal vocabulary and court procedures. (Older children
and adults did not always perform much better.) Children sometimes
think they know what a legal term means, but in fact misunderstand
its true meaning. For example, they may believe that 'to prosecute' is
'to hang' or 'to kill', and they may find the roles of the various legal
professionals and the jury difficult to comprehend. A six year old
told us that judges 'teach people dancing' and a ten year old said of a
jury, 'They ask the criminal questions, then he gives up and they sit
down'. An eight year old thought that a lawyer 'gives money to the
poor' and in a similar American study, some children believed that a
lawyer 'loans money', 'sits around', 'plays golf' or 'lies'. Amusing as
these responses may be, misconceptions about the role of a witness or
the purpose of a trial will undoubtedly contribute to pre-trial anxiety
and support workers must be alert to these difficulties.

When preparing a child witness for court, it is important not to
rehearse or to coach the child as this may significantly weaken the
child's credibility on cross-examination. Many child witnesses will
look for guidance and an experienced police officer told us that she
had to resort to saying 'Just tell them what you told me earlier' to

avoid this problem. Emphasise that the child should say if they do not hear or do not understand a question; and tell them that they must say 'I don't know' when they do not know the answer. (Children are aware, that in school, the response 'I don't know' is not usually a good answer.) The option of refreshing the child's memory with prior statements or taped interviews should be discussed with the police or the prosecutor in charge of the case.

The day of the trial

Witnesses need to be prepared for delays and for the possibility that the trial will not run on that day. Glasgow Sheriff Court must be one of the few which actually has a creche facility. Waiting rooms in most courts are not geared for children and accompanying adults need to come equipped with books or play materials in case of long delays. It may be worth asking the court officials if there is anywhere else that can be used to wait, such as an interview room, particularly if the child is distressed or can see the accused.

In terms of introducing measures designed to make the courtroom more informal (see above), these should be discussed before the trial with the other professionals involved, such as the police or the prosecutor but the final decision rests with the judge and requests will not always be successful.

After the child has given evidence most parents or guardians want to leave the court immediately. It may be helpful to offer support at that stage, depending on how the child has coped with the examination.

Postscript

There have been changes to the rules governing children's evidence and although these do not go far enough, they represent a step in the right direction. Obviously the rights of the accused remain paramount but victims must surely have rights too. Within the constraints of our adversarial system there are ways of introducing new technology to minimise unnecessary stress for witnesses without threatening the rights of the accused (see, for example, the Scottish Law Commission paper, 1988). When the question of children's evidence next comes up for public debate, it is very important that those social workers involved with child victims add their voices to the argument because lawyers have loud voices and appear to be eternally resistant to change. Pressure for reform must come from those working at the sharp end who realise that justice is not always being done within our present system.

9 Play based investigative assessment of children who may have been sexually abused

David Glasgow

Introduction

This chapter concerns a particular sort of work undertaken with a child who may have been sexually abused which is intended to assist legal proceedings. 'Investigative assessment' is intended to be distinct both from interviews conducted by statutory agents and also formal play therapy. Although some goals and qualities are shared with both of these, a well-planned and conducted investigative assessment may contribute more than either to a child's long-term well-being. The principle underlying investigative assessment is that the use of techniques drawn from 'therapeutic' practice can improve the quality of evidence submitted to court (and so more effectively protect a child), minimise the distress caused by traditional interview techniques and also introduce at a very early stage communications to the child of a therapeutic value. It is not possible to describe the actual process of play based investigative assessment in any detail here, the aim is rather to describe some of its qualities and the functions it serves, particularly with reference to children under the age of 10 years. (For an account of one approach to play assessment see Glasgow, 1987.)

The actions of statutory and supportive agents in cases of suspected child sexual abuse must vary depending upon circumstances and the evidence, or 'indicators', upon which suspicion of child sexual abuse (CSA) is based. Although it is very difficult to specify 'rules' as to exactly what should be done and when, it is possible to identify ways of thinking about the information available and the sort of work with the child that might be appropriate.

Investigation of suspected CSA

Figure 9.1 illustrates two dimensions which are of relevance when considering action in suspected CSA. Taking 'formality' first; at the low end of this dimension lies the immediate response to that behaviour of children which may be indicative of CSA, at the time at which it occurs. In the middle of the dimension lie more planned investigations which may involve special observation of a child and also pre-arranged contact with them, but still undertaken by those people with whom the child is familiar. At the high end of the formality dimension lies the investigations which accompany a statutory response. These may include interview by the police and/or social services, medical examination and referral to a child 'expert' for a formal assessment. The line marked A indicates a case in which, too early, a statutory response is overconcerned with detective and investigative priorities. This child is likely to be over interviewed and distressed. Line B illustrates a balanced progression from concern to action with a concurrent progression towards detective and investigative priorities, but continuing to take into account therapeutic and supportive priorities. This does not only mean being 'kind' to the child; it means understanding the information they are able to produce and its role in child protection proceedings. Such an approach is likely to produce better quality evidence in the long run. Line C illustrates the situation which becomes progressively formal but without acknowledging detective and investigative needs. An extreme example of this is where a professional takes a child or family on for therapy knowing that child sexual abuse is possible or probable, without involving statutory agencies.

There is the danger that the position on the formality dimension of the response of professionals may be incongruous with the degree of disclosure or the evidence upon which suspicion is based. This not only involves the possibility that a response may be *under formal*; as in the case where someone, perhaps a teacher, suspects that a child has been abused but only ever addresses the issue with the child when and if it arises (this may be appropriate but should not continue indefinitely). *Over-formality* of response can be equally damaging, even if a child has been sexually abused. Interviews and medical examinations occurring without less formal information gathering

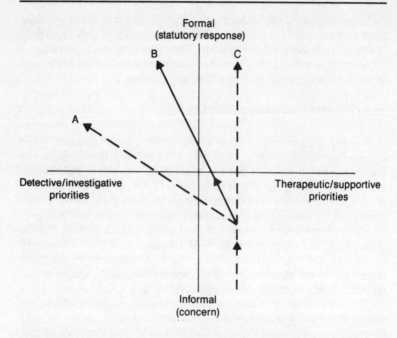

Figure 9.1 The dimensions of detection versus therapy

can not only be unduly distressing but may actually render a disclosure less likely. In the worst cases a child who has actually been abused may be more isolated and less likely to obtain help after an uninformed and premature investigation. It is also obvious that such an investigation is likely to alert the perpetrator(s) of the abuse to the possibility that there is a risk of discovery. A perpetrator's probable response to this would be to increase the sanctions operating on the child to inhibit their disclosure, whether this be bribery, blackmail, threats or violence.

The orthogonal dimension of detection . . . therapy/support merely reflects the emphasis of different individuals involved in working with suspected or actual child sexual abuse. The position on this dimension will reflect the priorities of an agency; i.e. the police force place a high priority on detection, whilst a psychotherapist is likely to place a higher priority on therapy with the child, but will also be influenced by the personal perspectives and skills of a particular person. It is also important to appreciate that no individual should fail to acknowledge the objectives pertaining to both ends of this dimension and wherever possible take both into account in all decisions and actions.

Typically, in a particular case of CSA, it is likely that the behaviour of professionals will progress 'up' the formality dimension from the low formality end towards the high formality end, (although if it becomes apparent that fears seem to be unfounded, level of vigilance, monitoring or investigation may become less formal). There also tends to be a concurrent progression from the therapy/support end of the other dimension towards detection. There may well be a trigger event, the occurrence of which promotes action involving a very high level of formality and emphasis on detection, involving criminal investigation and child care proceedings (see figure 9.2).

As indicated above, this chapter is concerned with investigative assessment of children in cases of suspected child sexual abuse. With respect to figure 9.1, its characteristics are that of a high formality action, probably, although not necessarily, occurring in conjunction with Child Care Proceedings. It is, in ways which should become apparent below, qualitatively different from 'interviews' which may be conduced with children suspected of having been sexually abused. It may be regarded as complimentary to medical investigations with which it can usefully be compared.

Medical evidence of CSA

Criminal investigation of CSA tends to emphasise the importance of medical, 'corroborative' evidence of abuse and unfortunately this as sometimes influenced those involved in child care proceedings to share a similar emphasis. In fact, most children who have been sexually abused do not present with physical evidence (Kerns, 1981; Rogers, 1982). Moreover, even where clear medical evidence exists, it is rarely regarded as conclusive proof of abuse and even more rarely does it implicate a particular perpetrator. This is consistent with Finkelhor's (1984) observations that those who sexually abuse children tend to avoid penetration which would be likely to leave strong evidence of abuse, if not actually identifying a particular person as the perpetrator.

The tendency to emphasise physical corroboration has also promoted the belief that the task is one of diagnosis rather than a forensic investigation which draws on evidence from many sources. This and related issues are discussed in the context of the Cleveland crisis in Glasgow and Bentall (1989). The crucial point is that child sexual abuse is not a diagnosis (for contrasting view see Corwin, 1988) and that to regard it as such may cause professionals to behave as though the identification of a particular child as having been abused is one which obviates or overshadows the need for further, particularly behavioural, assessments.

Behavioural evidence of CSA

The purpose of an investigative assessment is not to 'obtain a disclosure'. What a child says about sexual abuse to a person who subsequently describes this in court may well be disregarded as hearsay (although child protection proceedings tend not to stick rigorously to the rules of evidence in this respect). Thus, if children themselves do not give evidence, a problem arises as to how a court can take their comments, feelings, behaviour and needs into account. There are two closely related possibilities which may solve the problem.

1 It is possible for an 'expert' to take what the child says into account, along with all their other behaviour, thus forming an opinion on whether or not they have been abused and by whom. Opinion evidence is often presented in child care proceedings, although the court must be satisfied that the person offering the opinion has special skills or knowledge not shared by others in court. Expert witnesses who give evidence on the behaviour of children tend to be psychologists or psychiatrists. There is however no reason for the expertise necessarily to be theirs alone; if other professionals can demonstrate expertise, their opinion evidence may be accepted.

2 A child can produce material which is acceptable as evidence in court. For example, he or she may write a note or draw a picture giving information about abuse. It is important that the circumstances surrounding the production of the material are communicated to the court so that reasonable inferences can be drawn. If a contemporaneous record of an investigative assessment is made, this itself may be admitted as evidence and also made available to other experts in order that they can form opinions and present them in court. The best form of record is, of course, video-tape and if an adequate assessment has been conducted and recorded in the first instance, this may save both court time and, more importantly, multiple assessments of a child. It also allows the court to have direct access to what the child has actually said.

An investigative assessment may therefore fulfil either or both of the above functions. The adequacy with which it does so will depend on how well it is planned, conducted and the resources available. It is conceivable that it could be part of a joint investigation conducted by a police officer and social worker. Traditionally however, this tends not to be the case: joint investigations are much more likely to take the form of interviews rather than structured, play-based, assessments.

The distinction between interview and assessment is a very important one. Interviews are an adult invention designed to facilitate a rapid exchange of information. Closely related to this are the processes of interrogation and cross-examination which have the additional function of testing the accuracy and reliability of information which emerges. These are entirely inappropriate methods of obtaining information from children. This is partly because children's verbal abilities differ markedly from those of adults, and partly because whereas adults have come to anticipate interview situations and the degree of 'performance' required, a child will experience them very differently. The verbal behaviour of children is characterised not only by a limited vocabulary (this factor obviously becomes increasingly important the younger the child), but also to a very different pattern of conversation to that of adults. A simplistic and judgemental description might be an absence of 'efficient' dialogue. Children tend to be very tolerant, probably dependent, on pauses, silence and repetition; characterisics which sometimes lead to frustrated interviewers and distressed interviewees. Furthermore, the sophistication of children's speech is often dependent on the degree to which its content is related to the child's current environment. Thus, if elicited in a situation in which the subject matter relates to something the child can actually see or do, the child's verbalisation is likely to be more clear, mature and informative. All these points tend to support the need for adults to adopt a style of communication which is much more 'low pressure' than are traditional, adult oriented, interview techniques and is also facilitated by play materials. Through suitable play materials a child may be able to directly experience activities and recreate events, thus prompting a more accurate, relevant and informative communication.

In addition to the above, it is important to note that an interview has a particular social meaning for a child. Not only do they rarely experience interviews, and are therefore unskilled in the conventions involved, but they are likely to believe that an interview is a strong indicator that someone, (possibly themselves), has done something wrong. This leads them to adopt an uncomfortable and defensive position, and motivates them to give the adult what the child thinks they want. This obviously increases the probability of distorted or entirely false information arising from the contact with the child.

Resources necessary for adequate assessment
Skill

One of the reasons that courts have difficulty in identifying exactly who can legitimately give an expert opinion on child sexual abuse in child care proceedings has already been alluded to. The essential skills for an investigative assessment do not belong exclusively to any one profession. Further, it is important to state that the current situation could, and perhaps should, change, with courses and training focussed on child assessments leading to a recognised qualification which would satisfy the courts that a particular person possesses the necessary skills to undertake an assessment.

There are three strands of training which are important. The first is a good knowledge and understanding of development/child psychology. The second is experience of direct work with individual children involving supervision by a qualified person. This is quite different to working with children in general settings and someone who has many years experience 'working with children' may not have the skills to conduct and structure individual sessions with a particular child. The final strand is, again, supervised training but this time involving children who may have been sexually abused. Far too often, for those who are to have direct contact with children who may have been sexually abused, training consists only of a short course of primarily, theoretical and didactic teaching, followed by no 'apprenticeship' phase. The ideal way to acquire child assessment skills is by observing sessions conducted by a skilled practitioner followed by the trainee conducting sessions which are themselves observed, with each session being planned jointly by the trainee and practitioner.

Time

There is often less need for investigation of child sexual abuse to be completed very quickly than one might think (although it may well be that with the introduction of the Children's Bill, time becomes even more of a premium than it is at present). A thorough assessment will take at least three to five sessions although the intersession intervals can be shortened, depending on the urgency of the particular case, in order to make optimum use of the time available. One of the most common mistakes committed by those interviewing or assessing children is to use only a single session which lasts far too long and has the quite unrealistic goal of identifying or excluding child sexual abuse by the end of that particular session. This is very likely to lead to a situation in which the child is uncomfortable, distressed and highly sensitive to any cues the adult may give regarding their expectations. Thus, again this may lead to distorted or entirely inaccurate information, particularly if in conjunction with the above situation the investigator uses leading questions. Although several short sessions may be more difficult to arrange than one long session, if the same amount of time is dedicated to each, the former will be much more productive and allow much more careful planning.

As a rough guide to the duration of sessions it is sensible to spend about 30 minutes with the child aged five and under and up to 45 minutes with a child aged between five and about ten years. This should not be taken to mean that older children can be interviewed for much longer periods, because distress and discomfort are likely to lead to distortion in information, even in adolescence and adulthood.

Setting and resources

The least appropriate setting for the assessment of children (particularly those under ten years) is any kind of office and the ideal is a small playroom containing toys which act to facilitate communication. There are no 'hard and fast' rules about what does and does not facilitate communication and indeed this may vary between children and investigators of different levels of experience.

Materials best avoided:
a Toys which encourage aggressive play such as balls, toy soldiers and certainly weapons, etc. Although it may be *therapeutically* relevant that a child feels particularly angry and aggressive in the context of an assessment, this phenomenon can be quite disruptive. It can also be that a child becomes distressed and frightened by such feelings and so, although anger and aggression should be recognised by an investigator, they should not be encouraged.
b Materials which encourage regression (i.e. behaviour characteristic of a younger age than a child's developmental age) such as sand, water, paints, etc. Some investigators do use these materials skillfully and successfully, but for the relatively inexperienced it is best to avoid regressive behaviour in a child during an assessment. Again this is because, although a child is certainly communicating something about their emotional state, the emphasis of an investigative assessment is on communication about actual events.
c Activity oriented materials, such as games and moving toys can also interfere with communication and tend to contribute little to assessment.

Facilitative materials:
A recurrent theme has been that of communication. Materials which
are valuable in assessment, because they share the characteristic of
facilitating communication, include:

a   Paper and crayons, useful because they can produce a permanent
    record of a communication from a child. Although spontaneous
    sexually explicit drawings are rare, requesting a child to draw the
    person or activity which is not clearly (but may be) related to
    sexual abuse can be very illuminating. As indicated above, it is
    essential that a record should be kept of how a drawing which is to
    be used as evidence in court was elicited.
      If (non-sexually explicit) drawings are put on the wall they also
    serve the very useful purpose of making the child feel more com-
    fortable. This is because they give the child the clear message they
    are in a setting shared by other children, and may even give them
    the feeling that they are not alone in their experiences, perhaps
    that of abuse. This can only facilitate the investigative process.
b   Soft toys and small figures similarly, have the important role of
    generally reassuring the child that the place they are in is a good
    place for children to be. In addition, they also have the essential
    function of providing a means through which the child can act out
    things he or she may have difficulty describing or as indicated
    above, can describe only if their verbal account is supported by
    the manipulation of objects.
c   Sexually accurate dolls serve the specific function of allowing a
    child to act out sexual activity. They should, however, only be
    used in very specific circumstances and as part of a structured
    assessment involving other materials. Particular recommenda-
    tions for their use may be found in Jones and McQuiston (1986),
    Glagow (1987).

Planning an assessment

Unfortunately there is evidence that this essential process is often
neglected or omitted entirely. It is very important that, before conducting an asessment, an investigator should gather some basic information about the child they are to see. Of considerable significance is
the level of the child's cognitive development, which may be evaluated through school performance or more informally through talking to those familiar with the child. If the investigator has a good
understanding of child development they will be able to anticipate
the level of sophistication and skill at which they can pitch their communications and activities. Generally speaking it is a much more
serious error to overestimate a child's abilities than it is to under-

estimate them, and therefore if there is any doubt it is wise to do the latter and then adjust the assessment as necessary. Obviously, any clear signs of development delay are highly important and must also be taken into account.

It should also be established whether or not a child suffers from any physical handicaps (particularly those involving speech, hearing and vision) or emotional difficulties. A child with emotional problems will need particular care and will probably have difficulty displaying the attention span commonly occurring in children of similar chronological age.

An attempt should also be made to outline a child's care history, particularly brief descriptions of places they have lived and the significant caretakers in each. This allows a thorough investigation of the child's feelings towards both people and places, and also assists in a reliable identification of context and perpetrator of abuse (if it has occurred).

Despite the universal condemnation of over-interviewing children, unfortunately, it remains the case that many children are interviewed several times by different agents. Before undertaking a formal assessment, it is important to be aware of any previous interviews and investigations the child may have experienced and where possible detailed accounts of these obtained. This is because, along with factors described below, earlier interviews, particularly if they are poorly conducted, can corrupt or distort the evidence drawn from a subsequent investigative assessment.

Validation and distorting factors

A good assessment will show evidence that a child's comments have been accepted by the investigator whilst at the same time, a process of validation has occurred with particular reference to factors which may distort evidence of abuse and the identity of the perpetrator.

Suggestibility

Both adults and children vary in the degree to which they are suggestible (Cousins, 1988; King and Yuille, 1987) and, therefore, in the degree to which they will modify an account of events according to what they perceive the demands of the investigator to be. A sophisticated assessment will make some investigation of how suggestible a child is. This should take place either before or after but not during any disclosure. It is important to be aware that just because the child is somewhat suggestible, and, for whatever reason, modifies his/her account at the suggestion of the assessor, this will not cause a false accusation. It does require that the assessment is even more careful than usual and renders interpretation of the child's comments and behaviour more difficult.

Fantasy

An assessor must be aware that children do produce fantasy material and that this may emerge during an investigative assessment. This is not to suggest that a child will fantasise about the occurrence of abuse but that fantasy may distort their account of it. Fantasy can appear either as fears which tend to involve such things as 'monsters' and 'bogey men' (which in some cases represent a perpetrator), or may take the form of wish-fulfilment in which a child may distort an account of abuse such that they themselves are very powerful and controlling or are 'saved' from abuse (Pynoos and Eth, 1984). An example of this involved a child describing being rescued from an abusive situation by 'a white kangaroo'. In another case, a child described themselves 'beating up' their adult abuser and then jumping out the (2nd floor) window and running to the police. Both children had been abused, but their accounts were distorted by the presence of wish-fulfilment fantasy which served to render their experiences less distressing by denying their total helplessness. The general ability of a child to describe and act out everyday life events should be investigated early in the assessment process by asking the child to describe and illustrate non-abusive scenes from their everyday life. The accuracy with which they are able to do so may be confirmed by reference to those familiar with the true situation.

Prior history of abuse

It is important that an assessor should not terminate the assessment solely on the basis of apparently having identified an abuse situation. This is because children can have histories of multiple abuse in different settings and also because earlier sexual abuse can distort a child's account of more recent abuse or, in older children, may result in unfounded allegations which very closely mimic real abuse both emotionally and in content. Thus it is important to investigate whether the child has experienced anything prior to the events currently being described.

Common mistakes

1 The mistake most commonly made is that of allowing a session to last too long, leading to distress and the child becoming motivated

to accede to the perceived demands of the adult in order to terminate the session. Typically, overlong sessions are also interrogative in quality.

2   Leading questions are very difficult to avoid completely but should not be used during the majority of the assessment. The most dangerous questions are forced choice and hypothetical questions, both being very likely to lead to inaccurate response from a child. It is also important to be aware that one may 'lead' a child non-verbally. For example, using sexually accurate dolls to represent the family and then asking a child 'which of these were involved in x' effectively precludes the child identifying any person other than those so represented. Any form of leading within the context of 1 above, i.e. an over-long assessment is particularly dangerous. It is only through training which involves supervised practice that the use and impact of leading questions can be minimised.

3   The use of language which the child is unlikely to understand or may misinterpret is unfortunately quite common in interviews and assessments. It may be that the vocabulary is simply too sophisticated, or that technical or euphemistic terms are employed. An example of the latter is when an investigator, having invited a child to describe being undressed by a cousin then asked 'did he touch you down there?'. Investigators may also wrongly assume that a child is using language in an adult way. This is particularly relevant where sexual expressions or slang are used and invalid assumptions made about them, for example a child saying 'shag' was not using the term as a verb but as a noun or a general term of abuse.

4   Sexually accurate dolls are often inappropriately relied upon as a means by which the child can identify an alleged perpetrator. The identification of the person(s) who abused the child should not simply be a label, particularly one such as 'daddy'. It is important that identification can be achieved to the positive exclusion of others and confirmation of identity achieved through the general description of appearance and role in the child's life, etc. This is in fact much better achieved with drawings, where an 'identity parade' of significant adults can be identified by the child. The reliability with which the child makes these identifications can be tested, and then questions asked along the following lines, 'is the person who touched your willy here?' (*After* the child has indicated that this is what has happened.) If the child responds in the negative, a drawing can be added and then identification requested. If in the positive, then they can be invited to point to the person involved. This is much preferable to the limited and clumsy identification made based on sexually accurate dolls.

5   A closely related difficulty with the sexually accurate dolls occurs
    where investigators over-interpret actions demonstrated by the
    child. This is particularly common with respect to the placing of a
    penis inside the vagina or anus being understood as necessarily
    meaning penetration. Two points are relevant here. The first is
    that sexually accurate dolls neither have labia nor buttocks and it
    is therefore unclear whether 'inside' is in fact anatomically inter-
    nal. Also, a child who has experienced anal or vagina abuse may
    feel as though they have been penetrated when, in fact, they have
    not and the resultant sensation of hurting 'inside' may well be
    represented by the placing of a penis inside the orifices.

6   There is often little distinction made between identifying a child
    as having been sexually abused and identifying those responsible.
    The term 'responsibility' must be used to mean the person or per-
    sons who committed the abusive acts (or who were present when
    they were committed or were aware of them being committed).
    Occasionally parental responsibility, (i.e. that responsibility of
    care parents have towards their children) is confused with respon-
    sibility for the abuse. The judgement of whether parents have
    failed to discharge parental responsibilities because of a 'failure to
    protect' their child from sexual abuse is entirely different to that
    of responsibility for abuse. In fact, the former is probably not one
    an expert opinion should address, unless particularly asked so to
    do, or there is clear evidence of disregard for a child's well-being,
    particularly with respect to sexual abuse.

7   Occasionally an investigator explicitly invites a child to fantasise
    by saying something along the lines of 'let's play pretend with
    these dollies' or 'let's make up a story about bedtime'. The dan-
    gers of both are obvious, and although the child may subse-
    quently disclose sexual abuse, the impact of this is undermined by
    the behaviour of the investigator.

Conclusion

An attempt has been made to describe an approach to investigating
child sexual abuse, its place in the forensic process of child protection, the resources and training necessary for adequate assessment
and typical faults exhibited by interviews and assessments evaluated
by the author. It must be emphasised that the decision to undertake
an investigative assessment rather than a traditional interview should
be made as soon as possible; ideally before any contact with the child
has been made. Far too frequently children are 'interviewed' and,
only when this fails, is a more appropriate assessment considered as a
possibility. Very often in such circumstances the former prejudices
the latter, and may even prevent adequate child protection. This only

becomes apparent during child care proceedings which, quite rightly, are held in camera and so such failures are generally debated only within that forum. The introduction of 'joint investigation' between the police and social services (Holdaway, 1986) must be regarded as only the start of a process of improving and refining approaches, skills and techniques.

10 What use are statistics—policy and practice in child abuse

Mai Walton

Many social workers take the view that statistics are useless, irrelevant to their work and tell them nothing worthwhile. I would like to challenge this view. As a social work practitioner in child abuse, I too held that view but over the years, as my interests in policy and research have grown, my opinion has changed. I now believe that statistics can be of tremendous value in unlocking the policy–practice equation by revealing the link within and providing a view of what is really happening at the 'coal-face'. For example, since the early 1970s DHSS circulars of guidance to local authorities have consistently advocated increasing responsibilities in child protection work and the widening of child abuse registration criteria, but without ever grasping the nettle that this inevitably means an increase in time and costs. In 1976 registers were largely geared to non-accidental injury but the 1980 circular LASSL (80)4 marked a watershed in policy by advocating wider registration criteria covering physical injury, or reasonable suspicion of injury, physical neglect, failure to thrive, emotional abuse and children in the same household of a known abuser. This document, however, referred to these categories as 'those features which are likely to cost little or nothing'.

Had statistics been available nationally it would have been possible to chart the impact of this policy by comparing the increase in cases by the number of staff available to cope and then to argue for an increase in resources where necessary. In fact no national statistics existed at this time and it was not until 1988 that the cry for national statistics was heard and their value recognised in revealing the effects and outcome of policy decisions. What happened, instead, was that the burgeoning responsibilities in the child protection field were simply absorbed into existing budgets, staff establishments and individual workloads and, as a result, other services suffered. No real quantitative calculation of the impact of the policy was made. Nor were the qualitative aspects fully considered in terms of the stress and overload often engendered for workers.

Statistics for statistics sake, however, are pointless. Use, is the operative word and whilst senior managers may be more inclined to their use, team leaders and social workers can take hold of this information which is, too often, repeatedly relegated to the bottom of the in-tray. Locally produced statistics can be used to argue for reduced caseloads and in planning our own work and service to clients. By plotting the increased workload, the time involved and the opportunity costs, that is, the other services which have to be foregone to accommodate this increase, valuable, substantive information can be produced which allows us to move from a generalised view and feeling that work pressures have increased, to a specific picture of the pressure and its results. Balancing feelings, and suspicions, with facts should see an upswing in the credibility of any representations made to senior management. A common criticism of social work is that it is too woolly and unspecific. Regular use of statistics and research to substantiate our views can obviate this and allow ourselves, and social work, to be taken more seriously. In addition statistics can allow us to evaluate our own behaviour, service provision and help determine what does or does not work.

What can statistics tell us?

The necessity and value of statistics in child abuse is now being officially recognised and the DHSS has begun to collate figures nationally. The NSPCC (Creighton, 1984) has kept statistics for many years based on the areas where they administer child protection registers, covering about 10% of the child population of England and Wales. The NSPCC statistical reports tend to confine themselves to dealing with the incidence of abuse in these areas and to describing the salient demographic features such as age of child, financial and socio-economic status of the family, age of parents and housing situation. In addition, the NSPCC use their figures as a basis from which to estimate the incidence of abuse nationally. Whilst acknowledging the necessity of this type of information the misgivings of some practitioners about the relevance of statistics to their work is well

founded. New DHSS statistics (DHSS, 1988a), although still in their
infancy, again simply paint a demographic picture of child abuse,
which, although interesting as such, tells us little about practice. For
example, the DHSS reports 39 300 children on registers in England
at 31 March 1988, 3.5 children per 1000 of the population under 18
years of age. They also describe some of the characteristics of these
children — younger rather than older children featured and 15 000
were under five years of age. More boys than girls were represented
in the age group 0–4 years, but as age rose girls featured more predominantly. They also describe the type of abuse suffered, one quar-
ter physical abuse (9000), a seventh sexual abuse (5100) and a tenth
(4200) neglect. Furthermore 13 300 children were registered because
of 'grave concern'. These figures then gives us a number by which
we know how many were abused and percentages which allow us to
compare proportionately the types of abuse in relation to each other,
but not in any detail.

They tell us that 63% of the children were not subject to any legal
order. This allows us to deduce that 37% were. But, these figures do
not tell us what number or percentage of children were subject to the
different forms of legal order. The latter is an example of how little
official statistics presently tell us about agency response and the
translation of policy into practice; precisely the areas which concern
social workers and their line managers. Similarly a recent DHSS
(1988b) survey reported that 83% of authorities now have, according
to their directors, satisfactory joint working arrangements with
the police. I am sure practitioners would beg to differ! It can be
difficult for directors to keep in close touch with practice in their
departments and social workers and team leaders can use statistics
to inform them. This of course assumes that directors both wish
to know and are prepared to present objective information to national
policy advisers.

A current statistical research project into child sexual abuse being
undertaken by the NSPCC and Greater Manchester Authorities
Child Sexual Abuse Unit (CSAU, 1988) will be used to demonstrate
the wider scope of child abuse statistics and their present and future
uses. The CSAU works with ten local authorities and the study
gathers research data from them all. As such it is the first study of its
kind in drawing up a cohesive geographical area which contains
demographically similar authorities, but which are dissimilar in
policy and practice. Its objectives are to establish the incidence of
child sexual abuse and examine the response of agencies over a three
year period. Information is gathered by questionnaires administered
at the time of the initial case conference and six monthly review meeting. Feedback is given annually.

Like the DHSS, the CSAU statistics illustrate the characteristics of children; those sexually abused within the family, but they also paint a broader picture by describing the characteristics of the families and of abusers in detail. For example, in Greater Manchester from March 1987 to February 1988, 261 children were registered as having suffered abuse or being at grave risk of sexual abuse. Of this total, 183 had actually been abused, and 78 were at risk. Of those actually abused, 152 were girls (83%) and 31 boys (17%), a ratio of 5:1 which is similar to an NSPCC research briefing which examined registrations from 1977–82. It is however lower than that of Mrazek's British study (Mrazek et al., 1981) which found a ratio of 6:1. Other studies in America have found a lower ratio 2.5:1 (Finkelhor, 1984) but these fluctuating ratios still point to the preponderance of female victims in spite of increased reporting of the abuse of boys, particularly regarding sexual abuse within the family. Baker's prevalence study (Baker and Duncan, 1985) interviewed 2019 people over the age of 15 and questioned them about their experiences of sexual abuse. This study is probably the most comprehensive in Britain to date. It found that most respondents who were abused were abused after the age of 11. It does not tell us about the remaining 39%. The CSAU study found that the youngest child registered as sexually abused in Greater Manchester was a female aged 1 year 5 months. The average age of 'actual' registrations was 10.2 years for females and 9.2 years for males. 47% of children were under 10 years old. As these are the children's ages at registration the obvious conclusion is that abuse began at an earlier age and figures for the duration of the abuse confirm this by demonstrating the relationship between lengthening duration with the increasing age of the child; for example, in the age group 10–14 years 45% of children had been abused for over five years.

CSAU statistics concentrated in detail on the type of abuse suffered. In total 95% of children suffered contact abuse, that is, penetration, fondling and oral sex and masturbation, in contrast with Baker's study — 49%. Additionally 40% of the Greater Manchester study suffered more than one form of abuse and 36% were penetrated in some say. Methodological differences between the studies do exist with Baker's respondents having to rely on memory which, for some, was quite distant. Abdoulraman and Gladwell's (1988) study of referrals to a regional child psychiatry unit from 1975–85 found similar figures to the CSAU study.

Again it is the breadth of the CSAU statistics that gives a finer picture than is deducible from current DHSS statistics which at present are a very narrow baseline but which will hopefully broaden in years to come. At present they tell us little about abusers whereas the CSAU figures tell us that 93% of abusers were male and 7% female moreover, of the male abusers 39% were fathers, 15% step-fathers and 11% male cohabitees. In other words 65% were men in a position of trust and in a parenting capacity.

These statistics portray a child abuse landscape and provide useful knowledge of what is happening within it. Unlike the, as yet, generalised official statistics they allow us to compare our situation with other studies and findings which can be reassuring, but also point to differences which should be further explored.

In practice, statistics can be used in conjunction with other research to provide a conceptual framework to aid assessment and in planning intervention more accurately. An example would be to use Finkelhor's (1986) 'four traumagenic factors':

1   the exent to which victim's sexual development is damaged;
2   the extent of betrayal felt;
3   the extent of stigmatisation felt;
4   the extent of powerlessness felt;

alongside statistics which reveal the child's age, relationship to abuser and type of abuse suffered. Both would help the practitioner to predict more accurately the degree of trauma experienced, the likely extent of problems and to pinpoint the nature of the problem. In doing so the worker can more appropriately decide on the type of help needed and for example prepare foster parents in more detail for the range of behaviours and difficulties likely in a child of given age abused in a particular situation. Statistics and research applied in this way can therefore help scale risk, validate the worker's response or indicate the need for a change of strategy.

Equally they can help in situations where practitioners are called upon to substantiate their views in decision-making, for instance in the court or case conference setting. Myths about sexual abuse still abound, not least the ones about it only occurring in large chaotic families where it is the norm and is accepted. Statistics can be used to refute notions such as this by showing that sexual abuse occurs in all types of family (for example, the CSAU study revealed that 64% of children abused lived in families of three children or less). This then can enhance the critical decision making which takes place.

But it is at the agency response level that statistics can come into their own, again by showing how things are currently being dealt with and in allowing scrutiny leading, hopefully, to an improved future response. They can aid by providing hard facts from which to plan the volume, type and range of service provision needed, both on a national and local basis. Presently official statistics tell us little about agency response. The recent DHSS and Social Services Inspectorate (1988b) survey on inter-agency co-operation in dealing with child sexual abuse has begun to tackle these aspects and ask specific questions about what actually happens, for example, with regard to the medical examination of children. Recently, concerns have been voiced about the medical examination being a form of further abuse to children. Children have no choice in being abused and are rendered more powerless. Medical examinations can mirror this abuse by denying them a choice about whether a child wants an examination and about who should carry it out. Gender and the abuse of power are key issues in sexual abuse itself and are no less so in our response to it. Given that most children are abused by a man, the prospect of medical examination by a male can render the child further trauma. DHSS statistics, whilst differentiating between the type of doctor used, that is, paediatrician or police surgeon, are less clear in differentiating the gender of the doctor. By and large official statistics are only asking generalised questions and therefore cannot provide sufficiently comprehensive or specific information with which to guide. There appears to be no planned strategy but rather a reluctant reactivity on the part of policy makers. The CSAU statistics, on the other hand, highlight the necessary trend in Greater Manchester for children to be examined by a female should they so choose. By looking more closely at agencies' response we can begin to question whether departments are providing a child centred service or merely paying lip service to the philosophy. Surely it behoves us to determine whether our principles are carried through into practice. If we believe that therapy for abused children begins with investigative/therapeutic interviews, we need to know what front-line workers are actually doing. In other words, is the espoused policy fact or fiction, do the input and outcome match up? Again using CSAU statistics, if we truly believe that sexual abuse is an act perpetrated against a child who cannot consent, why is it that 35% of cases involving vaginal intercourse still result in charges of indecent assault only. The law states that consent is a defence only if the victims is over 16 years of age which most of the registered children will not have attained. Nor can they consent to abuse. What the figures show are the value judgements still being made about child sexual abuse and the culpability attributed to children.

Social workers tend to hold strong views about the 'wrongs' to children and the 'system's abuse' that can result when good practice tells us one thing and legal constraints work against this. Statistics can provide valuable information if we are to argue credibly for legal reform to improve the lot of children. The CSAU study showed that 59% of abusers had not been charged with offences at the initial case conference stage due to lack of corroborative evidence.

Detailed statistics which provide concrete examples and factual data can be useful in flagging up other issues of concern and in highlighting training needs. Many sexually abused children in Greater Manchester disclosed their abuse to their teacher and many also had

school-focussed problems. Whilst this had generally been accepted,
the emerging figures provided more particularised information to
support the call for training for teachers in their high-profile role in
the detection and monitoring of child abuse (Wattam, 1989).

Statistics that are collated by locality also raise issues about policy
variation regionally and nationally, and whether the degree of variation is acceptable. Questions can be asked about whether the differences are the result of differing ideologies, politics, definitions, interpretations or resources. The answers tell us that inequity is the result
because these differences result in varying decisions, often being
arbitrarily made. Service to children and families is then unfairly distributed with some children in similar circumstances being registered in one authority and not in another. Given that registers act as
gatekeepers and informal rationers of service, some children will be
missing out on provisions such as nursery places. Statistics can help
unravel this puzzling process, and register totals provide a good
example of how a beginning can be made.

Simplistically they tell us how many children are in the register at
a given time. Importantly they show us a picture of policy variation
the extent of which allows us to hypothesise about the reasons why.
This in turn should allow for the testing of hypotheses and some
problem resolution. At our present level of knowledge these totals
will not give any explanations about cause. What we can do is hypothesise that totals vary because of the way policy is framed and executed. CSAU research confirms this. An example being that two
'nearest neighbours' in the study had nearly four times as many
registered children. Their totals vary not only due to demographic
factors, but also due to the use of differing definitions, type of
register, unit of registration and discretion to register.

Registration criteria are an operational definition of child abuse.
As early as 1976 the DHSS commented:

> the considerable problem of forming a reliable estimate of the
> incidence of non-accidental injury cannot be overcome by
> register systems alone, for instance criteria for inclusion are
> themselves a problem.

The problem was varying registration criteria which affected incidence as represented by registration totals. Varying incidence is
partly a function of varying criteria. Criteria are often determined,
not so much by examining society's values about how children
should be treated, but by competing demands for limited resources
and priorities. As a result criteria are excluded or too narrowly
defined because departments would be overloaded, or because of ill-
thought-out views about cultural norms. Alternatively criteria can be
very woolly in wording.

Definitions of 'grave concern' or 'reasonable suspicion' need to be more specific, again because of their effect upon totals and how we then interpret these figures. Variation is exacerbated by the many interpretations placed upon unspecific criteria which, in child protection work, is compounded by the number and variety of professionals involved. As Graham Allison (1969) in analysing the Cuban missile crisis explained:

> what each analyst sees and judges to be important is a function not only of the evidence about what happens but also of the conceptual lenses through which he looks at the evidence.

The analogy with the inter-agency aspects of child protection work is obvious, when one considers the number of different analysts or professionals involved at case conferences, and the different numbers and permutations of conceptual lenses through which the evidence is viewed. It is no wonder that competing explanations and conflict is the result.

The DHSS recommends that 'actual' and 'at risk' cases are differentiated on the register. Register totals generally do not differentiate. Unless they do so they are not a true reflection of actual abuse. The type of register kept varies. Some authorities use 'at risk' registers to chart cases of grave concern whilst others do not. A few keep 'at risk' registers separate from the monitoring system of child protection. Register totals show the extent of muddled thinking and policy making here. Most authorities expounding no 'at risk' policy do in fact register children under the 'same household' criteria. The result of this disparity is to undermine the accuracy of incidence figures by inflating or deflating totals. Furthermore, it detracts from our ability to make detailed comparative analysis. Statistics therefore can expose these configurations of policy and permit the question 'should "at risk" cases be registered?' In turn the fundamental question about whether registers protect, or not, surfaces. If registers are designed to protect should not 'at risk' cases be included?

Disparity in the unit of registration reveals policy problems. Guidance from the DHSS refers to the child and most areas register the child, although a few still use the family as the unit of registration. Some authorities register only the child abused, others include 'at risk' siblings. Some register all the children in the household. A minority under the 'same household' category register the youngest child only. The influence of this workaday matter on incidence should not be underestimated. Consistency is the key to more meaningful statistics. There is a school of thought that would argue for a register of abusers as well as a register of children but objections about civil liberties and wrongful inclusion are raised. This is a comment on the way society views the civil liberties of adults against the civil rights of children and demonstrates how much more reluctant we are to transgress the rights of adults as opposed to the rights of children. Finally, discretion to register contributes to the muddle. Subjective decisions are often justified on the basis of scarce resources, by stating that certain categories of registration would 'swamp' workers, rather than on the basis of a child's needs. Some authorities only register if it serves a 'useful purpose' and as the latter is rarely specified one can only assume it is synonymous with lack of clarity on the worker's part or discomfort with professional authority and the social control aspects of work in this field. Workers who are not comfortable with their legal and professional authority will reframe information, not register and become dangerous by arguing that their relationship with the family will be damaged. Some authorities do not register children in care. Some do not register where parents are co-operative. This discretion to register increases in the face of ambiguity and complexity. Clarity is the watchword, criteria need to be specific. Recently the DHSS has been unequivocal in recommending the registration of all children meeting the criteria.

What statistics do not tell us

The contextual map is incomplete and recent DHSS statistics are merely a starting point, a springboard for the future. They can only provide data about how many children in their location are registered, criteria or type of abuse and limited information about agency response.

At present child abuse statistics are not studies of prevalence. Nor are they complete studies of incidence because, firstly, owing to under-reporting not all cases of child abuse come to the notice of official agencies; secondly, not all cases reported, investigated and proven arrive on registers; thirdly, particularly in relation to child sexual abuse, 'stranger' abuse, or abuse by someone having care and control outside the home, rarely comes to the attention of the NSPCC and social service departments. In fact the Cleveland report discourages social services department involvement in 'stranger' abuse cases.

Interestingly *Working Together* (DHSS, 1988) prefaces the criteria for registration by stating that consideration needs to be given to the fact that children may be harmed by 'an acquaintance or a stranger'. In short this means that these children are not included in official statistics. Police statistics for sexual abuse are often higher than social services statistics and do cover stranger abuse. Police and social service department statistics of children actually abused need to be combined for a true figure to be arrived at. In truth the size of the problem is not known. The CSAU research has shown how much more useful statistical research can be when it seeks to examine the wider aspects of child abuse and child protection policy.

What statistics generally are not providing are the finer details such as age and type of abuse. We do not know how many referrals are investigated, how many of these are proved, how many proved are case conferenced and the reasons why not. Neither do we know empirically the reasons why cases are registered or not.

We do not know the average duration of registration. Nor are we clear about when and why deregistration occurs. Such information could describe successful intervention. No figures are available for reregistrations. This rightly leaves us open to the criticism that there is little difference between those children registered and those who remain unregistered either in the country at large or as a result of a case conference.

There is little, co-ordinated information about the legal response to children and their abusers. We know little about the one-third of children currently registered because of 'grave concern', but not what the latter actually is. Nationally we have no baseline information about how agencies are responding nor any ongoing evaluation of local authority social work intervention in this field. As a result the pursuance of minimum standards as advocated by the DHSS has little meaning.

It is important to have more information because of the inherent injustices in register systems which demand that they be administered in a fairer, more consistent fashion.

What is needed

Collaboration between the police and social service departments, Home Office and DHSS is required for accurate incidence figures, and in determining a better legal response for children.

Research confined to describing characteristics should differentiate between children abused or 'at risk' in order to provide more accurate data and enhance our ability to scale risk. Research should extend to agency response and be used to illustrate how agencies are currently operating. Differences need to be critically examined, such as the number of investigations viz the number of registrations. The chairing of case conferences and the decisions made bears further scrutiny and the prospect of parental participation needs evaluation. Generally speaking there is a lack of basic information about what happens in local authority child protection work as opposed to the work of voluntary agencies with specialist resources.

National criteria would represent a step forward and represent a national working definition for child care agencies, but steps would have to be taken to ensure their implementation by local authorities as some authorities resent the fact that child protection work, as a small percentage of their overall workload, disproportionately demands a great deal of resources. Adoption of uniform criteria would clarify and refine statistics, make them more reliable, eradicate superfluous variation and begin to lay a baseline of accepted practice.

Why statistics?

Statistics are, among other things, concerned with increasing knowledge and expertise, with improving service and a better response to clients. They provide the opportunity to improve skills and enhance provision by posing questions and allowing speculation. For example, why should the number of girls on registers increase with age? Possibly because of increased disclosures of sexual abuse. Similarly the numbers of young children registered as sexually abused probably attests to increased awareness and professional skills.

Statistics can harness information about policy and practice which might otherwise remain hidden in departments or lost in case files. Research renders it accessible. It is also useful and usable to both practitioner and policy-maker.

Statistics are like paintings. Using the broad-brush approach a contextual, generalised picture can be painted. Alternatively a fine, detailed approach can draw out the minutiae of practice, for example, how many joint interviews between police and social worker were undertaken in sexual abuse cases. Furthermore do they really make investigation easier for children or easier for the professionals? Statistics permit analysis and bring to the fore these fundamental questions which need to be answered in the reactive world of child protection work in order to bring about a more proactive and thought out response.

Rather than arguing that statistics are useless the argument is for more and better statistics. Statistics for statistics sake are pointless but those which are purposeful and are used purposively can enhance our work with children and families. In fact they are a necessary and an integral part of it.

11 Legislation and child sexual abuse — considerations and proposed changes in the law

Norma Martin

Introduction

It may seem an historical coincidence that one century after the Prevention of Cruelty to Children Act of 1889, we are approaching the end of an era in child care law. The Children Bill (House of Commons, 1989), which at the time of writing is progressing through Parliament, promises to transform the legislative framework for the 1990s and beyond. The implications of the Bill are wide-ranging. It marks a subtle philosophical shift from 'rights' to 'responsibilities' in describing the legal relationship between parents and children. For child welfare professionals, the Bill contains new concepts, a new terminology and new procedures to deal with. On the institutional front, there may be no Family Court, but significant jurisdictional changes for the courts are vaunted.

So, where does the problem of child sexual abuse fit into this programme of legal reform? First of all, the point must be made that the Children Bill relates only to civil proceedings. As far as the criminal law is concerned, the legal issues posed by child sexual abuse relate to questions of proof and evidence, rather than the substantive law, and reform in this context has produced only an ad hoc and limited response.

Secondly, the report by Lord Justice Butler-Sloss (1988) into the events in Cleveland in 1987 may be seen as the catalyst for the Bill, but it should be noted that this area of the law has been thoroughly reviewed over the last five years. Indeed, the recommendations of the Cleveland Report in relation to the law do not differ substantially from the proposals in the White Paper of 1987 (Cm 62). The moral panic around Cleveland may have influenced, and even precipitated, political action but its significance in terms of the Bill's contents should not be over-estimated.

To present a summary of the law on child sexual abuse in England and Wales is no simple task. By the time this chapter is published, it is expected that the Children Bill will have become the Children Act, 1989. But although it will have passed onto the statute books, implementation of the new Act is not anticipated for a further twelve to eighteen months. Let us hope that this will be in one fell swoop, and that the precedent of the Children Act of 1975, which rather limped into force, will not be followed. Furthermore, the Children Bill at present is only a skeleton, which requires much fleshing out by as yet unpublished regulations and rules of court, and this makes it impossible to provide a detailed commentary on the changes. So, caught on the cusp, this chapter attempts a comparative approach, placing an account of the current law alongside speculation, in fairly general terms, as to the future.

Criminal versus civil proceedings?

As noted above, there are at present two ways in which the law can be involved with children who are victims of sexual abuse: namely, civil and criminal. The relationship between the two poses theoretical and practical issues. In particular, the use of criminal proceedings in such cases has been questioned.

In general, the objectives of the criminal law are to punish the offender and to deter others. The police and Crown Prosecution services are the agencies responsible for the management of criminal proceedings. In a criminal trial, the onus of proof is on the prosecution to establish guilt beyond a reasonable doubt. If satisfied and a conviction is obtained, then sentencing depends on the nature of the offence and the individual case, and may range from a conditional discharge to a probation order or imprisonment. Conditions such as attendance at a clinic or participation in therapy sessions may be attached to a probation order, thereby combining treatment with punishment.

By contrast, the civil law centres on the protection of the child by way of care proceedings. Such proceedings are typically initiated by the social services departments of local authorities, or the NSPCC. A lower standard of proof (on the balance of probabilities) is applicable, and care proceedings may result in either a care order, when the local authority decides where the child should live, a supervision order, where the child lives at home and the local authority's role is supervisory, or no order.

In the light of these objectives, criminal and civil proceedings appear as complimentary responses to the problem. To suggest there must be a choice between the two may also be false in many cases because of the differential standards of proof. If the abuser does not confess, then the nature of child sexual abuse means that there may be insufficient evidence to warrant prosecution let alone conviction, yet still adequate grounds for bringing care proceedings. For practical reasons, therefore, the use of criminal sanctions against the wrongdoer cannot be the law's primary response.

Aside from these practical considerations, it may be argued that criminal proceedings against abusive parents are highly problematic. This argument challenges the moral legitimacy of retribution by defining the abuser as not fully responsible for his actions, blaming instead individual pathology or family dysfunction. The criminal law is seen as a blunt instrument. Punishment does not only hurt the abuser, but also the innocent. The victim may hold herself responsible for the break-up of the family and experience feelings of guilt. Finally, the effectiveness of criminal sanctions, particularly imprisonment, in stopping the abuser from reoffending, is questioned.

Nevertheless, incarceration does offer short-term protection, and more significantly, criminal prosecution and punishment may possess symbolic value, as a statement that society regards the sexual abuse of children as wrong. The intervention of the criminal law may help the child to acknowledge that it is the abuser who is guilty in the eyes of the community. There is no reason why punishment and treatment must be mutually exclusive options in dealing with abusers — some would argue that the authority of the law may even facilitate therapeutic intervention.

If, on balance, the arguments against decriminalisation appear the stronger, this does not entail the consequence that criminal proceedings must be embarked on in every case. The discretion to prosecute may still balance the public interest in law enforcement against the child's interests. This may be what Lord Justice Butler-Sloss had in mind when, in the penultimate paragraph of the Cleveland Report (Butler-Sloss, 1988) she asked, 'whether different arrangements might be made in suitable cases for those abusers who admit their guilt, who co-operate with the arrangements for the child and who are prepared to submit themselves to a programme of control'.

On a more practical note, where two sets of proceedings are to take place, should care proceedings be deferred pending the outcome in the criminal trial? Home Office Circular 84/1982 states that care proceedings should not be automatically adjourned where there is no reason to believe they will prejudice the trial, e.g. where the defendant intends to plead guilty. This approach has been confirmed and extended by the courts. In *R v Exeter Juvenile Court ex parte H; R v Waltham Forest Juvenile Court ex parte B* [1988] 2 FLR 214, the President of the Family Division stated that the paramountcy of the child's welfare should be the guiding principle for the juvenile court, and that delay should be avoided. Accordingly, it was held that the juvenile courts were justified in refusing the parents' request for an adjournment. But if the magistrates should adjourn, then the local authority may still consider wardship. The presumption that delay is prejudicial to the child's welfare will be given statutory effect by Clause 27 of the Children Bill, which also gives the courts powers to draw up a timetable for expeditious disposal of care applications.

Identification and investigation

English law imposes no positive duty on any person or body to *report* suspected cases of child sexual abuse. This is in clear contrast to the position in the United States. There the initial legislative response to the discovery of the so-called 'battered baby syndrome' in the 1960s was the passing of mandatory reporting laws which bind professionals, such as doctors and teachers. According to the DHSS Review of Child Care Law in 1985, reporting laws are not necessary here because of the public sector nature of health, education and social services provision and their welfarist ethos.

The law does impose a positive duty on the local authority for the area where the child lives, or is found, to make enquiries if it receives information suggesting there are grounds for bringing care proceedings (s.2(1) Children and Young Persons Act (CYPA) 1969). However, it is relieved from this duty if satisfied that enquiries are unnecessary. s.2(2) CYPA 1969 places local authorities under a statutory duty to bring care proceedings where grounds are believed to exist, unless this would be neither in the child's, nor the public's, interest.

There is no express correlation between s.2(2) CYPA 1969 and the general preventive duty imposed on local authorities under s.1(1) Child Care Act (CCA) 1980. Thus there would appear to be no legal requirement that preventive work be attempted, or exhausted, before care proceedings are instituted.

Reform

Clause 39 of the Children Bill will strengthen the local authority's duty to investigate. In future, the duty will be triggered by referrals, or where there is cause to suspect a child is at risk. The technical reference to 'grounds for care proceedings' is dropped and replaced by a more general reference to harm and the risk of harm. The duty itself is intended to be more active — the purpose of the enquiries is to assess what action is needed to safeguard or promote the child's welfare.

There are no independent powers of entry to premises ancillary to this investigative duty. But lessons from previous child abuse inquiries have been incorporated in the specific direction that where access to a child is refused, then the local authority should consider applying for an emergency protection order, or other legal order.

In the event of the local authority deciding not to pursue legal action but to follow-up and monitor developments, then it will be required to fix a date for a case-review. This stresses an element of continuing accountability.

The Children Bill places greater emphasis on inter-agency co-operation by providing that other local statutory bodies, such as health and education, as well as voluntary agencies, are to assist social services with their investigations if so requested, if compliance would not be 'unreasonable in all the circumstances'.

Considerable discretion remains vested in local authorities in discharging the duty. The duty to act is qualified by 'so far as it is both within their power and reasonably practicable for them to do so'. The loose reference to 'action' ensures flexibility in response: it would seem to encompass not just the initiation of care proceedings but also the provision of preventive services under clause 15.

The administrative system for investigating suspected cases of child sexual abuse

Authority for the procedures to be followed in all child abuse cases does not derive from statute, but from a series of departmental circulars. The first was issued by the DHSS in 1974 following the Maria Colwell inquiry, while the most up-to-date, *Working Together* (DHSS 1988c), was published simultaneously with the Cleveland Report. The essential components of the child protection machinery are Area Child Protection Committees (formerly Area Review Committees), inter-agency case conferences and Child Protection Registers (formerly Child Abuse Registers). Registers and conferences have been criticised from a civil liberties standpoint. The operation of the system is said to involve judgements about parents and their children taken in their absence, behind closed doors, without any rights to challenge or 'appeal'. Two recent cases have attempted to open up the administrative procedures to judicial scrutiny through the avenue of judicial review.

In *R* v *Harrow LBC ex parte D* (*The Independent*, 1 December 1988) a mother sought judicial review of a local authority's refusal to allow her to attend a case conferrence which resulted in her children being placed on an 'at risk' register. The court refused the application on the basis that the purpose of the conference was not to reach a verdict on the allegations of ill-treatment by the mother, but to obtain advice on the next step. The court also noted that the *Working Together* guidelines, while recommending that parents should be kept informed, did not elevate that to a 'right' to attend and make submissions. Moreover, the Cleveland Report indicated that professional opinion was divided on the question of parental participation, so the decision to exclude the mother could not be said to be unreasonable and unfair.

By comparison, in *R* v *Norfolk County Countil ex parte M* (*The Times*, 27 February 1989) the decision of a case conference to record a person's name as an alleged abuser on a register, was found to be susceptible to judicial review. A thirteen year old girl had alleged that a plumber (M) working at her parents' home, had sexually abused her. At the subsequent case conference, the decision was taken to enter both names on the register. The local authority argued that conference decisions and registrations are merely internal, clerical acts and part of their confidential records. The court pointed out that entries on a register could be inspected by a fairly wide (albeit defined) section of the public, including the police, probation service, education and welfare agencies and doctors. Mr. Justice Waite went on to describe the register as 'a blacklist', with 'dangerous potential as an instrument of injustice and oppression'. It was held that there had been a breach of natural justice because M had been denied the opportunity of advance warning, prior notification, and of being heard by the case conference.

The notion of fair dealing, or procedural propriety, where a person's rights or vital interests are affected by an administrative decision, lies at the heart of the *Norfolk* case. The ruling may be interpreted as initiating a process of super-imposing legal accountability on the investigative system. However, the concept of procedural justice is limited — it cannot be used to directly challenge the merits of an administrative decision. Further it was stated in the *Norfolk* case that judicial review will be unavailable where the procedures followed represent 'a genuine attempt, reasonable in all the circumstances, to reconcile the duty of child protection with the duty of fairness to the alleged abuser'.

The protection of children in emergencies

There are a number of overlapping statutory provisions which authorise the removal of a child from its home, and detention in a 'place of safety'. The most frequently used power is s.28(1) CYPA 1969. It was the excessive reliance on these place of safety orders (PSO) that contributed to the crisis in Cleveland in 1987 and publicly exposed the deficiencies in the legislation.

Place of Safety Order: s.28(1) CYPA 1969

Any person may apply for a PSO under s.28, although in practice, most orders are obtained by local authority social workers. The applicant must satisfy a single justice that he has reasonable cause to believe that any of the primary conditions for care proceedings under s.1(2) CYPA 1969 is satisfied. The order authorises the detention of the child for up to 28 days.

Critique

s.28(1) does not specify that PSOs are to be reserved for genuine emergencies. Consequently in Cleveland (as indeed elsewhere), PSOs came to be used in a routine fashion, as a prelude to the commencement of care proceedings, even in cases where it was not really necessary to remove the child before the court hearing. Further, such orders may be granted informally. Technically anyone of the 24000 magistrates in England and Wales is competent to issue a PSO, and it seems that in Cleveland some magistrates were approached at their own homes at night.

PSOs are generally made ex parte, i.e. in the absence of the parents who have no right to challenge or appeal the decision. Without the opportunity to test the local authority's evidence by hearing the parents' story, there has been concern that justices accede too easily to applications by social workers, under the belief there is 'no smoke without fire'.

Finally, before the Cleveland crisis developed, there had been a move away from granting the full 28 day order, and magistrates were becoming reluctant to make orders lasting more than 8 days. But when the crisis peaked, there was a shift back to the maximum duration because of overloading in the juvenile courts and because social workers were seeking sufficient time to facilitate 'disclosure work' with the children. When combined with denial of access for the duration of the order, this fuelled distress and resentment among the Cleveland parents.

Recommendations and reform

Lord Justice Butler-Sloss expressed concern that the social workers in Cleveland had acted under serious misapprehensions as to the nature of PSOs. They should not have been used as a routine stage in case-management, nor to facilitate disclosure work; they do not confer on local authorities the power to curtail access, or authorise repeat medical examinations for forensic purposes.

The Cleveland Report (Butler-Sloss, 1988) endorsed the proposals for the replacement of place of safety orders by emergency protection orders, as outlined in the Government White Paper (Cm. 62, 1987). Those proposals have become Part V of the Children Bill.

Emergency protection orders, like PSOs, will be obtainable on application by 'any person' to the court. In general, this will be a full bench of magistrates but out of court hours a single magistrate will suffice. The purpose of EPOs is evident from their title, and spelled out in clause 36(1). In future, the court may only make the order if satisfied the child is likely to suffer reasonable harm if not removed from his/her current situation or detained in it. (The latter situation would cover the case of a child who is already in hospital.)

Once in force, the order will compel the production of the child, prevent its removal from any safe place, and give the applicant parental responsibility. The extent of that responsibility is defined as limited to taking such action as is reasonably required to safegurd or promote the child's welfare (clause 36(3)).

Emergency protection orders will not confer the right to enter premises where the householder refuses his consent. Where entry is likely to be refused, a warrant must be obtained under clause 40. This replaces s.40 CYPA 1933, and is similar in that the new warrant must also be executed by a police constable. Clause 40 contains an additional power specifically recommended by the Cleveland Report (Butler-Sloss, 1988), that is an order to disclose information as to a child's whereabouts.

The maximum duration of EPOs is shortened to eight days, with a further extension of up to seven days available once only, on application to the court. For the extension to be granted, the court must be satisfied that the child will suffer significant harm otherwise, and that the applicant has reasonable grounds for not being ready to proceed (clause 37). This clearly imposes significant time constraints on local authorities in preparing their case, and has obvious resource implications.

One element in the Bill was not foreshadowed by the Cleveland Report, and that is the right of parents, children and others to challenge the order after 72 hours. The details will depend on rules of court but it is expected to be restricted to ex parte orders. This right was advocated by Louis Blom-Cooper, QC in his reports into the deaths of Jasmine Beckford and Kimberley Carlile (Brent Area Health Authority, 1985; Greenwich Area Health Authority, 1987). Its inclusion in the Bill is a response to the perceived unfairness of an unchallengeable order which both restricts the child's liberty and infringes parental 'rights'.

Medical examinations and contact

The Cleveland Report described these as 'grey areas' in the present law, where the relative rights and responsibilities of parents and local authorities are unclear.

Before and during the Cleveland crisis it seems that some social workers and doctors were under the impression that PSOs gave the local authority the right to consent to the child's medical examination. The Report said this was an incorrect interpretation of the law; the effect of a PSO is only to transfer the right to decide where the child lives, and all other parental rights, including the right to consent to medical examination and treatment, remain vested in the parents.

DHSS Circular (88)2 (DHSS, 1988d) states that where a doctor has reasonable cause to believe that medical treatment may be needed, he may examine the child for the purpose of assessment for such treatment, even where the parents do not consent. But while he may administer urgent treatment, non-urgent treatment must be delayed pending the local authority bringing care proceedings. If an interim order is obtained this transfers parental rights to the local authority and enables them to give consent.

Post-Cleveland, then, the legal position is complex, and far from being black or white. The solution in the Children Bill is to empower the courts to give directions as to the medical or psychiatric examination of the child. This will place control over the number of such examinations firmly with the court, which will be able to override parental refusal.

What will happen if the child refuses to consent to a medical examination? The position is unclear. It can be argued that clause 36(4) does not affect the general law, so that following the case of *Gillick* v *West Norfolk and Wisbech AHA* [1980] AC 112, older children have independent rights to consent to medical examination and treatment, provided they are sufficiently mature to understand their nature. But a report in *The Times*, 24 April 1989 indicates that ministers are unwilling to permit children the right to refuse in the belief this will enable abusers to get away with their activities. Medical evidence is rarely clear-cut in sexual abuse cases, and the prospect of unwilling children being compelled to submit to medical examinations, and restrained by force if necessary, is highly disturbing.

Access was a further pressing issue which emerged from Cleveland. Here also the Report pointed out that PSOs do not confer on
local authorities the power to curtail access, save where the safety of
the child demands this. The Children Bill provides that the court will
be able to give directions on the contact which is to be allowed
between the child and its parents. ('Contact' is the new terminology
for 'access'.)

How will the new provisions be interpreted and applied in cases
of suspected child sexual abuse? The answer cannot be found simply
in the statutory provisions; it will also involve social work practice.

The comments of Lord Justice Butler-Sloss in the Cleveland
Report may give some enlightenment. The Report states:

> . . . sexual abuse of children is a problem best managed in a
> planned and considered manner. Responding on an emergency
> basis is rarely required and is not likely to be helpful . . . Child-
> ren's interests are rarely served by precipitate action.

In other words, investigations into allegations of sexual abuse may
take place over a different, and longer, time-scale than those into
physical abuse and applications for emergency protection orders
should not become an automatic response.

Care proceedings

The term 'care proceedings' describes a number of alternative procedures whereby a child may become subject to the compulsory care
of a local authority. There are three main routes into care: via s.1
CYPA 1969, a parental rights resolution under s.3 Child Care Act
1980, or in family proceedings. This section will concentrate on care
proceedings under the 1969 Act, since this is the most likely basis for
intervention in a child sexual abuse case, and allows for comparisons
between the present law and the provision in the Children Bill.

Under s.1(2) CYPA 1969, the applicant must prove that one or
more of seven 'primary conditions' relating to a child is fulfilled and,
secondly, that the child is in need of care and control which he/she is
unlikely to receive unless the court makes the order. It must be
stressed that the secondary 'care or control' test is not a formality,
but a separate requirement. Four of the primary conditions may be
relevant in sexual abuse cases, and will be considered in turn.

i   s.1(2)(a):

> the child's proper development is being avoidably prevented or
> neglected, or his health is being impaired or neglected, or he is
> being ill-treated.

This is the most relied on in practice, since its scope is broad and covers all types of child abuse, including sexual abuse. Since it is phrased in the present continuous tense, it does not cover fear of future harm, where none has yet occurred, no matter how imminent. In cases where a child is simply at risk, the local authority must resort to wardship unless care proceedings can be brought under s.1(2)(b) or (bb).

ii   s.1(2)(b): it is probable that para. (a) *will* be satisfied

> having regard to the fact that the court or another court has found (it) is or was satisfied in the case of a child or young person who is or was a member of the household to which this child belongs.

This covers potential harm to other children in a household where one child has already been abused. It will authorise the removal of siblings from the home, though the risk must be assessed in respect of each child individually. 'Household' means people rather than locality.

iii   s.1(2)(bb): it is probable that para. (a) *will* be satisfied

> having regard to the fact that a person who has been convicted of an offence mentioned in Schedule 1 to CYPA 1933 is, or may become, a member of the same household.

The Schedule covers virtually every offence of a violent or sexual nature against a child. The victim must be a child, but need not be in the same household. 'Conviction' includes a finding of guilt which resulted in a probation order or a discharge. Risk to this particular child must still be shown.

iv   s.1(2)(c): the child is exposed to moral danger
The concept of 'moral danger' is notoriously imprecise, but must surely cover sexual abuse.

Reform

The Children Bill aims to simplify the law by providing a single procedure to replace the present complex routes into care. The specific conditions set out in s.1(2) are to be reformulated and replaced by new general conditions (clause 26).

The preconditions for making a care order will be:

1   that the child has suffered significant harm, or is likely to suffer such harm; and
2   the harm or likelihood of harm is attributable to
   a   the standard of care given to the child or likely to be given if the order were made, being below that which it would be reasonable to expect a parent of such a child to give to him; or
   b   the child's being beyond parental control.

The threshold for intervention by the courts is therefore 'harm'.
There is an extension beyond the existing criteria through the inclusion of 'likely harm'. The burden of proof is, of course, on the local
authority. There must be a causal link between harm and the absence
of reasonable parental care, and the care is tested by reference to
objective standards.

'Harm' is further defined in clause 20(8) as meaning ill-treatment
or the impairment of health or development; development is then
defined as meaning physical, intellectual, emotional, social or behavioural development and ill-treatment as including sexual abuse and
forms of ill-treatment which are not physical. So the term 'sexual
abuse' will be in the legislation, but no further elaboration is provided. Sexual abuse is one of the categories of registration and is
defined in the *Working Together* guidelines (DHSS, 1988c) as:

> the involvement of dependent, developmentally immature child-
> ren and adolescents in sexual activity which they do not truly
> comprehend, to which they are unable to give informed consent,
> or that violate the social taboos of family roles.

But this definition, too, depends on imprecise concepts, so interpretation by the courts of the terms used in Clause 26 will be inevitable,
and much litigation thereby anticipated for 1992!

The Lord Chancellor has stressed that it is wrong to conceptualise
the requirements set out in clause 26 as 'care grounds' or as reasons
for making an order; instead they should be seen as the *minimum* circumstances which justify court intervention into family life. They are
conditions precedent to the making of an order: whether an order
will be made will be governed solely by the welfare principle.

This principle, that the child's welfare is the 'paramount' consideration, is set out in clause 1(1). For the first time there is a welfare
check-list in clause 1(2) — this specifies the more important matters
which may affect the child's welfare. These include the ascertainable
wishes and feelings of the child concerned considered in the light of
age and understanding; its physical and emotional needs; the likely
effect of any changes in circumstances; age, sex, background and any
other characteristics which the court considers relevant. Of particular relevance in abuse cases will be (e) any harm suffered or the risk of
harm; (f) the capacity of parents or others to meet the child's needs;
and (g) the range of orders. Note that the menu of orders will not be
limited to care or supervision orders, but include the new private law
orders under clause 7. The residence order which specifies with
whom a child is to live, may be used as an alternative to a care order,
or combined with a supervision order. This may open up more use of
the extended family network.

Finally, clause 1(4) will require the court to consider whether making an order would contribute positively to the child's future. This may well mean that local authorities will be expected to indicate their plans for the child.

The reformulated care proceeding will overcome many of the technical limitations of the existing law, but can hardly be described as simple. On paper at least, they should enable local authorities and the courts to protect children better than under the present system.

Wardship

The fact that many of the Cleveland cases were eventually heard under the wardship jurisdiction is indicative of its resurrection since the 1970s. It is the oldest procedure for dealing with the welfare of children, its origins lying in the royal prerogative. There are a number of reasons for its discovery by local authorities in recent times.

Firstly, the advantage of wardship over care proceedings under the 1969 Act is that no 'grounds' as such have to be proven. The welfare of the child is the 'golden thread' which runs through the wardship jurisdiction and guides the court. This means that wardship has a vital role as a safety net, to supplement the narrowly drawn statutory code.

Furthermore, the High Court has much wider powers than a juvenile court, and can tailor orders to the needs of individual cases. With the welfare of the child as its major tenet, the High Court may issue an injunction to exclude the alleged abuser from the home.

There are procedural advantages in terms of the hearing too. The High Court takes a more relaxed attitude to the rules of evidence than a juvenile court. Evidence is exchanged in affidavit form in advance, followed by oral examination at the hearing. It has also been said that judges are better able to assimilate and weigh conflicting evidence from expert witnesses.

The disadvantages of wardship to local authorities include the cost, the delays associated with it, and the fact that the local authority loses control over the child, for the court becomes the guardian of the child, and any major decision must be referred back to it.

Reform

The Cleveland Report (Butler-Sloss, 1988) voiced admiration for the wardship jurisdiction and recommended a continued role. However, the Children Bill greatly restricts the wardship jurisdiction in relation to care cases. Under Clause 69, a local authority will only be able to use wardship with the consent of the court, and consent will only be granted where the remedy sought cannot be obtained by other means, and in its absence the child will suffer significant harm.

Reservations have been expressed by eminent commentators that this is premature, that until the new grounds in clause 26 are tried and tested we cannot be sure that they will be adequate to protect *all* children. The Lord Chancellor rejects this argument on the basis that the statute is comprehensive, and that the need for wardship as an altenative to care proceedings has been rendered redundant. Furthermore, the provision of concurrent jurisdiction under clause 67 means that the High Court and its 'Rolls Royce' procedure will still be available for difficult or complex local authority cases. This debate will no doubt continue after the Bill comes into effect, but let us hope the Lord Chancellor is right.

Evidence

As noted above, wardship has become the preferred forum for sexual abuse cases because of the complex forensic issues involved. Sexual abuse may be proven by means of clinical findings, express disclosure by the child, or by interpretation of the child's behaviour by experts. It is all highly problematic. Medical evidence, for example, may be non-existent or equivocal, and subject to conflicting medical opinions. The interpretation of behavioural factors may also be contested by the expert witnesses. Furthermore, where diagnosis is based upon a disclosure interview with a child, the therapeutic function of such interviews may conflict with the forensic needs of the court to such an extent that its evidential status is compromised.

Some guidance as to the evidential value of diagnostic interviews has been offered by the judiciary. The courts have expressed concern over the use of leading and hypothetical questions and cross-examination by the interviewer. This may seem rather perverse since these are the interviewing techniques employed daily by lawyers in the court-room. Cues and prompts such as anatomically correct dolls must also be used with caution — the courts have worried that they may corrupt or taint the child. Prejudgement by the interviewer is also significant — it should not be assumed that abuse has occurred, and the possibility that there was no abuse should not be ruled out. It is the unprompted and spontaneous comments of the child which are of most value — in the words of Mr Justice Bush, 'In the end you have to look for a remark that is not forced or led' (*Re X* [1989] 1FLR 53).

Many interviews have been recorded on video-tape and controversy has surrounded the inadmissibility of such tapes as evidence. Any doubts now appear to have been overcome and Mr Justice Latey in the case of *Re M (A Minor)* [1987] 1FLR 293 suggested that where abuse is only suspected, a video-recording of the interview should always be made. Since the precise questions, the answers, the gestures and the body movements, vocal inflections and intonations all play a part in interpretation, the video-tape will permit second opinions where there is a dispute.

These problems are not susceptible of solution by way of legislation, so it is not surprising that the Children Bill does not address the matter. The Cleveland Report did contain a number of recommendations, in particular that the child should not be subjected to repeated interviews, nor to the probing and confrontational style of 'disclosure' interview. It also recommended that the consent of the child should be obtained before video-recording.

The courts, after initial scepticism, have become more constructive, and the interviewers too have modified and refined their techniques in response to judicial criticism. As experience develops, by trial and error, no doubt increased reliance on video-recordings will become more common in sexual abuse cases.

Using the criminal law

There are a large number of criminal offences for which a person who has sexually abused a child may be prosecuted. Although the definition of incest depends upon a biological relationship (and therefore cannot be committed by a step-father), the law does not otherwise distinguish between the victim being the suspect's child, rather than a stranger or another family member. The particular vulnerability of children to sexual exploitation is recognised by a number of specific offences, for example under the Sexual Offences Act 1956.

The problems with using the criminal law to protect children lie not so much with the substantive law but with the special rules in relation to children's evidence. There have been reforms but most commentators would argue that they have not gone far enough.

The first problem is in relation to the competence of child witnesses. Children between 10 and 12 years and upwards, will be questioned by the judge to see if they understand the difference between right and wrong, and the solemnity of the oath. If it is felt that they do, they are allowed to take the oath and give their evidence. This is sworn evidence.

Where the child is of 'tender years', s.38(1) CYPA 1933 permits the child to give unsworn evidence. The court must be satisfied that although the child does not understand the nature of the oath, she does understand the duty of speaking the truth and 'is of sufficient intelligence to justify the reception of the evidence'. The difficulties lie with the abstract concept — the duty of speaking the truth — since in practice this excludes most eight year olds, and all under-fives from giving their evidence.

A further problem is in relation to the problem of corroboration. s.38(1) CYPA 1933 also provided that the unsworn evidence of a child had to be corroborated, and this was accepted as a matter of practice for the sworn evidence of children too. s.34 of the Criminal Justice Act 1988 has now abolished both these rules but this does not affect the common law requirement that the corroboration warning must be given in cases of sexual assault. So it looks like two steps forward, one step back for children.

The other much-vaunted change brought in by the Criminal Justice Act 1988 is the establishment of the 'live-link', the cross examination of child witnesses by closed-circuit television (s.32). This has been operational in selected Crown Courts around the country since 1 January 1989. The 'live-link' is the high-technology response to the problem of the child being too intimidated to speak, when confronted by his/her alleged abuser in the court-room. It is limited to children under 14 as witnesses in trials on indictment for assault, cruelty to children, or a wide range of sexual offences. This leaves open the possibility that the child may still have to give live evidence at the committal proceedings in the magistrates' court. The 'live-link' is expensive, and less expensive, 'low-tech' solutions could be applied more readily. This would include the use of screens or curtains to separate the witness from the accused. It would also extend to the lawyers and court officials dispensing with their wigs and gowns, a prior visit to the court by the child, and the child being accompanied throughout by a supportive adult.

The Criminal Justice Act 1988 does not deal with the question of competence, so the use of the 'live-link' is further limited. The question of pre-recorded video-tapes is also missing from the 1988 Act but is presently under consideration by a Home Office Committee, headed by Judge Pigot, QC (due to report in July 1989). What is needed, however, is not more piecemeal reform in dribs and drabs, but a more fundamental review of the whole question of children's evidence in criminal proceedings.

Conclusion

The law on child sexual abuse is complex and frequently controversial. On the civil side, reform has been on the agenda for some time, and the changes to emergency protection and care proceedings contained in the Children Act 1989 will overcome many of the current problems. There is less cause for optimism as to future developments in relation to criminal proceedings. And in the end, no matter how sophisticated the legal framework becomes, it cannot by itself offer a long-term solution to the problem.

Bibliography

Abdoulrahman, H. and Gladwell, S. (1988) 'Sexual abuse referrals to a regional centre for child psychiatry', *Child Abuse Review*, 2 (1).

Abel, G. et al. (1984) 'Complications, consent and cognitions in sex between children and adults', *International Journal of Law and Psychiatry*, 7.

Abel, G. et al. (1986) *Treatment of Child Molesters*, mimeo, 722 West 168th Street, Box 17, New York, 10032.

Adcock, M. (1988) 'Levels of context', *The Association for Family Therapy Newsletter*, 8, 21-2.

Allison, G. (1969) 'Conceptual Models in the Cuban missile crisis', *American Political Science Review*, 63.

Angelou, M. (1984) *I Know Why the Cage Bird Sings*, London: Virago.

Aries, P. (1973) *Centuries of Childhood*, Harmondsworth: Penguin.

Baker, A.W. and Duncan, S. (1985) 'Child sexual abuse: a study of prevalence in Great Britain', *Child Abuse and Neglect*, 9.

Baker, A.W. and Duncan, S. (1986) 'Child sexual abuse', in Meadow, R. (ed.), *Recent Advances in Paediatrics*, London: Churchill Livingstone.

Becker, J. (1988) 'Treating the perpetrator', *Intervening in Child Sexual Abuse*, audiotape, University of Glasgow.

Bentovim, A. and Bingley, L. (1985) 'Parenting and parenting failure: some guidelines for the assessment of the child, his parents and the family', in Adcock, M. and White, R. (eds), *Good Enough Parenting*, London: British Agencies for Adoption and Fostering.

Bentovim, A. et al. (1988) *Sexual Abuse in the Family: Assessment and Treatment*, London: John Wright.

Blagg, H. et al. (1988) 'Inter-agency cooperation: rhetoric and reality', in Hope, T. and Shaw, M. (eds), *Communities and Crime Reduction*, London: HMSO.

Blagg, H. and Stubbs, P. (1988) 'A child centred practice? Multi-agency approaches to child sexual abuse', *Practice*, 2(1).

Blatner, A. and Blatner, A. (1988) *Foundations of Psychodrama, History, Theory and Practice*, New York: Springer Publishing Co.

Bray, M. (1989) *Susie and the Wise Hedgehog go to Court*, London: Hawksmere.

Brennan, M. and Brennan, R. (1988) *Strange Language*, Wagga Wagga: Riverina Literacy Centre.

Brent Area Health Authority (1985) *A Child in Trust: The Report of the Panel of Inquiry into the Circumstances Surrounding the Death of Jasmine Beck-ford*, London Borough of Brent.

Brittan, A. and Maynard, M. (1984) *Sexism, Racism and Oppression*, Oxford: Basil Blackwell.

Broussard, S. and Wagner, W. (1988) 'Child sexual abuse: who is to blame', *Child Abuse and Neglect*, 12(4).

Butler-Sloss, E. (1988) *Report of the Inquiry into Child Abuse in Cleveland*, London: HMSO.

Campbell, B. (1988) *Unofficial Secrets*, London: Virago.

Carver, V. (ed.) (1978) *Child Abuse: a study text*, Milton Keynes: Open University Press.

Chadwick, K. and Little, C. (1987) 'The criminalisation of women', in Scraton, P. (ed.) *Law, Order and the Authoritarian State*, Milton Keynes: Open University Press.

Children's Legal Centre (1988) *Child Abuse Proceedings: The Child's Viewpoint*, London: Children's Legal Centre.

Cheetham, J. (1972) *Social Work with Immigrants*, London: Routledge and Kegan Paul.

Cm. 62 (1987) *The Law on Child Care and Family Services*, London: HMSO.

Cohen, S. (1981) *The Thin End of the White Wedge*, Manchester: Manchester Law Centre.

Cohen, S. (1985) *Visions of Social Control*, Cambridge: Polity Press.

Cohen, S. (1988) *Child Abuse Procedures; The Child's Viewpoint*, London: Children's Legal Centre.

Coombe, V. and Little, A. (eds) (1986) *Race and Social Work: A Guide to Training*, London: Tavistock.

Cook, R. (1987) *The Cook Report on Child Pornography*, transmitted on Central Television, 29 July 1987.

Corwin, D. (1988) 'Early diagnosis of child sexual abuse: diminishing the lasting effects', in Wyatt, G. and Powell, G. (eds), *Lasting Effects of Child Sexual Abuse*, New York: Sage.

Coulter, J. (1979) *The Social Construction of Mind*, London: Macmillan.

Cousins, P. (1988) 'Interrogative and imperative suggestibility', Paper presented to 'Current Issues in Clinical Psychology Conference', Chester.

Creigton, S. (1984) *Trends in child abuse*, London: NSPCC.

Creighton, S. and Noyes, P. (1989) *The File Report: Child Abuse Trends in England and Wales, 1953–87*, London: NSPCC.

CSAU (1988) *Child Sexual Abuse in Greater Manchester: a Regional Profile*, Joint NSPCC/Greater Manchester Authorities Sexual Abuse Unit.

Dale, P. et al. (1986) *Dangerous Families*, London: Tavistock.

Dawson, J. and Johnston, C. (1989) 'When the truth hurts', *Community Care*, 756, 30 March 1986.

De Young, M. (1982? 'Innocent seducer or innocently seduced?', *Journal of Clinical Child Psychology*, 11.

DHSS (1988a) *Surveys of Children and Young Persons on Child Protection Registers*, London: HMSO.

DHSS (1988b) *Child Sexual Abuse: Survey Report, Interagency Cooperation in England and Wales*, London: HMSO.

DHSS (1988c) *Working Together: a Guide to Arrangements for Inter-agency Cooperation for the Protection of Children from Abuse*, London: HMSO.

DHSS (1988d) *Medical Examination of a Child Subject to a Place of Safety Order*, London: HMSO.

Dingwall, R., Eekelaar, J. and Murray, T. (1983) *The Protection of Children: State Intervention in Family Life*, Oxford: Blackwell.

Dominelli, L. (1988) *Anti-Racist Social Work*, London: Macmillan.

Donzealot, J. (1980) *The Policing of Families*, London: Hutchinson.

Ennew, J. (1986) *The Sexual Exploitation of Children*, Cambridge: Polity Press.

Erooga, M. and Masson, H. (1989) 'The silent volcano: groupwork with mothers of sexually abused children', *Practice*, forthcoming.

Faller, K.C. (1984) 'Is the Child Victim of Sexual Abuse Telling the Truth', *Child Abuse and Neglect*, 8.

Faller, K.C. (1988) *Child Sexual Abuse; an Interdisciplinary Manual for Diagnosis, Case Management and Treatment*, New York: Columbia University Press.

Finkelhor, D. (1984) *Child Sexual Abuse: New Theory and Research*, New York: The Free Press.

Finkelhor, D. (1986) *Sourcebook on Child Sexual Abuse*, New York: Sage.

Flin, R., Davies, G. and Stevenson, Y. (1989) 'Children's knowledge of court proceedings', *British Journal of Psychology* (in the press).

Flin, R., Davies, G. and Tarrant, A. (1988) *Children as Witnesses*, Report to the Scottish Home and Health Department.

Flin, R. and Tarrant, A. (1989) 'Preparing child witnesses for court', *Social Work Today*, 18–19, 2 February 1989.

Garfinkel, H. (1967) *Studies in Ethnomethodology*, Englewood Cliffs: Prentice Hall.

Gelles, R.J. and Lancaster, J.B. (eds) (1988) *Child Abuse and Neglect: Biosocial Dimensions*, New York: Aldine de Gruyter.

Glaser, T. and Frosh, S. (1988) *Child Sexual Abuse*, London: Macmillan.

Glasgow, D. (1987) 'Responding to child sexual abuse: issues, techniques and play based assessment', Mersey Regional Health Authority, Marketing Department (available from author).

Glasgow, D. (1988) 'Child sexual abuse is not a diagnosis', unpublished paper, Liverpool.

Glasgow, D., and Bentall, R. (1989) 'What do expert witnesses in child sexual abuse think they are doing? Diagnosis and the sexually accurate doll "test" as professional myths', *The Liverpool Law Review*, **V** (1).

Goodman, G. and Jones, D. (1988) 'The emotional effects of criminal court testimony on sexual abuse victims', in Davies, G. and Drinkwater, J. (eds), *The Child Witness — Do the Courts Abuse Children?*, Leicester: BPS Publications.

Goodwin, J., Sahd, D. and Rada, R.T. (1982) 'False accusation and false denials', in Goodwin, J. (ed.), *Sexual Abuse: Victims and their Families*, Boston: John Wright.

Gordon, L. (1989) *Heroes of Their Own Lives*, London: Virago.

Greenwich Area Health Authority (1987) *A Child in Mind: The Protection of Children in a Responsible Society*, The Report of the Commission of Inquiry into the circumstances surrounding the death of Kimberley Carlile, London Borough of Greenwich.

Hall, S. and Jefferson, T. (eds) (1978) *Resistance Through Rituals*, London: Hutchinson.

Hartman, C.R. and Burgess, A.W. (1988) 'Information processing of trauma', *Journal of Interpersonal Violence*, 3(4).

Hearn, J. (1989) 'Sexual violence and sexualities toward young people', *Sociology*, 22.

Hedderman, C. (1987) *Children's Evidence: The Need for Corroboration*, London: Home Office Research and Planning Unit, Paper 41.

Heger, A. (1989) 'Medical evaluation of sexual abuse', in Murray, K. and Gough, D. (eds), *Intervening in Child Sexual Abuse*, Edinburgh: Scottish Academic Press.

Holdaway, S. (1986) 'Police and social work investigations: problems and possibilities', *British Journal of Social Work*, 16.

Hooper, C.A. (1987) 'Child sexual abuse: getting him off the hook', *Trouble and Strife*, Winter.

Horowitz, M.J. (1976) *Stress Response Syndrome*, New York: Jason Arouson.

House of Commons (1989) *The Children Bill*, House of Commons Bill 104.

Independent Second Opinion Panel (1987) *Child Sexual Abuse: Some Principles of Good Practice*, North Regional Health Authority.

Jampole, L. and Weber, M. (1987) 'An assessment of the behaviour of sexually abused and non-sexually abused children with anatomically correct dolls', *Child Abuse and Neglect*, 11.

Jansen, M. (19837 *Silent Scream: I am a Victim of Incest*, Philadelphia: Fortress Press.

Jehu, D. (1987) *Beyond Sexual Abuse: Therapy with Women who were Childhood Victims*. Chichester: Wiley.

Jehu, D. (1989) 'Mood disturbances among women clients who were sexually abused in childhood: prevalence, etiology, treatment', *Journal of Interpersonal Violence*.

Jewett, C. (1982) *Helping Children Cope with Separation and Loss*, Boston: The Harvard Common Press.

Jones, D. and McQuiston, M. (1986) *Interviewing The Sexually Abused Child*, National Centre for the Treatment of Child Sexual Abuse and Neglect, Denver.

Jones, D. et al. (1987) *Understanding Child Sexual Abuse*, 2nd edn, London: Macmillan.

Kelly, L. (1988) *Surviving Sexual Violence*, Cambridge: Polity Press.

Kempe, R.S. and Kempe, C.H. (1978) *Child Abuse*, London: Fontana/Open Books.

Kerns, D. (1981) 'Medical assessment of child sexual abuse', in Mrazek, P. and Kempe, C. (eds), *Sexually Abused Children and their Families*, New York: Pergamon.

King, M. and Yuille, J. (1987) 'Suggestibility and the child witness', in Ceci, M., Toglia, M. and Ross, D. (eds), *Children's Eyewitness*, New York: Springer.

Kitzinger, J. (198) 'Defending innocence: ideologies of childhood', *Feminist Review, Special Issue*, 28, London: Routledge.

La Fontaine, J. (1988) 'Child Sexual Abuse: An ESRC Research Briefing', ESRC, London.

Lambeth (1987) *Whose Child?*, London Borough of Lambeth.

Langley, D. (1984) 'Metaphor in the search for self', *Changes*, 2 (3).

Lewis, C.S. (1981) *The Lion, the Witch and the Wardrobe*, Oxford: Bodley Head.

Bibliography

Lorde, A. (1984) *Sister, Outsider*, London: Crossing Press.

Masson, J.M. (1984) *The Assault on Truth: Freud's Suppression of the Seduction Theory*, Harmondsworth: Penguin.

McEwan, J. (1988) 'Child evidence: more proposals for reform', *Criminal Law Review*.

McFarlane, K. et a. (1986) *Sexual Abuse of Young Children*, New York: Holt, Rinehart and Winston.

Macguire, M. and Corbett, C. (1987) *The Effects of Crime and the Work of Victim's Support Schemes*, Aldershot: Gower.

Macguire, M. and Pointing, J. (eds) (1988) *Victims of Crime: A New Deal?* Milton Keynes: Open University Press.

McKay, R.W. (1974) 'Conceptions of Children and Models of Socialization', in Turner, R. (ed.), *Ethnomethodology*, Harmondsworth: Penguin.

McLeod, M. and Saraga, E. (eds) (1988) *Child Sexual Abuse: Towards a Feminist Professional Practice*, London: PNL Press.

Metropolitan Police and Bexley Social Services (1987) *Child Sexual Abuse Joint Investigation Programme, Final Report*, London: HMSO.

Metropolitan Police (1989) *Force Response to Child Abuse within the Family: Principles and Code of Practice*, 2nd edn.

Miller, A. (1985) *Thou Shalt Not be Aware: Societies Betrayal of the Child*, London: Pluto Press.

Miller, A. (1987) *For Your Own Good: The Roots of Violence in Childrearing*, London: Virago.

Milne, A.A. (1927) 'The Old Sailor', *Now We Are Six*, London: Methuen.

Miner, J. and Blythe, E. (1988) *Coping with child sexual abuse: a guide for teachers*, London: Longman.

Moreno, J.L. (1987) *The Essential Moreno*, ed. Jonathan Fox, New York: Springer Publishing Co.

Morgan, J. (1988) 'Children as Victims', in Macguire, M. and Pointing, J. (eds), *Victims of Crime: A New Deal?* Milton Keynes: Open University Press.

Morrison, T. (1986) 'Beyond the sum of its individuals', *Community Care*, 4 September 1986.

Morrison, T., Bentley, M., Clark, P. and Shearer, E.L. (1989) 'Treating the untreatable — groupwork with intra-familial sex offenders', *NSPCC Occasional Paper*, forthcoming.

Moynihan, D. (1965) *The Negro Family: The Case for National Action*, US Department of Labour, Washington, DC.

Mzarek, P., Lynch, M. and Bentovim, A. (1981) 'A recognition of child sexual abuse in the United Kingdom', in Mzarek, P. and Kempe, C.H. (eds), *Sexually Abused Children and their Families*, London: Pergamon.

Nagel, W.H. (1974) 'The Notion of Victimology in Criminology', in Drapkin, I. and Viano, E. (eds), *Victimology*, Mass: Lexington.

National Association of Victim Support Schemes (1988) *The Victim in Court*, Report of Working Party.

Nelson, S. (1987) *Incest: Fact and Myth*, 2nd revised edn, Edinburgh: Stramullion Cooperative Ltd.

Oaklander, V. (1978) *Windows to our Children*, London: : Real People Press.

Official Solicitor (1988) *The Investigations and submissions of the official solicitor to the Supreme Court*, London: Penderel House.

Parish, M. (1953) 'Description of applications and review of techniques', *Group Psychotherapy*, **6** (1–2), 74–77.

Parton, N. (1958) *The Politics of Child Abuse*, London: Macmillan.

Parton, N. and Martin, N. (1989) 'Public Enquiries Legalism and Child Care in England and Wales', *International Journal of Law and the Family*, **3**.

Pearson, G. et al. (1989) 'Policing racism', in Morgan, R. and Smith, D. (eds), *Coming to Terms with Policing*, London: Routledge and Kegan Paul.

Pithers, D. (1988) 'The Ozymandis reaction and the prison of Narcissus: are some sexually abused children untreatable', unpublished manuscript.

Pollner, M. (1975) 'The very coinage of your brain: the anatomy of reality disjunctures', *Philosophy of the Social Sciences*, **5**.

Pynoos, R. and Eth, S. (1984) 'The child as witness to homicide, *Journal of Social Issues*, **40**.

Reader's Digest (1985) *You and Your Rights (Scotland)*, London: Reader's Digest Association (English edn available).

Riley, J. (1985) *The Unbelonging*, London: Women's Press.

Rodney, B. (1987) *Racism and Resistance to Change*, Liverpool: Merseyside Area Profile Group.

Rogers, C. (1982) 'Child sexual abuse and the courts: preliminary findings', in Conte, J. and Smore, D. (eds), *Social Work and Child Sexual Abuse*, New York: Hawthorn.

Ryan, W. (1976) *Blaming the Victim*, New York: Vintage Books, Revised Edn, Random House.

Sampson, A. et al. (1988) 'Crime, localities and the multi-agency approach', *British Journal of Criminology*, **28** (4).

Saraga, E. and McCleod, M. (1988) 'Abuse of trust', *Marxism Today*.

Schafer, S. (1977) *Victimology: the Victim and his Criminal*, Virginia: Reston.

Schutz, A. (1978) *The Phenomenology of the Social World*, trans. Walsh G. and Lehnert, F., Evanston: Northwestern University Press.

Schutz, A. (1972) 'Don Quixote and the problem of reality', in *Collected Papers*, II, Broderson, A. (ed.), The Hague: Martinuus Nihoff

Scottish Law Commission (1988) *The Evidence of Children and other Potentially Vulnerable Witnesses*, Discussion paper 75.

Sgroi, S.M. (1982) *Handbook of Clinical Intervention in Child Sexual Abuse*, New York: Lexington Books.

Shearer, E. (1988) 'Child sexual abuse: issues for treatment work with families', *Child Protection*, **3** (4).

Smith, D. (1978) 'K is Mentally Ill', *Sociology*

Spencer, J. and Flin, R. (1989) *The Evidence of Children*, London: Blackstone.

Striker, S. and Kimmel, E. (1978) *The Anti-Colouring Book*, London: McClure-Hindman Books.

Stubbs, P. (1985) 'The employment of black social workers', *Critical Social Policy*, **12**.

Stubbs, P. (1987) 'Professionalism and the adoption of black children', *British Journal of Social Work*, **17** (5).

Stubbs, P. (1988a) *The Reproduction of Racism in State Social Work*, PhD thesis, University of Bath.

Stubbs, P. (1988b) 'Relationships with the police: intermediate treatment and the multi-agency approach', *Youth and Policy*, 24.

Stubbs, P. (1989) *Police–Social Work Relations in Child Sexual Abuse: an Account of the Rochdale Pilot Project*, NSPCC Occasional Paper, forthcoming.

Summit, R.C. (1983) 'The child sexual abuse accommodation syndrome', *International Journal of Child Abuse and Neglect*, 7.

Triseliotis, J. (ed.) (1972) *Social Work with Coloured Immigrants and Their Families*, Oxford: Oxford University Press.

Walker, A. (1983) *The Colour Purple*, London: Women's Press.

Walker, C.E., Bonner, B.L. and Kauffman, K.L. (1988) *The Physically and Sexually Abused Child*, London: Pergamon Press.

Waterman, C.K. and Foss-Goodman, D. (1984) 'Child molesting: variables relating to attribution of fault', *The Journal of Sex Research*, 20.

Wattam, C. (1989) *Teachers' Experiences with Children who have or may have been Sexually Abused*, NSPCC Occasional Papers, No. 4.

Wattam, C., Blagg, H. and Hughes, J.A. (1988) 'Report of Joint University of Lancaster and NSPCC Conference, Research in Child Sexual Abuse, 1988', *Social Work Today*, Forthcoming.

Wells, J. (1985) 'Bruises are not obvious', *Community Care*, 10 January 1985.

Wells, J. (1988) 'Pin People', *Practise*, London: NSPCC.

Whitcomb, D. et al. (1985) *When the Victim is a Child*, Department of Justice, Washington.

White, E. (1984) 'Listening to the voices of black feminism', *Radical America*, 18.

Winnicott, D.W. (1964) *The Child, the Family, and the Outside World*, Harmondsworth: Pelican.

Wolfe, S.C. (1984) *A Multifactor Model of Deviant Sexuality*, mimeograph, North West Treatment Associates, 315, West Gale Street, Seattle, Washington 98119.

Wyre, R. (1988) 'Working with sexual abuse', SACCS Conference, Telford, 25 October 1988.

Index